WHEN
YOUR PARENTS
GROW OLD

When Your Parents Grow Old

INFORMATION
AND RESOURCES
TO HELP THE
ADULT SON OR
DAUGHTER COPE
WITH THE
PROBLEMS OF
AGING PARENTS

Jane Otten and Florence D. Shelley

Funk & Wagnalls
New York

Manufactured in the United States of America

Library of Congress Cataloging in Publication Data
Otten, Jane.
When your parents grow old.
Bibliography: p.
Includes index.
1. Old age assistance—United States—Directories.
2. Old age assistance—Information services—United
States. 3. Aged—United States—Family relationships.
I. Shelley, Florence D., joint author. II. Title.
HV1465.087   362.6'0973   76-10697
ISBN 0-308-10256-8

10 9 8 7 6 5 4 3

To our parents,
who loved us
and taught us how
to love others

FOREWORD

This book is intended as a resource for those who are wrestling with the difficult problems of their parents' old age. It was written at the suggestion of our friend Sylvia M. Pechman, who thought there was a need to bring together whatever information was available for adult children to use in caring for their aging parents.

To make our information sound, we interviewed many specialists in the field of aging and read much of the professional literature. To make it practical and relevant, we listened to the expressed concerns of our friends and acquaintances and of the old people and their children whom we interviewed. What we learned, together with our own family experiences, contributed to the content of this book.

Most of the professionals we interviewed are listed in the Bibliography. Where anonymity was requested, we have respected it. There are many more experts than we have quoted and many more agencies than we have mentioned. We apologize for our omissions. Local services are proliferating now, and families are fortunate in that they will find more, rather than fewer, resources for help than those we have cited.

David A. Affeldt, general counsel to the Senate Special Committee on Aging, reviewed the section on taxes. Attorneys Ira S. Siegler and Seymour L. Mantell advised and reviewed on the section dealing with wills and estates. Dr. Joseph G. Slavin, a practicing psychologist, and Margaret Rafner, a geriatric social worker, gave early encouragement and suggestions. Directors of services to the aging of three major philanthropic organizations—Ben Kaplan, Alice Murphy, and David Sambol—highlighted for us some of the common problems adult children face as their parents age. Sara Rose Stivelman researched California services for us.

In particular, we would like to thank the doctors—Robert N. Butler, Edward Fischel, Ira Bernstein, Robert Stivelman, Harold Rifkin, Steven Mattis, and Maclyn McCarty—who took time from their busy schedules to educate us in the fields of their specialties, and Dr. Joseph Ney, who read the manuscript.

A number of directors of the National Council on the Aging shared their knowledge with us: Walter M. Beattie, Jr., Mother M. Bernadette, Ollie A. Randall, William R. Pothier, O. J. Gates, David G. Salten, Edwin F. Shelley, and Ellen Winston among them. Jack Ossofsky, present NCOA executive director, and Geneva Mathiasen, former executive director, were especially helpful.

If there are errors in this book, it is we who are responsible and none of those with whom we spoke. The opinions and viewpoints are our own.

The information here is as accurate as we have been able to make it. But because laws, regulations, and practices change, and new information develops, we urge you always to check local officials, lawyers, doctors, and other authorities for specific technical or professional advice and for procedures which apply to your problem.

We had some difficulty with one small but important aspect of this book: which pronoun to use when we referred to the word "parent." To use "he or she" and "him and her" each time would have been too awkward. Traditional usage and custom persuaded us to use the masculine pronouns, and, accordingly, throughout this book, we use "he," "him," and "his." Obviously, however, whatever we write applies equally well to a female parent. Doctors and other professionals have also become "he" for the same reason.

We must, of course, thank our husbands and our children,

who read the manuscript critically and whose suggestions improved this book.

We also thank our patient and skillful typists: Laura Otten, Sonia Kugler, Jeanette Dombrowski, Joan Rasnow, Grace Gaffney, and Carol Dassau.

CONTENTS

INTRODUCTION

This is a book to help you when you find yourself faced with the problems of your parents' old age. The problems may be chronic, or they may erupt suddenly. You may be at a time in your own life when you don't need any more problems. All kinds of conflicting emotions appear: love, affection, guilt and anguish, frustration, sadness.

Where can you find the supportive services you and your parents need? How can you deal with your parents' emotions and your own? How have others felt and what have they done when they've faced the same problems you're facing?

For each individual family, aging is a personal matter. It can be a glory or a nightmare. For those who are obliged to call on others for help—on their children, other family members, and friends—the process can be demeaning, bewildering, and painful. For those called upon to help, it can be equally distressing.

If you are the one who is summoned to act, to answer the emergency calls, to deal with the finances and the doctors, to organize the drill and deal with the consequences of your action, this book should help you find the resources which are available to make your task less difficult and painful. There is no single simple solution suitable for everyone, but there is help available for you to find your own solution, the one best for you and your family.

The factors in determining what is right for whom are freighted with complex considerations. How each family solves its problems will rest not only on the resources to which it has access but the style and customs to which it adheres. There are class differences, economic differences, ethnic differences, and religious differences in how families behave.

Many of the aged are poor, largely because incomes are sharply cut after retirement. Half of the over-sixty-five couples living together have incomes of $6,000 or less; half of the widows, widowers, or unmarried aged living alone have incomes under $2,500 a year. One-fourth of older families have annual incomes of more than $10,000, and 3.5 percent of more than $25,000. The average income for all older families is just over $8,000. In the over-sixty-five group, one out of every eight family heads and one out of every sixteen individuals works full-time.

Over eight out of ten older persons have chronic health problems for which they are receiving medical care. Yet almost all of this group manage to maneuver and move around well on their own.

No matter what your parent's chronological age is, his requirements will vary depending on his physical and mental health, his vigor and attitude, his income or lack of it, his family situation, the kind of community in which he lives. Economic, social, medical, housing, and transportation patterns which are suitable for one stage in the later years often become unsuitable as one or another component changes. Solutions that are satisfactory for problems under one set of circumstances similarly become inappropriate as new conditions emerge.

The very poor, the families on welfare, are accustomed to the intervention of public agencies, the services of social workers, subsidized, inexpensive food, public medical care, government-supported housing, or provision of other basic needs. The very rich can buy the physical services and supports they require to ease the burdens of deteriorating physical and mental health. But the vast majority in the middle, independent people of moderate income, are unaccustomed to looking to outside assistance. They are frequently ignorant of the resources available to them.

Rich or poor, aged people have many common needs—and family problems have many common elements. There are things that money can't buy: love, attention, tenderness, a willing ear, a visit. And there are human feelings that override class and other distinctions. Not the least of these is guilt. Guilt appears to be the feeling that most troubles the adult child dealing with the problems of aging parents. (How people feel as they become increasingly involved in their parents' lives is the subject of the first chapter.)

Thus, despite unique differences in individual needs and situations, many problems break down into broad categories in which general approaches and suggestions can be of help. And cutting across all categories of need are many outside resources which were not available fifty years ago, ten years ago, or even five years ago.

Extended longevity and the growth in the older population (in 1900 only one out of every twenty-five Americans was sixty-five or older, while today they make up about one-tenth of our national population) have resulted in a much greater awareness of the needs of the elderly. Federal government programs for the aged are expanding rapidly—social security, medicare, medicaid, the provisions of the Older Americans Act, for example. In addition, state and local governments have established relatively new services for the aged, and both public and private agencies in many cities and counties offer counseling and therapy services for the aged and their families. (Interviews with the representatives of these agencies and the experience of ordinary people lay the basis for Chapter 2.)

More physicians are studying the physical health of the aged, and more psychiatrists and psychologists are examining their mental health. Even political scientists are analyzing the voting patterns of the over-sixty-five group, weighing their actual and potential influence as a voting bloc. Geriatrics—the study of old age and its diseases—and gerontology—the study of the aging process—are relatively new areas of research and specialization, yet within the last few years they have generated a growing body of knowledge about older people. (How to deal with the medical problems associated with aging—as, for example, selecting, communicating, and cooperating with a doctor—are among the matters covered in Chapter 6.)

All this growing interest in the aged is producing substantial across-the-board resources for families and their aging relatives. New approaches to housing, health, social, and educational needs are being translated into new operating programs in communities across the country. It's true, however, that these programs will probably be found most commonly in areas where the aged are concentrated. Six out of every ten older people live in metropolitan areas, 35 percent in small towns, and 5 percent on farms. One out of every four lives in three states—California, New York, and Pennsylvania. Well over half of the total national aged population live in these three states and seven others—Illinois, Texas, Ohio, Florida, Massachusetts, Michigan, and New Jersey. The small-town aged and even those in some metropolitan areas may not have access to a broad range of supporting services.

But new approaches to the economic problems of older people, offering specific direct and indirect financial benefits, transcend geographical lines. Federal and state help for medical bills and lower taxes benefit the aged from coast to coast. Lower transportation fares, reduced admission prices to theaters and other places of recreation and education are also widespread. It's true that it may not always be simple to take advantage of these opportunities. Sometimes individuals just don't know about them. Sometimes they do know about them, approach them, and founder in red tape and bureaucratic hassles. Often, lately, money sources have shrunk and many programs are operating with small staffs and minimal activities.

The span of aid and assistance for the aged and their families is nevertheless very different today from what it was when your grandparents—and even your parents—automatically took an aged, impoverished, or lonely parent into their home and assumed total care because there was no other answer. The concept of the family's responsibility for its members was largely automatic then, as was the concept of the three-generation family living in the same residence. There were no choices and no aids to choice—unless the "poorhouse" could be considered a choice. Today there is a range of choices for care of the elderly.

In addition, in those not-so-far-off times, there was at least lip service given to the belief that old age was a respectable condition, even one to be venerated. The older person had worked hard throughout his life, had skills and talents to offer, had made his contribution to his family and society. This was an achievement which merited some rewards. Attitudes toward the old have changed now. We admire more the young and vigorous; we respect future potential more than past performance. Old age, to many younger people today, is a fearsome stage, almost a loathsome one.

Still another factor, mobility, makes the process of caring for aged parents a very difficult one. Until World War II, succeeding generations of a family remained in the same community, living in a traditionally homogeneous fashion. It was relatively easy to keep an eye on aging parents or relatives who lived only a short distance away; if circumstances required, it was easy to move them to a more suitable residence—perhaps your own— still within their familiar surroundings. But the dispersion of the past thirty years has separated the generations in many families, and adult children often must arrange for the care of parents who live many miles away and whose life-styles are very different from those of their children.

What does all this mean to you when your aged parent's problems become a problem to you? It means you and your parent are in a tough situation, but it also means there's a lot of help available.

The process of dealing with a troubled older person to whom you are connected with bonds of love and loyalty is rarely rosy, and sometimes painful. But if you are armed with information, if you understand your feelings and those of your parent, if you are able to achieve a certain clarity of purpose, the process can be better than it might otherwise be. This, we hope, is what our book is all about.

CHAPTER 1 FACING UP

According to the law, parents are responsible for minor children, while adult children are responsible for parents only in very special circumstances. But according to custom, religious mandate, and the inner commands of filial duty, respect, affection, and love, children usually do not forsake parents in their old age.

Old age is not merely a chronological state. It comes to some sooner than to others. The process of aging, from which none of us escapes, diminishes our strength and capacities, frequently our resources. For the chronically ill, the mentally or physically incapacitated, the financially impoverished, the socially excluded, becoming old can be degrading, isolating, and destructive. Among all the other losses may also come the theft of autonomy, or control over one's own life. In the long run, that may even be the most painful loss of all.

Most aging adults, with reason, hang onto their autonomy as long as possible, sometimes longer than appears to others to be suitable. Most pyschiatrists believe that all people, including the old and the sick, are entitled to control over their own lives. They have a right to choose how to live and how to die. Even loving children have no right to impose on frail parents solutions the parents themselves are unwilling to accept—even if the children have no doubt that these solutions are in the parents' best interests.

But each of us with a parent in pain or need knows that life is not that simple. The demands made on us, the decisions we are forced to confront, the pressures imposed on us by circumstances, our inner emotions, and outside expectations, tear at us, fragment us, drain us of energy, of time, and, worst of all, of good feelings.

Feelings That Intrude

Feelings surround all the actions we take—the logical ones, the necessary ones—and all the actions we avoid. A family that has everything straight—all its inner relationships, its medical and financial plans, its action program for crisis and emergency—is not the typical American family. The professionals in the social service agencies know this because it is they to whom desperate people turn when crisis strikes and there is no plan ready to put into operation. And the decisions that are made under pressure and without professional assistance frequently are not the best possible decisions and may prove difficult to live with. The feelings that intrude on all these actions have to do with guilt as well as love, fear as well as understanding, egos pitted against egos, sibling rivalries, hostility, resentment, duty, affection, need for approval—a whole tangle of family history and relationships which often seem to bubble underneath or even explode at the very time it would be most constructive for love, patience, and logic to prevail.

So, when you get your first emergency call from a stricken parent, or when the demands of dealing with a continuing difficult situation wear on you, don't be surprised if some of these feelings rise up in you and in others of your family, sometimes seeming to overwhelm.

You and Your Parents: Something Changes

Let us assume your parents have been living an independent life. They are in an apartment or a house, in a retirement community or a heterogeneous neighborhood, living near you or not. They may work at paid or volunteer jobs; they may have retired. They have certain interests which they pursue. You and they are continuing a long-standing pattern of living. Your lives are separate, meshing for holiday and other visits back and forth. You maintain regular communication through informal visits and phone calls if you live near them, through letters, photographs, and phone calls if you don't.

At some point, sharply or gradually, the situation changes. In regular phone calls or visits, over a period of time, you begin to sense from a parent some new failing or infirmity and you hear some new fears. Your seventy-eight-year-old widowed father may indicate that he's finding it more difficult to climb the stairs in his two-story house. Your mother may call to report that she is very worried about your father, who has been growing more and more depressed and now refuses to leave the house at all. Or you may receive a sudden announcement. Your father has been taking care of your mother, who is suffering from a chronic, irreversible disease. He dies. Or your mother calls frantically to say that your father has had a stroke and will be hospitalized for a very long stay. She does not drive, nor is she able to maintain their home without his help.

These are the large signs that foretell the end of an independence you and they have been enjoying. Some new and great responsibility begins for you. You will be called upon to make new decisions, take new actions. And your parents will be called upon to exchange some independence for necessary care.

What Happens Is Determined by Attitudes

What happens from now on will depend to a degree on factors which you may not be able immediately or ever to change—your financial condition and your parents', the geographical location of their home in relation to yours and those of your brothers and sisters, their actual condition and the kind of medical care they need. To a large degree, also, the decisions you and your parents make at this point will also be influenced by cultural attitudes.

Among some groups—Jews, Chinese, and Catholics, for example—there is a long tradition of the extended family. The Amish build an addition to the main farmhouse for the traditional purpose of housing an older generation. Suburban split-levels are often advertised now as "mother-daughter" houses. If you are religious, you will automatically accept the mandate to honor your father and mother. Cast me not off in time of old age, says the Bible. If you are not affluent, economic conditions may dictate that the elderly become part of your household; they may care for your children while you are out working. Rich or poor, religious or not, you may well wish to become involved. When these attitudes prevail, you expect without question to take on the burden of caring for your parents. But there is still an internal searching and decision-making process you will have to go through, and the decisions you reach may not be any better or worse with or without money, with or without convenient geography, with or without strong cultural or religious precepts. Feelings can subvert the process of making a decision and forestall reaching one which might be the most practical and effective.

Suppose, for example, your mother is still telling you that your wife spends too much money or that your husband spends too much time playing golf or watching television. Or your father is consistently and loudly critical because you haven't required that your children adhere to his and your religion and they are dating—and mating—with partners of a different faith. Caring for parents who are still critical, still supervisory, will make it more difficult for you than otherwise to contribute efficiently to their needs. You will have to surmount not only their attitudes but your possible resentment of them. Or, if you have lived separated from them for a long period of time and with little communication—either by your design or theirs—it will be difficult for you to enter into the problem situation, make the required decisions, and then carry them out.

Suppose your father has had a massive stroke and will recover only a small part of his former faculties. Your mother has led a sheltered life, never assuming any responsibilities. What now? Will you take over your father's role in maintaining your mother's dependency, or will you try to help educate your mother to assume the new responsibilities she must face?

Decision Making and Family Tensions

The need to make decisions, the ability to make decisions, and the authority to make decisions are often at the center of family disputes, of feelings of guilt or of frustration. How this is resolved often grows out of the whole history of the previous family relationship. If you are from a family with strong familial tradition, it may be unthinkable to consider putting an infirm parent into an institution. You may have different feelings if your parent becomes so incapable, incontinent, or infirm that it seems irresponsible to turn your entire household into a hospital or sickroom and deprive your spouse and children of the right to independence and joy in living. Everyone has needs and rights, including you. All this has to be balanced in the decisions that must be taken, the responsibilities assumed or shared.

Sharing Responsibility

The complications are not related to the parent–child relationship alone. The burden is more easily divided if all the people who would logically be a part of the enterprise live within the same general area, but even closest relatives who are separated by geographical distances can still participate in many ways—through advice, through help in finding information and making arrangements, through financial advice and support, through regular telephone calls.

But remember that bringing other people into the caretaking process may likely produce its own problems. Brothers and sisters and other close relatives all have individual ideas of how matters should be handled. Each has his own agenda, his own life history, his own current life, and his own psychological baggage to bring to the problems of caring for older relatives. Bickering, tension, and stress are not uncommon in the best of families suddenly forced to cope with new situations.

A suburban rabbi reports a typical plea for counseling from a member of his congregation: "Help me. What should I do? I hate everybody. My father died last year, and my mother is in chronic heart failure. She really can't live alone. I don't work. My older sister lives in Florida. My younger sister teaches in Brooklyn and has two teenagers at home. My brother says, 'You're the one who got the dowry, so you take care of Mother. You're home all day. But don't put my mother into a nursing home. I'll never forgive you. No, I can't take her to my house.

My wife can't bathe her or stay home with her all day. I'll send you some money. No, I can't have dinner with you on Sunday. I have an important appointment.' So, of course, I took her in with me. And as soon as I did, they all disappeared. They are too busy or too far away. And it isn't fair."[1]

Which Child Takes the Responsibility?

In some families it is taken for granted that the daughter or daughters will take physical care of the parents, while sons offer financial and "moral" support. Whether it is the youngest or the oldest, the married or the unmarried, the richest or the poorest, depends on the particular patterns in the family.

The personalities of the adult children are very important in how responsibility is assumed. Sometimes a child feels very close to a parent and does not resent the extra burden of care. Sometimes taking responsibility is the logical outcome of a history of devotion to the needs of a parent. Sometimes the child feels guilty about his past feelings: his neglect of the parent, his lack of devotion, his lack of affection. If he feels this way, he may act suddenly to win approval from a parent toward whom he always felt hostile, whose approval he never thought he could win. The child who feels the most guilty is often the one who seizes the caretaking responsibility, while the most self-centered child may find it the easiest to break away from loving care of his parent. Very few children, however, are so alienated from their parents that they will turn their backs completely.

It is important to realize, however, that many older people don't want to accept the realities of their lives—it's too painful to admit that they can no longer cope on their own with transportation, household activities, managing their own affairs. It's too destructive to contemplate a health situation which deprives them of the ability to live an independent life. Thus, they will often try to ignore infirmities and continue to live as they have been living. Some will do this, also, in order not to burden their children. And they will struggle keenly between their need for help and assistance, on the one hand, and their desire to be independent, on the other.

You and your parents—and your siblings—must try to sift

these things out, perhaps through many conversations over a period of time. A hasty decision is probably a bad one.

You and Your Parents: Dependence and Independence

As your parents age, you will sense the need for change of some sort in their lives, or some incident will point it out to you sharply. If it appears that your mother is having more and more difficulty walking four blocks to the nearest grocery store, this is a sign that the shopping situation needs some review. If your father's eye doctor tells him he should no longer drive at night, this requires some new arrangements.

But on whose part? Who is to make the decisions? This is a sticky area. Is it up to you to tell your parents that they have to revise their habits, up to you to take over with your proposals? Will your parents abide by a decision if you try to force it on them? Or should you wait—even though the signals are clear to you—until they are equally clear to your parents and they ask your advice? How will you feel if they insist on maintaining a pattern which you feel is dangerous?

Experts differ as to which course you should take. Some believe you should intervene if you feel it is the loving, caring thing to do. Others believe that respect for autonomy is the most important rule.

With conflicting professional advice, you'll have to run your own course. Do what is comfortable for you and acceptable to your parents, as long as no serious danger is involved in allowing them to deal with their inconveniences and burdens. If the grocery bag is too heavy, the walk for the newspaper too long, the frustration of straightening out a bill or a credit too overwhelming, in all probability you'll finally be asked to intervene. Meanwhile, a little annoyance keeps the blood circulating.

Most of us have experience with generational problems, having observed how our own parents dealt with our grandparents. We may have a layman's notion of sophisticated psychological and psychiatric attitudes, about what is appropriate or inappropriate behavior. And we tend to measure ourselves by this complex bundle of internal emotions and opinions we carry with us. Professionals in the geriatric field—

whether they are social workers or psychiatrists, agency heads or institution administrators, counselors, or researchers—seem to agree that adult children tend to feel obliged to "take over" if their parents begin to falter, and to feel guilty if they fail to do so. Yet, in our interviews, we heard again and again that the quality of life as it is regarded by the person living it is the best indicator of what should be done and when.

Your parent is living in a ghettoized neighborhood, once safe, but now dangerous. What should you do? He has friends and activities in the neighborhood and is willing to "risk it" in order to maintain the integrity of his daily life. Should you insist, to soothe your own guilt, that he move to a "safe" neighborhood, a sterile existence in your parent's eyes, a life that is prolonged but empty? Parents thus transplanted can become a real burden to their families—and to themselves.

No, say the experts. Leave him where he is if that is what he prefers. But ask him, Are you getting worried about the neighborhood? Would you like to stay where you are? Would you like to move closer to me? Would you like to live with me? Don't ask that last question unless you are willing to share your home. And don't decide that you are willing without thinking through all of the consequences for you, your spouse, your children, and your parent. And don't be surprised if your parent prefers independence in his second-class neighborhood to becoming a second-class citizen in your first-class home.

Survival Techniques

A director of services to the aging in a large city warns about breaking down the defense mechanisms people have spent a lifetime constructing. If your seventy-eight-year-old mother still insists on getting down on her hands and knees to scrub her kitchen floor, don't bug her about it. The exercise is good for her—and so is her feeling that she can still do what she always did. If your eighty-one-year-old father still feels he must walk to the newsstand every day, rain or shine, to buy his daily paper, don't hassle him about it.

When your mother ceases to be interested in her kitchen floor, and your father in the act of walking to get his daily paper, they will both cease to be interested in living. If either falls and breaks a hip in the process of performing these chores which are essential to their spirit and morale, don't overreact. Many aging hips have been broken on bedroom and bathroom floors under more protected circumstances.

"You can't knock down your parents' survival techniques and expect survival," the social worker says. "Your parent may deny the need for help and become hostile. Don't be surprised if that happens."

Housekeeping and independent living may indeed become too overwhelming. Then you should ask, Do you want to leave?

Leave? To where? To what? Here is where the parent, if mentally capable, must participate in the solution. "Children have no right to jump in, take over, and direct all the traffic," says a New York City geriatric specialist. "When they do, they trade one set of problems for another."

It is important to remember that your parent will usually have ambivalent feelings when a change in living considerations is under discussion. If you can recognize some of these feelings—which he or she may not be able to verbalize—that will aid you.[2]

Guilt Is Real

Guilt may appear irrational to the outsider, but it is real and authentic to the person experiencing it. According to Washington psychiatrist Robert Butler, it isn't useful to remonstrate with someone, to tell him not to feel guilty. "That is counterproductive," he says. "Guilt feelings are inevitable." From infancy on, the child demands total care from parents, "but kids don't want to give that kind of care to parents."[3] When parents reach the stage where they need care and the child does not fulfill the demand, the child feels guilty.

Guilt has been called the great civilizing force of mankind. Without it, Freud believed, men would be more greedy, violent, and cruel. It is not pretty to think of ourselves as kind, caring, and responsible only because we are repressing gross and terrible impulses. Beyond this primitive core, however, there is much more involved. Sometimes our guilt derives from feelings of not having lived up to our parents' expectation of us, or from our feeling that we haven't honored our mother and father, or that we haven't lived up to our own idealization of ourselves.

Overreacting

We all feel guilty and vulnerable, and this is when we most frequently overreact. We do so particularly when death separates two parents. The most common overreaction cited by professionals dealing with families who have lost a parent is the tendency to move the remaining parent out of his or her home immediately. Come live with us, or Brother John, or Aunt Sue. Come live in this apartment on the next block. You don't have to do anything. We'll take care of everything for you.

This is a seductive appeal to a newly bereaved person who may or may not have been dependent in many ways on the lost mate but is certainly in shock. Grief-stricken and bewildered, the survivor is rushed away from home, friends, familiar surroundings, activities, and, perhaps, a job, in the interest of doing "the best thing" for mother or father. He or she will not be left alone, but will be in a caretaking arrangement. The caretaker will not experience guilt at the thought of the bereaved's loneliness and will eliminate the necessity of traveling far to give aid and comfort.

Yet, according to geriatric psychiatrists, the bereaved person is being denied individuality, self-determination, and simple human rights, including the right to grieve. The opportunity to try to make his or her own adjustment to the new situation has been removed, as has the right to assess the adjustment after a time and come up with his or her own new equation for living. And you, the guilt-ridden caretaker who has summarily applied the solution, have bought yourself a bundle of troubles.

Role-Reversal

You have also brought to its peak the process of role-reversal which has probably been going on for some years between you and your parents. When you were a small child, your parents were the authorities. They directed you; you respected their wisdom and judgment and had confidence in their ability to make "better" decisions than you. But probably sometime along the way your parents asked you for information, for an opinion, for a judgment. Or, perhaps, unasked, you offered guidance to them. This is part of the beginning of role-reversal, and it generally happens as all parent–child relationships evolve. Sometimes this process achieves a tenable balance—both parent and child give and take in an adult fashion. Sometimes the parent remains a strong authority figure. Sometimes the child takes over completely the role of parent to the parent.[4]

Often a "loving" child can be ruthless, domineering, and controlling, insistent on assuming the parent role. This happens frequently if the child feels guilty.

When adult children overdo this matter of role-reversal, most geriatric specialists feel, they are usurping their parent's decision-making rights and are increasing the parent's dependency. Typically, this happens more frequently with women than with men. Fathers are more frequently left to "adjust." Mothers are moved for "their own good." This attitude may be a hangover from earlier days, when women were regarded as weaker, dependent, and less able to cope on their own. With new attitudes toward women, new attitudes may come toward widows. It is wise to remember, as one psychiatrist says, that "you can't transplant an old plant or an old tree without ill effects. Sometimes the transplant doesn't take."[5] Statistics show a higher mortality rate among older people who are removed from familiar surroundings.

When Role-Reversal Is Required

Obviously there does come a time when role-reversal is required, and a child must make a critical decision: when a parent has a stroke or other disabling disease, when there is chronic brain disease, where there is a physical handicap that prevents self-help and, instead, demands constant outside care and attention. Or a parent may recognize his limitations and seek care himself. Given severe mental or physical deterioration, a caring child will act even if there is resistance from the parents. But the determination should be made only with the advice of

an objective outsider or outsiders—a physician, psychiatrist, social worker, or clergyman.

Money and Guilt

Guilt has another face. A sixty-five-year-old man appeared in
the social service department of a suburban county agency. He
was overcome with anguish. For years he had supported not
only his wife and children but also his mother. Suddenly—or so
it seemed to him—he had turned sixty-five and was required to
retire from his white-collar job. His pension and social security
barely covered expenses for his wife and himself, and inflation
threatened to push them into the ranks of the poverty-stricken.
He felt he had no right to deprive his wife in order to sustain
his mother, but was overwhelmed by a feeling of having failed
his parent. His anguish derived from a feeling that he "should"
continue to care for his mother, his guilt from the knowledge
that he "couldn't."

People with money can have guilt problems, too. Using
money to buy services for one's parents is certainly a way of
dealing with their very real needs—but it is also a way of dealing
with one's own guilt. "Giving money is no action," says a family
service counselor. "The person who is really coping with the
problems of the needful parent, making the decisions and carrying them out, is the major contributor."[6] In some families, it
may be accepted that the oldest child is responsible, and the
other children put all the responsibility on his or her shoulders.
They may give money, but nothing more—no time or energy.
And they will frequently criticize the decisions they have
avoided making. All this can lead to divisive family arguments
to which guilt—conscious or unconscious—is a major contributor.

We've touched on this tender area of feelings—guilt, anguish, and others equally painful—because so many of us share
these feelings, carry them inside us, are reluctant to air them
with our friends and families. If you have these feelings, you
aren't unique and alone; what you feel is real, and whatever
course you choose will be influenced by those feelings. It is up
to you to sort it all out. If you think professional help might be

of assistance to you, seek it out. It's available, and in the next chapter we tell you how to find it and use it.

A Last Reminder

You are in a new role in relation to your parents; you are probably looking over your shoulder at your children and wondering how they will behave toward you when you are older. You may suspect that the way in which you treat your parent now will affect how they will behave to you later. You are not going to be able to rewrite your whole life history in twenty-four hours and erase all the emotional trauma of your relationships with your parents. You should be cautious about taking away all their rights to their own lives; provide help and assistance only as it is requested or really required. You should not be so aloof as to cause harm or grief to them or regret or grief to yourself that neither you nor they can live with—but neither should you rush them into a dependency that is unnecessary and undignified.

You should simply deal with the present reality as thoughtfully and as competently as you can, given the circumstances. Remember always that, whatever happens, the best thing is to take one step at a time; don't overreact, don't overanticipate, don't overindulge. But don't stay clear out of everything, either, when a little tender, loving care can go a long way toward helping them and you—and your guilt.

CHAPTER 2 FINDING HELP IN THE COMMUNITY

Most people, at some point in their later years, enter critical situations where they need help or care that comes from outside their normal life framework. If your widowed father, living five hundred miles away from you, has a cataract operation, that's a minor problem that requires special assistance for a short time. If your eighty-five-year-old mother breaks her hip and can't live alone anymore because she needs a person in attendance whenever she walks, that's a major crisis that necessitates a complete change in her mode of life. As social worker Bertha G. Simos wrote, "The aging of an individual eventually results in a crisis for every family."[1]

There is help for problems such as these, whether they are small or large, and there's help to avert or plan for a crisis that may come. Public and private agencies in your parent's area, which have been substantially expanded in recent years, can help you with trained social workers and informed personnel. They can lead you to many avenues of assistance and support which the community has set up for older people and their families.

How much help is available varies from state to state and community to community, and depends on the amount of money local governments allot to services for the aging and how generous the local population is to the social and philanthropic agencies it supports. The chances are that no single community will provide everything that we will describe. Some will have many; many will have some. Sometimes a service will be open only to older people of limited means. But if you do look into what your community can give, you will at least have explored what help you can get from outside your own and your family's resources, and then you will know what you have to do on your own.

This chapter will cite the public and private agencies through which you can find or receive the help you need. Later chapters will include more detailed discussions of some of these sources for help for those readers requiring more extensive information on the more common problems adult children face in caring for their aging parents.

Make a Beginning

- *Talk to your friends.* They may have been through it. They can tell you about the good people they've dealt with, the ones who can get action. They know the dead ends. Their good and bad experiences can be guides for you.
- *Talk to your doctor and your parent's doctor.* They can help you define the problem and suggest appropriate agencies. A psychiatrist or psychologist may be able to counsel you.
- *Talk to your local religious leader if you belong to a congregation.* The major religious denominations sponsor a full range of social services. Your minister, priest, or rabbi can put you in touch with the right facility. He can also counsel you directly about your emotional and spiritual problems. Many religious leaders have been trained in pastoral counseling and can provide expert guidance on interfamily relationships.
- *Establish contact with a social worker.* Social workers are important links between families and the services or resources they require, and can help you deal with crises and make a plan.

The better informed you are, the better off you will be when you are evaluating the advice you receive and making your decisions.

Private Social Service Agencies

You may find that some of the best services for the aging are sponsored by the major religious denominations and philanthropic organizations. You don't need to be poor to seek the help of a social worker, you don't have to be Jewish to secure counseling from a Jewish family service agency, and you don't have to be Catholic to get help from Catholic Charities. Nor do you have to be an alcoholic or a Bowery bum to utilize the Salvation Army.

Most of these agencies, generally sponsored and maintained by a particular faith, have expanded to become social resources for the entire community. You will also find a Family Service Association, which has no religious affiliation, in almost every major metropolitan area, usually supported in part by United Way or United Givers funds. Help-giving organizations sponsored by religious groups may have a sliding fee scale related to family income, or they may suggest a small donation. Family Service Association fees are elastic, based on income. You will often find that many of these agencies have specialized divisions for services to the aged, whose staff not only can tell you about what help is available for your parent's special needs, and assist you in finding it, but sometimes arrange it for you.

Local Government Agencies

In addition, most localities have established, or are in the process of establishing, commissions or offices or agencies on aging. These are now functioning in all state capitals, as part of the state administration. They are in just about every city of any size, and in every county, even rural ones. These units have pulled together information about all the agencies and organizations in their area offering assistance and support of any kind to older people. Depending on their size, they will have a range of specialists on their staff who should be able to direct you to anything you need.

States, counties, and cities often publish directories of the services they offer to the aged. These can give you a general guide to the services operating in your parent's area and can lead you to more specific information. The local library may have these directories on file. If not, you can call or write to the local commission on aging or the state commission in your state capital, or to the one in your parent's area.

If you're calling from a rural area and can't find relevant

listings in the local phone book, ask the telephone operator if there's a statewide toll-free number you can call for the information you want. Many states with large rural areas have this service. Your call will generally be answered by a social worker or other trained person who can either give you the information you need or connect you directly with the agency where you will find it.

The Administration on Aging in Washington advises, "If you can't get the information you need in any other way, don't be afraid to call your mayor or city or county manager. If he can't answer your question offhand, your query may prod him into finding out just what does or does not exist in the community he is responsible for and motivate him to fill gaps he discovers."

Services of a Social Worker[2]

Any city with a population over 50,000 should have enough social services to help the aged people in its area, says the director of a city-county commission on aging in a large Western state. The problem, he says, is that these services are often not coordinated. You may need great patience to get through to medicaid, community health services, legal and protective services, and other offices in some localities. Usually you will meet with courtesy and helpfulness and will find the information you need, but you may have to spend many hours and make a long series of telephone calls before finding the right person or the information you're seeking.

There's frequent compartmentalization of information in local communities. A worker in the department of human resources may not know what the state's medicaid eligibility requirements are. The person who does know that may not know whether the state department of health can give geriatric evaluation services. The person who knows that may know nothing about the availability of Meals on Wheels, rental allowances, or minibus transportation.

For this reason, you might be best off working with a trained and experienced social worker. It's a simple question of efficiency and of finding with the least hassle the proper answer to the problem. Many middle-class people associate social workers with the poor, welfare, and relief programs. Social workers are trained to help people in crisis, no matter what their economic level. There is no stigma attached to using a social worker. Ask for help where you need it.

Experienced social workers in family and community service organizations, whether they're nondenominational or religiously based, can normally provide you with whatever information you need. They can answer your questions over the telephone because they know what resources are available to you locally. They are also prepared, however, to find with you any positive and actual help you may need. They know what your parent is entitled to from the federal, state, and local governments, and they can get you through all the red tape more easily than you can by yourself. When you are desperate and don't know what to do or when to do something, they can really help.

A social worker can be particularly valuable to you if you live in one place and your ailing parent in another. The social worker can look in on your parent regularly, check what needs to be done for his comfort and convenience, keep you informed, and then make the arrangements you cannot make becuase you're not in residence. If you can afford the fees or the donation this kind of service may require, you will have a degree of peace of mind which you could not otherwise have.

A social worker can help you in your relationship with your parent if this is a concern to you. If you and your parent and other members of the family aren't getting along too well, if you don't understand puzzling aspects of your parent's behavior and attitudes, if there's undue argument or frustration, a social worker will listen to all of you and will try to give you help and counseling.

A social worker can also help you with your feelings about your parent. They may not be obvious to you when you are deeply involved in a period of caretaking, but if they are unpleasant or negative, you will know somehow that you have them, and they may erupt at the wrong moment in a counterproductive manner. Professional counseling may relieve you of some of your anger or fear before these emotions become too large and damaging.

If you ask for it, a social service agency will usually assign a social worker to you and your family. The relationship can be effective if you know how to work together.

What You Should Expect from a Social Worker

- An attitude of warmth, understanding, listening, and accepting. Professional knowledge and experience about human behavior, family relationships, motivation, the social and physical problems of the aged.
- Skilled and sensitive questioning which will help you to describe the situation accurately.
- Help in getting through the bureaucratic channels, in establishing entitlements and benefits, in gaining admission to special programs, residential facilities, and institutions.
- Direct consultation and help for each family member and for the family as a unit while a common solution evolves.
- Help in putting everything together and making a workable plan.
- Emotional support and reassurance for you when you're taking actions that may be necessary but are painful; help for you to deal with this so that you don't tear yourself or your own household apart.

What a Social Worker Should Expect from You

- An honest description of your feelings about your parent and his situation: guilt, misgivings, reluctance.
- An honest description of what you believe your parent's feelings are, what he wants, and his reaction to what is happening.
- An accurate outline of your parent's financial, health, and living conditions.
- An objective description of your parent's personality.
- An honest assessment of the feelings and attitudes of other concerned and involved family members.
- The understanding that the social worker cannot solve the problem immediately. Good solutions take time.

Knowing the true facts of the situation, a social worker can help you put it together effectively. He or she will be able to sense whether you are, perhaps, hurrying a parent prematurely into an inappropriate situation or maintaining him too long in one which is no longer appropriate.

What a Social Worker Should Not Do

- Take over other people's lives.
- Sit in judgment on whether what you are doing is good or bad.
- Be cold and officious or "screen you out" without referring you to a person or agency better equipped to provide the service you need.

Don't expect a social worker to do what you must do yourself or to relieve you of a burden. The hard fact is that once your parent becomes "a burden," either in your mind or in your actual life, he will probably remain so in one way or another until his death. A social worker can help you ease the burden and can be at your side to give you strong help and reassurance with the steps you may have to take.

Help Before the Crisis Comes

Most people don't ask for help until they're in a crisis or are frustrated and fed up. Then they want immediate action, total solutions. This usually isn't possible or reasonable. Placements and supportive living arrangements take time. Many agencies have crisis intervention services, but it's better if you anticipate problems and begin to explore possible solutions with a professional counselor well before the time when the problem presents its acute face.

Obviously, you can't anticipate a heart attack or the onset of cancer or a disabling stroke. But when something like that occurs to your parent, you can surely begin to anticipate and think about the kind of extended care he will need afterward and the changes that may or must come into his life. Nobody wants to anticipate widowhood for a parent, nor the depressive state which sometimes engulfs a widow or widower after death terminates a longtime marriage. But the clues that come at the beginning of a depression can be quite obvious, and sensitive observers can take steps to fend off its intensification. In cases like this, a little advance exploring with a social worker can point out ahead of time some alternative approaches which you can then utilize when you need them.

What to Look for in the Telephone Book

Each community may have different kinds of agencies serving the needs of families and their aging parents, and names may vary slightly in each locality, but in general you will find private helping agencies under these titles:

In the white pages:
- Family Service Agency of (name of city or county)
- Community Service Society of (name of city or county)
- Catholic Charities Family and Community Service
- Jewish Family and Community Service of (name of city or county)
- Protestant Federation of Welfare Agencies (or by denomination: Methodist, Lutheran, et al.)
- The Salvation Army
- The American Red Cross
- Volunteers of America
- Mental Health Association of (name of city or county)

In the yellow pages, look under:
- Health and Welfare Agencies
- Social Service Agencies
- Senior Citizens
- Nursing Services
- Homes for the Aged

If you want information or assistance from a government agency, look in the *white* pages of the telephone book for the name of your city, county, or state government: for example. Portland or Multnomah County or Oregon. Then look within that for a listing for the service you need.

Some Typical Listings for Public Agencies:
- Agency, Commission, or Office on Aging
- Department of Social Services
- Department of Human Resources
- Department of Community Service
- Department of Welfare

- Department of Health
- Department of Housing and Community Development

If you need help with legal problems, call the state or county attorney's office or the corporation counsel in your city. Among the regular listings, look for a Legal Aid Bureau or Society. You'll also find listings, either under local governments or on their own, for food stamps, medicaid, and the Retired Senior Volunteer Program. Federal government agencies will be listed under U.S. Government. There's more detailed information in later chapters about phone calls for a variety of other assistance.

Help in the Home

One of the most common needs of older people is for help in their homes. Your parent may simply need a friendly phone call or a visitor on a regular basis, something volunteer groups in most communities can supply. He may need someone to come into his home for several hours at a time to do the marketing, some cooking, and a few household or personal chores. He may need the part-time service of a nurse. Or he may need someone to care for him full-time. The developing trend now, both through federal legislation and local action, is more and more to extend home services to older people; home care is regarded as more beneficial than institutional care in the great majority of cases, and it is less costly.

With the expansion of this concept, many communities are now working to provide chore and helping services of all kinds to older people. If their incomes are low enough this comes at no cost, or there will be some financial support from the state if their incomes fall within a surprisingly high range above what would qualify them for free services. You can find out easily what your parent's state is offering, and with what income requirements for recipients, by calling the local department of social services or human resources and asking about Title XX (new legislation to provide extra aid for the elderly).

Home Health Care

You may find, however, that your parent's income is too high to qualify him for locally supported services in his home. Then, if he needs help that goes beyond maid or house-cleaning services, there should be private agencies in the community that can provide it for a fee. Look in the *yellow* pages for specialized employment agencies catering to the needs of the elderly.

If the requirement is for a skilled or practical nurse who can give full- or part-time care after an acute illness or a hospital stay, the doctor will recommend a reliable nurse's registry. These are costly caretakers, however, to be used only on a short-term basis, if possible, unless medicare or private health insurance is paying for them.

Should your parent need help over a longer period of time because a chronic condition impedes his ability to meet all the demands of living alone, you may be able to find trained people to help out with the kind of care that's needed. This type of service should be available on a daily basis, or for several days or several hours a week. At best, it can be tailor-made to fit your parent's needs, and there are several levels of trained workers who can supply it. Home-care costs aren't cheap, but sometimes fees can be paid on a sliding scale, and sometimes a state or local agency will pick up part of the costs.

A home health aide will help with bathing, dressing, and personal needs and can perform light nursing services. She will also shop, cook, and do general housekeeping chores. A housekeeper will do all shopping, marketing, and housekeeping chores, will probably help with dressing, but not with nursing. A companion will shop and cook, won't give any physical care, but will try to answer some of the client's social and companionship needs. Fees for services at these levels of care are approximately the same and will depend on the going rate in the locality.

A licensed practical nurse will give injections and medications and will cook for the client. She will be more knowledgeable medically than the kinds of helper just described, more sensitive to the client's health condition and any changes which may occur, and can discuss these with the doctor. Naturally, her fee is higher. But be careful always to look for kind and compassionate people. School credentials and licenses alone are not adequate qualifications when caring for the elderly. In the long run, a warm and nurturing person may do your parent more good than one with impeccable clinical credentials, and may give you greater peace of mind.

There are several national groups with local offices around the country equipped to give this kind of home health care through a roster of trained personnel. Most prefer to supply workers for daytime, rather than for twenty-four-hour, help. Some may have a minimum requirement for the number of daily working hours. And you will certainly find local agencies giving the same kind of home-care services.

Visiting Nurses

The Visiting Nurse Association (VNA), in existence since the turn of the century, is a national voluntary nonprofit agency whose services include home nursing and health care. The VNA charges a fee, but sometimes, by agreement with the client or through contractual arrangements with local social service agencies or departments of health, patients need pay only part of it. Some VNA locals offer programs geared especially to provide custodial care to persons over sixty who have a chronic illness in a stabilized condition; the goal is to maintain older people in their own homes as long as possible. The VNA gives daytime service, generally on a part-time basis.

National Council for Homemaker—Home Health Aide Services

This is another nonprofit organization with about 1,800 affiliated local agencies across the United States. H–HHA offers no nursing care but will send a nursing supervisor to a case to make an evaluation of the kind of care that's needed. Its roster includes personnel trained to perform the duties of part-time homemaker, home health aide, housekeeper, or companion. A new trend in H–HHA locals is focused on supplying chore service: minor home repairs, heavy cleaning, yard and walk maintenance. H–HHA help is normally available in the daytime hours, although some local affiliates are moving toward arrangements for twenty-four-hour care, and some have twenty-four-hour emergency service.

H–HHA workers will care for a sick or disabled person under

the direction of a physician or public health nurse, market and prepare meals for special diets, manage the household, and provide routine care for an older person. As for fees, "Clients are expected to contribute to the cost in accordance with their ability to pay and the cost of care established by the agency at that time." Like the visiting nurses, H–HHA has contracts with public and voluntary agencies which will pick up some of the costs for the individuals they are serving.

Some H–HHA affiliates are adding new services: home-delivered meals, day-care centers for older people, transportation and escort services, convalescent aids.

Homemakers Home and Health Care Services

Operating in about 180 cities nationally, Homemakers Home and Health Care Services is not to be confused with H–HHA, although both provide some of the same kinds of services. This Homemakers is a private operation run by the Upjohn Company, a manufacturer of pharmaceuticals, which took over a number of independent homemaker agencies in 1970 and has added to them since then. The Upjohn Company itself runs some of these local units; others are run under franchise. Supervision, standards, and inspection conform to a national model, but fees differ according to those prevailing in each area, and services differ according to what else is available in a particular area. Services are medically oriented, with nursing services outweighing others, but housekeepers, home health aides, nurses' aides, and companions are available. Home-makers–Upjohn guarantees to replace a worker who is sick or goes on vacation, or whose personality conflicts with that of the older person for whom the worker is caring.

In major metropolitan areas you may also find local private employment agencies specializing in supplying similarly trained workers to care for older people. None of these services is cheap, and their quality will often depend on the standards of the particular agency and the caliber of the particular individual who comes to do the job. As with any other kind of employment, there will be workers who are reliable, attentive, and efficient, and workers who aren't. Some of these agencies will guarantee to replace a worker who is sick or who is on vacation. Often a philanthropic or social service agency in an area will know of a reliable employment service of this kind.

Because all agencies supplying home health care provide part-time service, you should think about using them not only for long-range care but for relief or respite care on a short-term basis. If you have been going to your parent's home every day to perform certain functions, or if your ailing parent lives with you, you can get a substitute through these agencies for part of a day, a week, or a month. You may need to go out of town; you may want to go on a vacation; you may just need a few hours' break. Think of these agencies as flexible, even if sometimes expensive, help.

"It pays to have someone who is impersonal come in from time to time," says the director of a large-city agency. "A daughter often can't persuade her mother to do something for the mother's good, but outside help might be able to. An impersonal, kindly person can do better with an older patient, and it gives relief to whoever is taking regular care of the patient."[3]

Don't assume, once you've made the proper caretaking arrangements for your parent, that you're finished and can relax totally. Follow-up is essential. Even if the person who is employed is reliable, she or he may not be compatible. You may have to try two or three different people before you've made the best choice, and, no matter how satisfied you are with your selection, be sure you have made arrangements for emergency backup help.

Telephone Reassurance Program

If your parent is independent and able to live at home without help, but is lonely, he may need a friendly telephone call or a visitor on a regular basis from time to time. These are aids almost any community, small or large, can supply. Volunteer workers in senior citizens' centers, many church and fellowship groups, and Red Cross units are organized to do this. You can arrange for someone to telephone your parent once a day or once every few days through the Telephone Reassurance Program, and for someone to visit once or twice a week.

One wealthy New York family tells a story about a grandmother in Minneapolis who refused to give up her big house and move close to either of her children (one on each coast), or to move to a warmer climate. The family was concerned that the heavy winter snows would isolate this independent eighty-year-old woman at a time when she might need help urgently. They paid a woman to telephone her each day, morning and evening, to check on her needs and whereabouts, although she resented the intrusion on her privacy. When the paid telephoner arranged for prompt snow shoveling and plowing with each new snow last winter, however, and had some groceries delivered on a bad day, the grandmother grudgingly agreed that having a telephone companion wasn't a bad idea. Now she has a new friend.

In some localities the police will call an older person living alone once every twenty-four hours, just to check on his well-being. Check the agency on aging in your parent's area or the local police department.

Meals for the Homebound or the Lonely

There are all kinds of reasons why older people who can afford to eat three good meals a day don't, but one of the major reasons is their tendency to make do with less and less when they are eating alone. The recently widowed woman, formerly a great dinner-party giver, suddenly becomes ill and depressed, and the doctor finds she's suffering from malnutrition. She will accept invitations, but not give them. She lives on cookies and crackers, a cup of tea, an occasional glass of milk. An elderly man, living in a single room in a big Eastern city, tells his children when they telephone from their Midwestern home that he's fine; he is, in fact, gaunt and hungry, becoming confused and frail for lack of proper nourishment. It is a good idea to check on the eating habits of very old people; you may be shocked to find that your parent is actually poorly nourished. (See Chapter 3 for more on this subject.)

Fortunately, most communities now offer help in two ways: through home delivery of Meals on Wheels for the frail and handicapped, or in social settings at a central community place for those who can leave their homes.

If there are Meals on Wheels or similar services in your parent's area, the telephone directory will list them, or check with your parent's clergyman, a nearby senior center, or the YMCA. These programs, designed to bring balanced, nutritious meals to homebound older people, are often supported by both federal and local funds. Sometimes Meals on Wheels delivers at noon two meals for that day—a dinner to be eaten hot on delivery and a cold supper for the evening. Sometimes only one meal is delivered. There's a modest charge for people who can afford to pay, but frequently the state will pay part of the cost. Food stamps can be used to pay for these meals.

Some communities have even started a "market on wheels," to bring the supermarket to the old person who can't get out himself to shop in a store. A truck, with its shelves and bins stocked with all kinds of foods, services neighborhoods where there are heavy concentrations of older inhabitants.

Help Outside the Home: Meals

Congregate or communal meals are for the older person who is capable of leaving his home and who needs the social exchange that breaks up loneliness and isolation. Offered through the National Nutrition Program for the Elderly, a solid meal once a day is provided for the solitary older person whose interest in cooking and eating has waned. The communal setting stimulates enjoyment of eating, and the substantial meal backstops the fragmented nutrition an older person tends to supply to himself. Administrators of the nutrition programs report that about one-third of the elderly people who enjoy communal meals are above the poverty level, and they even include some lonely millionaires. Those who can afford to pay for the meals, do, while those who cannot pay are given meals free. The dining rooms are housed in a variety of places—schools, churches, senior citizens' centers—in order to have them easily accessible for the older person. Often some form of sponsored transportation will bring the older person to the dining place and then return him to his home.

Transportation Help

Local governments and church and other groups offer a variety of transportation services to the aged. There may be regularly scheduled minibuses following planned routes to take older people for weekly shopping and recreational excursions and visits to senior citizens centers. Volunteer drivers, organized by some of these groups, will chauffeur for visits to doctors and other health-related trips and for other necessary expeditions.

Some communities have medicabs, health cabs, or invalid coaches, vehicles specially outfitted to permit a person in a wheelchair to be rolled in directly. They may have automatic lifts or steps so that the handicapped can enter without having to make any climbing movements. Hospitals and rehabilitation centers, the Red Cross, or a volunteer ambulance corps may offer these vehicles. Be sure to check on the availability of this service before you or other family members engage in cumbersome lifting for a handicapped parent. Communities will frequently have a dial-a-bus or a dial-a-cab service for older people, and a telephone call in advance will bring transportation to the door. Costs may not be too great because this special transportation for the aged is often partly supported by state money.

Senior Citizens' and Day-Care Centers

There are thousands of senior citizens' centers all over the country. Equipped to provide social and recreational opportunities for older people, they offer everything from the ubiquitous bingo game to organized travel, from adult education courses to volunteer and paid job connections. They're located in churches, in local recreation department buildings, in apartment houses and complexes. Look in the phone book under Senior Citizens' Centers or call the local office on aging to find a convenient center. Older people whose energy, abilities,

and social needs require continuing outlets are finding fulfill-
ing activities and companionship every day of the week. "It's
my lifeline," said one user of a Brooklyn senior citizens' center,
and many of her fellow participants feel the same way.

Day-care centers represent a new development that is beginning to take hold. They are especially valuable for the older
person who cannot be alone all day—whether he lives in his
own home or whether he lives in a household where other
family members work or are in school. These centers provide
the physical care and rehabilitation therapy required by older
people with chronic illnesses in order to keep them in their
homes and out of institutions as long as possible. The older
person is brought to the center each morning, either by the
person who cares for him or through the transportation arrangements day-care centers sometimes offer. He is returned
to his home at the end of the day. In his time at the center he
has had the benefit of its sophisticated facilities and services
and, in addition, some companionship and social activity.
There aren't too many in the country today, but their number is
growing as their value to both the older person and his family
becomes apparent. An increasing number of nursing homes
now offer day-care programs to residents in their localities.
In addition, more hospitals and rehabilitation centers are now
providing day care. Check into your community.

Housing: Where Can My Parent Live?

Proper housing for an aging parent is a universal and over-
riding concern. It can also be a problem you will face more than
once as your parent's situation may change. A suddenly
widowed parent living in a seven-room suburban house may
need more manageable quarters; public transportation cutbacks and closing stores in a changing neighborhood may indicate a move to an area where these services exist so your parent
can continue to maintain independent living; physical incapacity may demand a setting with built-in services.

At any of these watershed points, you will want to investigate
carefully to find suitable housing. If your parent has no special
needs, you may find a solution through what the community

normally offers—an apartment in town within walking distance of necessary stores and recreational facilities, a suburban apartment with bus service at the door. But you may need to look for something designed more directly for the older person.

More and more now, you will find a variety of special housing for the elderly, ranging from totally independent living to arrangements for the most sheltered housing, sponsored by the local city or county government or privately operated.

In cities, suburbs, and surrounding areas, retirement villages and communities offer a homogeneous citizenry, an active social program, and maintenance for homes. There may be lifetime-care complexes, where the entering older person can move into a completely independent setup and then, as he requires more assistance, move through varying levels of support to complete care.

Residences designed for older people will sometimes be developed by private investors or religious and philanthropic groups, but they will often be city- or county-supported. Many are attractive new high-rise apartment buildings with accommodations in efficiency and one-room apartments for older people of both low and moderate incomes. Some are older buildings that have been renovated specifically to suit the physical needs of older residents. They may have wide doors, ramps, grab rails in bathrooms, efficiently arranged kitchenettes; some housing may be only for the physically handicapped. Residences for low-income tenants will place a ceiling on income and assets, and those for moderate-income residents may have higher financial limitations. There may or may not be a requirement for previous residency in the area. Monthly rents can range from a percentage of the resident's income to around $500, depending on the facilities offered and the size of the apartment. Many buildings maintain active recreation and social programs and may require that occupants take at least one meal a day in the apartment house dining room.

The local housing authority or community development agency will probably have information about just what housing arrangements exist in the area for older people. These agencies can probably also tell you, if your parent has a low income, whether he's eligible for a rent grant or subsidy. In addition, there may be a housing relocation authority to help with suggestions, especially if your parent needs to move quickly.

The local office or commission on aging will almost surely have a directory of all levels and types of special housing for older people, describing the facilities, requirements, and costs of each particular residence. The social service agencies can also help with information. Often a social worker from such an agency, or one who is in private practice, can investigate with you and advise you. Even if this necessitates paying a small fee, it would be worthwhile help.

You might especially want to have the assistance of a social worker if you're looking into a nursing home. These often appear better in brochures and on paper than they actually are, and even a visit or a series of visits may not reveal the true quality of the atmosphere and services you would want for your parent. Nursing homes are licensed by state departments of health, and your county or city health department will give you a list of all approved homes in its area. Then you can investigate.

You will find more information on all kinds of housing in Chapter 9, and on nursing homes in Chapter 4.

Legal Assistance

Older people, through confusion, loneliness, or simply lack of information, tend more than others to put themselves into situations where they may be victimized and require legal help. When you and your parent are some distance apart, you may be concerned that he not get himself into some legal bind or be duped because of negligence or ignorance. Perhaps the landlord is insisting on a rent increase of major proportions, despite local rent-control restrictions, or is changing the terms of the lease by eliminating free gas and electricity. Or perhaps a door-to-door salesman has convinced your parent to sign up for the purchase of an appliance or service with seemingly small monthly payments but expensive credit arrangements.

If there's a family lawyer at hand, he may be able to give the counsel which will straighten out the situation. If there isn't one, you and your parent can find competent legal help without much difficulty.

The local county or city bar association should have a lawyer-reference service which can give you the names of several reputable lawyers. When you telephone the service, you should indicate the area in which you need legal advice—a tax problem, making a will, advising on a contract—and you will be given the names of one or two lawyers who are knowledgeable in that field. Then you can select one and make an appointment for your parent or yourself. In large metropolitan areas, lawyers' fees for a client who is referred in this manner will normally range from around $10 to $20 for the first half-hour conference. Each bar association sets its own standard fee for this service. The lawyer will have his own fees for subsequent visits, and you or your parent must be sure to ask him during the first conference what that will be so that you will know exactly the cost of future legal services.

If your parent needs a lawyer but can't pay for services, there are several avenues to try. Look in the telephone book for a local Legal Aid Bureau or Society; these will give free legal advice, but may, perhaps, do so only for people below certain income levels. Law schools often have a legal assistance service which gives free advice, and there may be other legal services in your area, sponsored by local public interest or philanthropic groups, which can aid you.

In Los Angeles, for example, there is a walk-in clinic sponsored by the Jewish Family Service where a broad range of paralegal services is available to people who just walk in off the street: help in tracking down the Veterans Administration benefits accruing to a mother after her son died in the service; help in writing a letter concerning an inheritance that had been improperly distributed; help in telephoning a local company which refused to replace a faulty appliance. The major social service agencies can also help arrange for these paralegal services, or for proper legal counsel to defend an elderly person in an action or to bring suit when it is required. Your best bet is to call the local agency on aging, which will either have a legal and protective division for services to the elderly or refer you to such a service. Bear in mind that if legal services are free from any agency, they may be only for low-income people.

Financial Assistance

Your parent's local government may very well be able to help him financially or with some free services he may require. Older people who want to buy a new home or adapt an old one to their current physical abilities can, in many localities, get low-interest loans for mortgage or remodeling payments. If your low-income parent is living in a rented house or apartment, he might be eligible for a rent grant or subsidy. The local housing authority can tell you about this.

In many cities and counties, older people who are receiving supplementary security income (SSI) or other kinds of public-assistance payments, or whose social security or pension check is small, can qualify for additional free benefits: many kinds of care and assistance in their homes and a wide range of social and medical services. They might also be eligible for cash grants to help with their monthly living expenses. If your parent's only income comes from a social security or pension check which is delayed or lost, and if he is out of money, a local agency may lend him some temporarily to tide him over the immediate financial crisis.

Police departments in some localities have emergency funds to give to older people who have been robbed and left without cash.

Health and Medical Assistance (see also Chapters 6, 7 and 8)

The greater number of communities will offer a large spectrum of medical assistance in addition to that provided by private physicians and hospitals. Many will have city or county hospitals and clinics where patients are treated at no cost or for a small fee; some hospitals and clinics will give free dental care. There may be mobile medical units which will give free general medical care and refer patients to doctors who are specialists in certain areas.

Ear, eye, nose, and throat examinations are often available at no cost; this is true also of blood-pressure screening and chest X rays. Sometimes there is free emergency dental service. City and county health departments may provide services in many ways to older people who have chronic conditions: arthritis, blindness, deafness, stroke, diabetes, and others. If your parent suffers from such a condition, he can surely get counseling and specific aids in learning to live with his condition.

If transportation is the obstacle to medical care for your parent, you will probably find that some agency or agencies in his community will provide it either on a regular or a need basis for trips to a doctor, to a clinic, or to another health-related service (see page 34).

If your parent reaches a point where you are wondering whether he can still be maintained in his home, either for physical or psychological reasons, there may be a geriatric evaluation team organized by the state department of health or department of social services which will examine him thoroughly, make a diagnosis and a prognosis, recommend the proper environment for him, and map out a course of treatment and care.

To find any of these resources, call the local department of health.

National Health Agencies

It's likely that your parent has a specific medical problem; surveys show that most people over sixty-five should be or are under treatment for an average of three chronic conditions. For many of these, your parent can supplement his physician's medical treatment with help from local chapters of national health agencies specializing in research and assistance for particular diseases. (See the Appendix.)

Cancer Care, Inc., an activist arm of the National Cancer Foundation, helps with counseling, guidance, home care, and financial aid to advanced cancer patients and their families living within a fifty-mile radius of New York City. The American Cancer Society, through its local units spread across the country, gives similar assistance: dressings, rehabilitation services, financial help, counseling, transportation to and from treatment centers. It may also supply homemakers at no cost to the needy.

Other examples of national organizations whose local arms may be able to help you: the American Diabetes Association; the National Lung Association (formerly the National Tuberculosis and Respiratory Disease Association); the American Heart Association; the Arthritis Foundation; the American Foundation for the Blind; the Association for the Visually Handicapped. These may give nutrition counseling, tests, education in learning how to live with an illness or disability, equipment loans, and other services.

If you can't find a listing for these or similar organizations in your phone book, try the nearest American Red Cross office. They may be able to direct you. The Red Cross, as a matter of fact, may be able to help your parent in other ways, depending on the spread of services in each local chapter. Look into these possible helps from the Red Cross: transportation to doctors, clinics, rehabilitation services, shopping; Meals on Wheels; friendly visitors to the homebound; telephone reassurance to shut-ins. Some Red Cross chapters give courses to older people to train them as homemakers, home health aides, companion aides, nursing assistants, and patient-sitters. Your parent may be interested either as a potential trainee or as a user of trained personnel.

Don't overlook local chapters of fraternal, benevolent, and interest organizations, whether your parent is a member or not. Many have strong public-service-oriented volunteer programs, and you may find help there for transportation, friendly visitors, telephone reassurance, and other needs. Check out, for example, the Elks, Kiwanis, Rotarians, Junior Chamber of Commerce, Altrusa, or B'nai B'rith—depending on what groups are active locally.

Emotional Problems

In well-populated regions you will generally find community mental health or psychiatric clinics staffed by trained social workers, psychologists, and psychiatrists. They can give counseling to individuals and families for emotional and behavior

problems or simply for the difficulties of getting along together, which often intensify as the generations trying to get
along together grow older. These clinics are sometimes supported in part by United Way or United Givers funds, and their
fees are based on a sliding scale related to income. You can find
them by calling local social services departments or United
Way. You may even find a free mental health clinic in the
community.

Remember that social service agencies can generally give you
and your parent counseling by a trained social worker or can
refer you to a psychiatrist, psychologist, or social worker in
private practice who can work with you. In most cities and
counties, there is a Mental Health Association which can refer
you to qualified professionals, and the local hospital will have a
psychiatric staff from whom you can select someone to talk to.
And, obviously, you can get recommendations through your
doctor and your friends. There are also pastoral counseling
centers, staffed by clergymen trained in counseling and
therapeutic techniques. (Some medical insurance policies will
cover therapy and counseling costs under certain conditions.)

Well-populated areas will surely have some kind of counseling hot line—a telephone number you can call twenty-four
hours a day, seven days a week, for immediate information and
help or for actual crisis intervention. This would be listed in the
telephone book as Hot Line.

Widows and Widowers

Special needs arise when a long-married couple is suddenly
separated by death. Grief, loneliness, financial problems, estate
tangles face many newly widowed people, men and women
alike. Capitalizing on the experience of Alcoholics Anonymous,
several social service agencies sponsor counseling sessions for
the recently bereaved; these meetings are led by other widows
or widowers. The emotional support comes from people who
really understand what it's like, and the advice that is offered is
credible. Some of the groups provide practical help about legal
and financial matters, housing decisions, job counseling, and
family relationships.

To find a group in your parent's vicinity, look in the telephone book. The local mental health association, the Y's, the Family Service Association's Widows and Widowers groups are all possible avenues of support for your widowed parent. Some local divisions on aging have established a Widowed Person's Service. To ease the transition to an altered life; the retirement associations offer booklets which answer questions on dealing with grief, moving to a new home, preparing for life without a partner. (See the Appendix.)

Work and Recreation

You will find considerable detail about avenues to paid work, volunteer work, and recreational activities in Chapter 9, but here are a few tips which can lead your parent to sources in his community.

For paid or volunteer work:

- Check to see if there's a Senior Citizens' Employment agency in your parent's area, or a Senior Personnel Placement Office which has information about part-time, full-time, and seasonal jobs.
- For volunteer work, look up ACTION under U.S. Government in the local phone book or write to the address listed in the Appendix. Under this government-sponsored operation are the Foster Grandparent Program, Retired Senior Volunteer Program (RSVP), Service Corps of Retired Executives (SCORE), Volunteers in Service to America (VISTA), and Senior Companion program.
- ACTION and a Senior Citizens' Employment agency will know of other local volunteer programs organized for older people.

For recreation and enjoyment:

- The local department of recreation can tell you about cultural, recreational, and local volunteer activities in which your parent might be interested.
- Many public library systems will deliver books, records, and paintings to the homebound.

- There may be special radio programming with which your visually handicapped parent can connect. These bring news and feature programs to those who can't watch television or read newspapers. Many communities also have special television programs for the deaf.

Communication Aids

- By calling the local post office, your parent can get an order form for buying stamps or stamped envelopes by mail.
- Some local telephone companies have an economy service for people who don't make many outgoing calls but need a telephone for security or emergency reasons. The rate is generally about half the regular local monthly home telephone rate. The telephone subscriber may receive an unlimited number of calls for the basic monthly rate, but is charged at a low rate for each outgoing call. This system could be useful if your parent has to be economical with money but, at the same time, also needs checkup, reassurance, or just friendly calls.
- Almost all telephone companies can install mechanical equipment on the telephone of a person who has a hearing loss. The phone company puts an amplifier on the telephone receiver which the subscriber can adjust to the level at which he can hear. A flickering light can be added, also, to attract the attention of the eye when the bell rings. There's an installation charge for this and a monthly fee of around a dollar. The phone company can also install a telephone bell in rooms which don't have a phone, so that the person will hear the ring no matter where he is. There's a small monthly charge for this, too. Check the local telephone company to see what services it has and at what cost. These vary with the locality.
- Other states may have instituted a Senior Citizens Hot Line, like New York's, which operates toll-free, statewide, Monday through Friday, and is plugged into a tape recorder at all other times. The Hot Line connects the caller to the agency which can answer his question in any area of the needs of the aging.

- Rent-a-kid. Some communities have a roster of local teen-agers who will carry bundles home after shopping trips and do small chores and errands. Check the local commission on aging or the nearest high school.

National Organizations of Older People

A number of national organizations of retired and older people can give some kinds of support to your parent through the feeling of belonging to a group of peers. Since these organizations represent large numbers of very active, fairly enlightened senior citizens, association with them can, at a minimum, be a healthy experience. There might even be some more concrete benefits.

Most lobby actively before Congress and state legislatures on national and local issues affecting older people, an activity which may not help your parent in dealing with his immediate problems but which has certainly affected past legislation benefiting older people and will surely continue to do so even more impressively. Membership in any of these groups costs only a few dollars a year and definitely gives a sense of being in touch with other older people across the country through each organization's regular and upbeat publications. They offer such other benefits as reduced travel and car rental prices, information on retirement and nursing homes, and discounts on drugs bought through their pharmacies.

The American Association of Retired Persons (AARP) and its affiliate National Retired Teachers Association (you don't have to be retired to join) has the largest membership—close to eight million nationally. The National Council of Senior Citizens, composed of over three thousand older people's clubs across the country, is the next largest. Senior Advocates International is the smallest. If you'd like to find out more about these organizations and whether local affiliates exist in your parent's vicinity, write to the national office. All are in Washington, D.C., and all addresses are listed in the Appendix.

If your parent is interested in working with the professionals in the field of aging, he or she can become an individual member of the National Council on the Aging (NCOA). NCOA provides research information, technical assistance, and re-source services to other groups and organizations dealing with the aged. NCOA publications highlight current issues for pro-fessional workers in the field of aging, and periodically list a selected bibliography of current literature. National confer-ences bring thousands of professionals together with legislative and community leaders to stimulate positive social and political action for the aging population. If your parent enjoys putting intellectual and creative energies or organizational experience to work in this field, NCOA welcomes individual participation.

While NCOA is an umbrella organization, there are other specialized groups in the field which might be of particular interest. The National Caucus on the Black Aged is an advocacy organization to improve the quality of life for older black people. The Gray Panthers, a fairly new, highly activist organi-zation headquartered in Philadelphia, is represented in about two dozen cities. Members are both old and young. The group has the same lobbying goals as other national organizations of older people and, in addition, devotes much of its energy to combating age discrimination in such areas as housing and re-tirement policies.

Rural Area Services

Although a large proportion of the country's aged live in high-population, nonrural states, the proportion of the aged to the general population is greater in rural areas. In other words, there are proportionately more over-sixty-five people living in rural areas, with proportionately fewer younger people to help out.

In addition to a scarcity of helpful neighbors, rural regions have a great scarcity of doctors and of public transportation, essential needs of the old. In close to 150 rural counties, there is no doctor at all. More than 150 counties are without any public transportation. Religious and voluntary agencies, with their sometimes ample spread of services, may not exist in rural areas. And the services that come from the state may be more profuse in well-populated areas and, like the tree branches which stretch out farthest from the roots, slimmer in the rural reaches.

One positive factor, which doesn't exist in urban areas, is that there are proportionately more wives in rural areas than there are widows. This means that the incidence of two-person older families, where one person can care for the other, if needed, is greater than in the widow-heavy metropolitan areas.

Although many people in government and in farmers' organizations are working on such major problems of the rural elderly as transportation and housing, they have met consistently with great frustration, largely because funds aren't available. They are starting to take some small hope now from the fact that city people are beginning to return to the country; they know that services generally follow people.

Nevertheless, rural counties do have social, medical, and volunteer supporting services, even though they may not be so numerous or so accessible as their urban and suburban counterparts. If you have a parent in a rural community living alone or needing help and you live at a distance, you may be perplexed about whether to move your parent close to you. But investigation may show that you can get him the help he needs through the resources in his own locality. Specific help for specific problems can be sought from:

- Your parent's minister, priest or rabbi, who can counsel you about how to deal with nagging problems and may help you decide whether it's time to move your parent into town, into a supervised residential setting, or near you. He might help arrange for an able parishioner to make regular calls or visits to your weakened parent, perform some housekeeping or chore services, sleep overnight.
- The county social services, human resources, or welfare department, for information about medicare, medicaid, SSI, food stamps, local supporting services, and other state and federal government programs.
- The county health department, which will try to arrange for special care and help in the home, may have mobile units which bring certain health services to distant residents, and can provide other medically related services and facilities. Some rural counties often have a comprehensive health center, and more of these are being developed. "We're going in the direction of providing primary treatment and emer-

gency treatment centers with transportation to bring people to them," says Dr. George Bragaw of the U.S. Public Health Service.[4] The county health department should also know about nursing homes in the area, since these are licensed by state departments of health.

• Farmers' organizations such as the Grange, whose 5,500 chapters conduct a range of volunteer activities: transportation, reassurance telephone calls, and friendly visitors, Meals on Wheels, clinics for eye and hearing tests. Green Thumb, administered by the Farmers Union and operating in twenty-five states, trains older people and finds jobs for women as homemakers and nurse's aides, for men as carpenters, renovators, and refurbishers.

Cooperative Extension Service

The rural elderly can get a lot of help from the U.S. Department of Agriculture's Cooperative Extension Service, with which they have been dealing in one way or another for most of their lives. The well-trained and competent home economists who are part of the Extension Service have been working increasingly on programs for older people.

A county home economist is a good source for almost any kind of information you may need. "One responsibility of our home economists is to know what services are available in a rural community and to help people get to them," says Jeanne Priester, who works out of Washington for the Extension Service. She cites the Service's Community Resources Development units, whose role is to "get groups together, help them identify major needs in their county, and then help organize the things that are needed."[5]

The county home economist should be able to tell you about food stamps and financial and medical help for your parent. She should know what recreational activities are at hand, either through a nearby senior citizens' center or through church and interest groups. She may also know about opportunities for volunteer work and about educational courses your parent can take at a minimum cost. If there's organized transportation for older people in the area, she'll know about that, too. Many rural counties have a special transportation setup for older residents. Sometimes it's manned by volunteers in their own cars; sometimes it's an organized bus or minibus system. With most of these, the user pays a small charge and must call in advance to make his reservation for the trip he wants to take. Then he will be given door-to-door service.

The specific services Extension home economists provide are different in each state. All are trained to give nutrition education, counseling, and demonstration, and to help organize a household for the needs of the older person. Many, now, are teaching money management to older rural residents, talking about insurance needs and selection, wills and estates, the legal aspects of retirement, consumer education. In addition, they are providing preventive health service through eye and hearing examinations and blood-pressure screening. "Many of the needs of the elderly can be met with increased knowledge," Priester believes.

Through local units of the National Extension Homemakers Council, an organization of volunteer women advised by the Cooperative Extension Service home economists, the rural aged can often find other helps: congregate or community meals taken at a local site, Meals on Wheels brought to the home, transportation on a volunteer basis, daily reassurance phone calls either by volunteers or by other older people living in the area.

In some rural counties there's been a MAC program operating—Maintenance of the Aged in their Communities— with the cooperation of the Extension Service. These programs train paraprofessionals to go right into the homes of the aged, work with them and for them, teaching them to live independently in their own homes. Funding for MAC programs has been cut, but some are still in existence. Perhaps there's one in your parent's area.

Long-Distance Rural Help

If your problem-plagued parent is living in a rural area and you're living at a distance apart, you can make a telephone call or write a letter to try to get the information and help that you both need. There's a lot you can do long-distance, without being right on the spot. Remember about the statewide, toll-free telephone number you can call for help on the needs of older people. Remember that long-distance caretaking of older parents is a common phenomenon now, and helping agencies are accustomed to it. Most states and counties are prepared to provide some help, and between you and them you can work out a living pattern for your rural parent.

Follow-Up

Follow-up is essential for all the services you want and for all those you actually get.

Bureaucratic agencies are sometimes rigid, often disorganized. Employees might not look for loopholes or the small print unless you prod them. If a social security spokesperson tells you your mother doesn't qualify for certain benefits, don't give up until you have talked to a second and perhaps a third person. Records get lost; forms aren't signed. Your parent's doctor may have forgotten to sign the forms required to obtain certain services; if he has signed them, his nurse may have overlooked sending them on. People are busy and need to be reminded. Push for everything you would like to have. After you're told that you'll have it, watch to be sure you get it. Don't be afraid to be a pest.

CHAPTER 3
IMPROVING THE QUALITY OF YOUR PARENT'S LIFE

You cannot become the total focus of your parent's life, nor should you try. You are not the companion who has departed, the social and physical stimulus, the beginning and end of the day. But if you spend a part of your time organizing some reasonable way for your parent to interact with you and the family, with the community and a few friends, to live in a better place or improve his nutrition, his appearance, or his safety, then you can spend your own time free of the nagging feeling of having done nothing or of the repressed guilt that accumulates when you, in fact, do nothing. You can be an important influence in the quality of your parent's life. This chapter suggests approaches which can help you to make your parent's life better than it is.

Morale

Morale is a tricky thing. It is a reflection of each person's perception of himself and his world. Your parent's perception of his own world may be quite different from the way you perceive it, and arguing about it won't change the way either of you feels. But sometimes you can change the conditions which lower your parent's morale or create new conditions which will increase it.

In a study conducted some years ago in San Francisco, a group of elderly people listed the factors they believed influenced their morale. While these listings may not coincide precisely with your parent's view, they can be a clue if you're trying to improve the quality of his life. Factors which these elderly people considered as conducive to high morale, listed in order of importance, were entertainment and diversion, socializing, productive activity, physical comfort (other than health), financial security, mobility and movement, health, stamina, and survival. The most significant causes of low morale were financial or physical dependency, physical discomfort or sensory loss, loneliness, bereavement or loss of nurturance, boredom, inactivity, immobility and confinement, mental discomfort or loss, loss of prestige or respect, fear of dying, and problems of others.[1]

It's beyond your ability, no matter how much you care, to change some of these factors in your parent's life. But there are small things you can do which may be really big things for him and can raise his morale substantially.

Your attitude, of course, comes first. Try to see things from your parent's point of view. How you go about offering help will have a great deal to do with maintaining your parent's self-respect and dignity. If your mother has said, "Wait until it happens to you," perhaps you have affronted her by being insensitive to her dignity. Dignity is involved in many of the factors listed in the study. It has to do with self-image.

Respect, on the other hand, has to do with someone else's attitude toward you. If your mother is in good shape and you treat her like a simpleton by insisting that she read all the nutrition information that she probably knows already, she may be rightly offended. If your father is in full command of his business or professional life and you give him retirement advice out of a pamphlet, he may well think you're the simpleton. In each case, you would not have treated your parent with the respect you should have. If either of them were becoming frail or more dependent on you, the information and assistance might be more appropriate, but it should be given sensitively. The best-intentioned child in the world sometimes has an insulting way of talking down to an older parent.

A real-estate agent recently visited the home of an eighty-year-old woman who was preparing to sell. The agent spotted a sampler on the wall. Surrounded by cross-stitched flowers, the mottoes cautioned the elderly owner to keep her mouth shut, give advice only when asked, smile a lot, make no trouble for others, help other people, never complain, cook good things to eat, and have no opinions.

In posting these rules for herself, this elderly lady was acceding to the American stereotype which implies that good relationships between the generations depend on the graceful behavior of the older person. A child in trouble is almost always welcome in a parent's house, no matter how old the child or how old the parent. The nurturing role of the parent continues. A parent in trouble is not always that welcome in a child's house; his presence interferes with the child's ongoing life. When the child must become the nurturer, he often finds the role psychologically uncomfortable and physically inconvenient. Annoyance and condescension are the frequent unhappy results.

Communications Breakdown

All of us have experienced communications breakdowns in talking to other people. Sometimes one person hasn't concentrated on a part of the conversation; his thoughts were elsewhere. Sometimes one person truly hasn't heard something the other has said.

These two conditions are especially common in conversations between parent and adult child, who often don't want to hear what the other is saying and use wandering thought as a protective device to block it out. Sometimes the relationship at which the adult child and the parent finally arrive is one huge communications breakdown. It's a situation where built-in attitude confronts built-in attitude. They talk, but nothing is conveyed. Nobody is penetrating anyone's mind, nobody is exchanging anything.

How many of us, faced with complaints that seem incessant, tend to discount these complaints and insist that an act of will on our parent's part will make everything better? The emotion-laden confrontation between the impatient offspring and the tearful or wounded parent is not unfamiliar to many of us. Our inability to cope with the situation without feeling totally frustrated often turns us away completely. Even if we cannot make the situation perfect, we can, in some ways, make it better. Trying to make it better in reasonable ways is one method of dealing with our own guilt.

The way in which you talk and listen to your parent is very important. If you and he are communicating honestly, you can add a great deal to his life and take away a great shadow from your own. If you have been accustomed to frank and open dialogue since you were a child, you are probably continuing this now that you're an older adult. This makes everything much easier. So when your parent says, "I don't feel well," you know that he really doesn't feel well, and you can sympathize and make suggestions. You know he's not saying it because he's angry at you, or about something else, or as a device to gain the attention or sympathy he doesn't think you're giving him.

Bad communications between parent and child probably start early in the child's life. Sometimes they never get better. But since communications between you and your parent become more essential to him as he grows older and others with whom he was close move away or die, it's really important that you find good channels for talking to each other.

You may be glued into a pattern of communication which frustrates both of you. You may be like the Seattle lawyer who is concerned that his lonely mother doesn't leave her house much for recreation and rages at her over the long-distance telephone when she answers his first question with, "Well, I didn't go out of the house yesterday or today, either." Or you may be like the Milwaukee housewife who is miserable because of the intrusive behavior of her eighty-five-year-old father who lives with her. She says, "I wouldn't dream of telling him how I feel or of talking to him about it."

Perhaps your mother asks question after question about you, your spouse, and your children. She's prying, you tell yourself, just the way she always pried about your friends and your dates and your life. You clam up. Or you get angry. Perhaps your father complains about his doctor, talks ceaselessly about his health. You're bored and don't respond. Or you get angry. It's likely that the less you respond, the more they'll talk in the same vein. Beneath their monologues lies real fear that their futures may be dark, and an almost frantic need for reassurance and affection from you. They are trying to communicate it.

When You Talk to Your Parent

The eighty-five-year-old man was confined to his home. He could walk with difficulty from room to room. Poor eyesight prevented much reading or television, but his mind was keen, his reactions lively. His son, who lived nearby, came to visit at the same time as his daughter, who had driven in from a city 250 miles away. The daughter, saddened by her father's physical infirmities, said little. The son talked. He talked about his wife and his children, about two interesting law cases on which he was working, about several of his office colleagues, about recent encounters with law school classmates whom his father had known. The father listened, commented, responded, reacted.

"You're marvelous," the sister said to her brother after they left the father's home. "You tell him everything. Why do you do it?"

"I'm trying to bring some of the world to him," the brother said. "I know he can't get to it any other way."

Much of the world has left your parent, too, but you can bring part of it back. Talk to your parent about what's happening in the world; except in cases of extreme impairment, your parent will have as much interest as he had when he was younger. Nursing homes with good social programs find that discussion groups on current events and issues draw people out of their rooms and make even the most withdrawn older resident respond.

Give your parent news about your own family. Don't feel you have to protect him totally from your problems or those of your spouse or children. By bringing him the news of your life, you assure him he is still needed, still has the resources to be a parent, and, possibly, can even help with your problems. If he is very ill, you might not want to tell him something which will distress him. But otherwise keep him abreast of the details of your life. Not to do so reinforces his feeling that he is old and useless, out of the action. Your parent, who has known you for many years, will probably sense anyhow when something is troubling you, and your covering it up may prevent you from talking casually about anything else and will probably only increase his uneasiness.

But be cautious. "Don't flood your parent with terrible things," says social worker Judith Altholz of Duke University's Older Americans Resources and Service Program, "but don't keep him in a world of unreality. Given the facilities which the older person has for dealing with information, tell it on a selective basis. Most older people don't have the coping techniques anymore. If your parent has a memory loss, he will tend to get more upset than a younger person. Figure out what is important to him and what he needs to know about the world around him."[2] It is often better, in relationships where the dialogue is so often about problems and attitudes charged with emotion, to talk to your parent about impersonal subjects as much as possible.

Sometimes you will get a warm and surprising reaction from your parent. A fifty-year-old daughter telephoned her eighty-three-year-old mother with the sad news of her infant great-grandchild's death. The daughter was apprehensive about her mother's reaction, but the family had agreed that she should be told. The great-grandmother shared her daughter's grief and made a warm, philosophical response. Early the next morning she called back. "I was concentrating so hard on what you told me last night that I forgot to tell you something important," she said. "You have to take care of yourself now. Your children are reaching an age where they're going to need you."

Give your parent the opportunity to continue to be a parent to you.

Listening to Your Parent

It's good for your parent to talk to you, and you should encourage it. Most older persons, especially if they live alone, don't have enough relatives and friends to talk to. Your parent has things to say—about his past and yours, about what's happening to him currently, about what may happen in the future.

If he talks to you for half an hour and you really respond to what he's trying to convey, he may not develop that pain in his stomach that will make both of you worry.

Aging elders complain that no one listens to them. One of the reasons is that their conversation is frequently boring, often little more than a litany of complaints and grievances. Some of these may very well be real, but they also reflect an increasing turning inward on self, a preoccupation with aches and pains and with lack of attention and social contact. If a physical handicap begins to appear in an aging person, that doesn't mean that all the rest of him is falling apart. He can still be interested in the world around him and want to participate in it. Isolation will quickly turn him into a boring hypochondriac.

When he reminisces, don't cut him off. Older people may need to go over events that troubled them or that brought them joy. Recapturing parts of his past life can give meaning to his present one and, if you listen, perhaps to yours also. Recollection can be therapeutic. It can reinforce the happy aspects of his life and give him an emotional shot in the arm.

Good listening is a true skill, especially when the talker is a parent whose complaints, worries, nagging, accusations, constant repetitions, or even silence creates a communications barrier. You must respond to what you see as the reality of your parent's situation and not to the emotion he projects. Point out to him objectively and calmly what you think he can do about the things that trouble him. Suggest equally calmly what you or other family members can do. Don't allow a conversation to develop into a harangue, either from your lips or from his. Before your parent is a parent, he is a person. Try to treat him that way.

When parents are mentally impaired or very ill, communicating can be a difficult situation for the visiting child. With little or no response to continued remarks or questions, the child becomes tongue-tied, unable to conduct a monologue.

But only in very extreme cases of ill health does a parent not know his child is sitting there in front of him, and just the presence of the child is a satisfaction. "Some children were uncomfortable about visiting their parents and complained that there was nothing to do and they just sat there," said Bertha G. Simos in a study, "Adult Children and Their Aging Parents." "It was incomprehensible to them that they might be supporting their parents emotionally, merely by their presence and interest."[3]

The message is: Don't give up on communicating with your parent.

Visiting

Visit your parent as you would a dear friend. Bring a small gift sometimes—a newspaper or magazine article which would be of interest, flowers, or some special food. Don't poke into the kitchen and the refrigerator. Don't suggest that this old piece of furniture be disposed of or those curtains washed. This is your friend's home, not yours. Accept the offer of food or drink. Bring a child with you; bring a friend. Treat the visit as a pleasant social occasion. It could be one.

If your parent is active, he surely visits at your home. Make it a special occasion from time to time. Invite other people—your friends or his—for lunch or dinner or a holiday celebration. Your parent may be physically feeble, but if his mind is nimble he probably will not recount your cute baby sayings. He may rather be an interesting commentator on the events of the day. Your guests will enjoy his company, and he will certainly appreciate theirs. One eighty-five-year-old woman delighted a dinner party with her comments on Henry Miller's *Tropic of Cancer*. Don't be surprised if your parent has a few things to say on matters you've never discussed together before.

Sharing

Most older people would like to keep up with what's happening in the world and with new developments in fields that have always interested them. But it's difficult to do so on their own. The ready access to newspapers, magazines, books, and energetic people is gone. Television helps, but you can help even more. Bring your parent magazine and newspaper clippings that would amuse or interest him, bring books and records. If he likes to go out for recreation with friends, suggest movies, plays, concerts you think he would like. Or invite him to go with you on occasion.

If you live too far away for frequent visits, you can still maintain consistent and positive communication. Telephone regularly. Send clippings, magazines, books, and family snapshots as they emerge from the camera. Write a long letter every week or two, one your parent can reread over a cup of tea or before going to bed at night. You might want to take a small tape recorder when you do visit, show him how to use it if he's not familiar with the mechanism, and then send news-filled tapes from you and your family. Ask him to start recording the family history. Amusing cards, little gifts—all these things are forms of communication which, continued without too great lapses of time between them, contribute to your parent's good state of mind. And his state of mind affects yours.

Dealing with Your Parent's Marital Problems

"I don't know what to do," the fifty-year-old woman said. "My father just called from Florida. He was seventy-six last month. He told me he just took ten thousand dollars out of the bank and he's going to leave my mother. He says he's had fifty-two years of it and he can't stand any more."

"Did he leave her?" the listener asked.

"He can't," the woman's husband said. "He's in a walker. He can barely move across the room."

This is a true tale and a telling one, both tragic and comic. Its tragedy is in the length and depth of frustration which it expresses; its black comedy in the image of the old man struggling impossibly to leave his equally old wife.

Its message is that old people—no matter how old—have the same kinds of emotions, needs, and frustrations as younger people. Feelings don't stop with age; sometimes they intensify.

Many older people do not go off happily hand in hand toward the sunset. They frequently take with them, along the later stretches of the road, unresolved problems of earlier years, frustrations and irritations in their relationship which they have never worked out. The wife who still instructs her

60 IMPROVING THE QUALITY OF YOUR PARENT'S LIFE

husband when he is driving, the husband who still refuses to take a vacation, the couple who still scream at each other over the bridge table—these are common examples. In many cases, these patterns are so entrenched that the husband and wife aren't even aware of any frustration at the other's behavior; this is the way he is, and this is the way she is, each feels, and were either to act differently, the other would feel threatened. But sometimes sharp events—illness, a drop in income, retirement, or other psychological blows—can exacerbate the older person's behavior or make him more sensitive to that of his partner. Then the pot boils.

If you see tension, anger, and bickering between your parents, you may shrug it off with, "Well, they've always been like that." But if you begin to perceive that they're more "like that" than they were, or that there's a new intensity in their hostility, then you should not shrug it off. You may not be able to act as a marriage counselor yourself, but you can talk to them, probably separately, and suggest outside counseling. Older couples who want to straighten out their relationships can be helped by marriage therapy just as much as younger ones.

A marriage of many years can sometimes be troubled by the fact that one partner is aging at a different rate from the other. Your bald father may resent your mother's full head of hair, especially if it's dyed. If your mother has trouble controlling her weight, she may be envious of the fact that your father is wearing the same size pants he wore twenty years ago. Your father may still enjoy his daily golf game and afternoon walk. Your mother is no longer so energetic; she prefers now to sit and knit. She needs eight hours of sleep each night; he now requires only six. These differences may show in behavior. Perhaps one of your parents is determined not to "grow old" and works actively at postponing or masking the effects of aging. The other may be more accepting—or may feel defeated. If there's open resentment, you'll know it. You should try to defuse it, and help your parents defuse it, in a judicious manner. If resentment is festering beneath the surface, you'll sense that, too; it can be just as damaging and should be brought out into the open.

Differences in aging rates can sometimes create sexual problems between two people. But sexual blocks or difficulties can arise from other reasons as well. And the absence of sexual relations can surely be a problem for your single older parent.

In the last few years a flood of books, magazines, and survey reports have brought sex out from behind the closed door of the bedroom and into the open discussion and action area. These, of course, have had a liberating effect. Youngsters in their teens and parents in their forties and fifties are thinking more freely, talking more openly, and in many cases acting more comfortably about their sexual needs and concerns.

This liberation has percolated up the age ladder somewhat, and there's been enough publicity now to make us aware that sexual desire, activity, and satisfaction can continue until very late in life, bringing rewards comparable in value to those of younger years. If they don't continue, and there is still an existing partner, it may be because of mutual agreement, or one partner may be impotent or disinterested, or there may be emotional or physiological impediments which didn't exist before.

It's very unlikely that your parent will voluntarily indicate to you any sex-connected problem, whether it's frustration at not having a partner, frustration with an unsatisfying partner, or frustration with his own performance. But if you pick up any clues from your parent in this direction, you should think about exploring them further. You might judge whether or not you can bring up or pursue the topic by how you feel about discussing a possible sex-related problem of your own with your parent. If you have or could, then it's possible that the two of you could begin to talk about what's happening with him. With enlightened techniques and with understanding, sex problems at sixty-five can be overcome just as at thirty-five. A sex counselor, a marriage counselor, or a physician should be able to help. (For books to read on the subject, see the Appendix.)

Encouraging Interests and Hobbies

The casual hobbies of younger days sometimes become compelling and consuming interests for the older person. The businessman who automatically tore stamps off envelopes and stuffed them into shoeboxes may be an avid stamp collector and organizer after he retires. Needlepoint or knitting, which the younger housewife enjoyed as a casual respite from her many chores, can become a prime focus of the emptier hours when she is older.

If your mother clamors for knitting jobs for you and your family, keep the orders coming. Discuss the styles, colors, and measurements, even though you may have to do so endlessly, and even though nobody in the family needs any more sweaters or scarves. "My house is wall-to-wall mosaics now because my father-in-law does that all the time at the community center, putting those little chips together," one woman said to a friend at the supermarket. "That's all right," the other said. "Mine is wall-to-wall bargello pillows because that's what my mother-in-law does while she watches television." As long as your older parent *does,* that's healthy—and no matter what he's doing, encourage it. "Each aged individual is depressed at least part of the time," says psychiatrist Olga Knopf.[4] Knitting, needlepoint, and mosaics can help your parent fend off depression.

Encourage any of these occupations, even if you have to contribute time, effort, and planning to keep them going. You're maintaining your parent's good mental health, and whether or not you value the activity or the result, praise it. Older people seem to need more psychological stroking then younger ones. They have less activity in their lives, and support from fewer people in their close circle; spouses have died, sisters and brothers have died, and so have friends. "The welfare of the old is primarily a problem of their opportunities for meaningful occupations, which need not be work for pay," says Warner A. Wick, University of Chicago philosophy professor.[5] You can help make your parent's occupation—whatever it is—meaningful to him.

Anticipating Change

The prospect of change is very often a threat to any individual, but it can be particularly upsetting for older people. Change in habits, customs, living arrangements, independence may terrify your parent. And the possibility of change in his life, especially as it will affect yours, may frighten you also.

This is very natural. You may have reached a level in your own life where things are almost orderly. The demanding years of early professional advancement may have leveled off for you and your spouse. You are probably no longer tied to the full-time care and supervision of growing children. You may perhaps be feeling some lessening of the responsibilities which have been yours until now and are enjoying life in a new way. And then, suddenly, you feel the weight of a new and scary situation.

Or you may have been going through a period where some of the other facets of your life have been plaguing you—and now here comes something else to plague you further. Or you are already in a caretaking relationship with your parent. You have established the support system, and it has functioned well. And now a new development creates a strain on that system.

One of the problems of a situation like this is that very few people have thought about it in advance. The tendency of most people is to go along, living as they have lived. There are certain life events which are universally accepted as change makers—going away to school, the first job, marriage, the birth of a child, a move to another city—but one knows about these events in advance and anticipates them, preparing to meet them when they occur.

Yet the process of growing old, with the demands it may place on the aging individual and his family, is really no complete surprise, either. Some preparation is indeed possible, but nobody wants to think about it until he has to.

Try to anticipate the change, try to investigate and plan a little beforehand, try to have some options lined up for the time when you will actually have to deal with the new situation. Then you will have participated to a degree in the change. It will not be suddenly thrust upon you from the outside.

Discuss with your parent, if you can, how he would like to handle certain circumstances, should they occur. If he's widowed and alone, would he want to live with a child? If he's sick and can't manage by himself, what living arrangements would he prefer? What are his thoughts about his future? You can discuss these in a casual way, long before the necessity of making any decision arrives. Get a head start—even though you may never have to run the race.

Housing

The first time the thought crosses your mind or your parent's that the day may come when he will no longer be able to continue living under current arrangements is the time when you should begin to think about other arrangements.

Elderly people who have never married and have no children seem to be much more practical in investigating where they might live when their needs change. Some people with children also do their own spadework, visiting retirement homes and homes for the aged when they are still living quite independently. But, too frequently, decisions about where to live are postponed or avoided. If you are to avert a crisis situation in your family, then it is wise to start investigating alternative living arrangements before an event imposes a hasty decision on you and your parent.

For an older person, a move is a traumatic event, involving the severing of long-held emotional and physical ties, the sharp amputation of old habits and patterns, and the painful requirements of establishing new ones for survival. Gathering information beforehand so that you can discuss and plan in advance with your mother or father can smooth the way and make both the move and the adjustment easier.

A Time Frame

You and your parent can look at a move in two ways: as a permanent one or as one which may have to be replaced by still another—and perhaps another—as your parent's situation changes. It's generally best to try to look ahead to see not only this year's requirements but those of future years. Although no one should be rushed into the first step of a total-care situation—especially because only a small percentage of older people ever needs this kind of situation—it's better to envisage some future erosion of totally independent living and try to plan for some of the dependency which may occur.

Where and how your parents live will be of utmost importance in determining whether their later years will be enriched or lonely, independent or dependent, financially perilous or secure. No plan may be permanent, as conditions change, but each decision along the way will count. If both of your older parents are contemplating a new home, you should think about its suitability for the survivor when one of them becomes widowed.

Any new housing at an older age should be examined with an eye to your parent's physical and social requirements, not only at the time of the move but in terms of what will be needed over the next several years. Look for locations in a pleasant neighborhood within an easy walk of stores for basic shopping and close-by transportation for other needs and for recreation. Examine safety features—the absence of basements and tricky staircases. Consider proximity to family and friends. Other factors will come quickly to your mind and your parent's, and all of them should be applied whether he prefers to remain in the community where he's currently living or whether he chooses to move to another.

Moving to a New Community

If a move has been thought about long in advance—tied to impending retirement, a predicted change in income, or a desire to live closer to a child or other relative—then there will be time to consider some of the factors involved. If the necessity to move is suddenly imposed, then you may find the same considerations helpful, but your options fewer. Naturally, if your parent is remaining in his present area, he will know some of the answers already, but many of his new requirements will still need careful thought.

Classic errors can be avoided by some advance planning or tryout. The reality of living in a warm climate may be different from the dream. The concept of living in an apartment with built-in services, freed from having to shovel snow-covered walks or fix leaky faucets or put up screens, may not translate so well in actuality. The parent who decides he wants to move to another city to be near children and grandchildren may be looking for trouble. Proximity to his family, dear though it is, might not compensate for the loss of the friends, the social activities, and the rewards of the neighborhood he left behind.

It's a good idea to research a new state, and certainly a new community, in advance. A subscription to the local newspaper for several months will give some clues and insights into the local life and atmosphere. Local chambers of commerce are good sources of information. Some states will send a summary of state features related to retirement living. You can write the state office on aging to learn about types of housing, the cost of living, special advantages for those over sixty-five, job opportunities, and available services. Friends already living there can share their judgments.

A trial living period is the best test of what the future will bring. This may save your parent the disappointment or frustration of finding out, after the fact, that he doesn't really care for the new location or life-style. To do this, some people rent out their present homes and then rent for themselves a small residence in the preferred location. Although this may be somewhat more costly in the short run, it may be much less expensive financially and emotionally in the long run.

If your parent hasn't had an adequate trial period, you may find yourself getting frantic phone calls after he has sold his house in Michigan and gone to live in a sunny climate. "Why did I do it? I've made a terrible mistake. Your mother cries all the time. She's lonely and wants to see the children. I'm sick of playing golf. I should never have retired."

Or, "They said they have twenty-four-hour switchboard service, but I fell down last night and no one ever answered when I called. Finally a neighbor from down the hall came this morning. My left side is all bruised. I can't live here. Take me home."

Check very carefully into the new state's requirements for eligibility for public housing and other types of state benefits.

Help your parents to be realistic about costs—uprooting is an expensive process—and be sure they can afford what they would like to have. Because their financial flexibility is likely to be reduced as they grow older, every effort should be made to conserve some of their funds for emergency situations.

The Wide Range of Housing Choices

Public and private social agencies can tell you what is available for your parent's needs in the community where he now lives or the one where he has chosen to go. The local office on aging can provide you with comprehensive lists of housing for elderly people, ranging from apartments for independent living to institutions providing lifetime care.

The National Council on the Aging published a comprehensive directory on housing for older people in 1969. Although its listing of existing housing is out-of-date, its guidelines help to analyze all the factors that should go into suitable housing at different stages of an older person's life. Criteria to consider range from fireproofing to accessibility and transportation to medical care, recreation, and social services.[6]

There are several other excellent directories which detail the wide variety of housing for older people existing across the country. You'll find some at the local public library; others can be bought from the associations which publish them. (See the Appendix.) Although these describe facilities, services, and costs, they give no ratings or judgments.

What is appropriate will depend on whether independent living is still feasible, or whether minimal to extensive care is required. Following is the range of potential options.

Independent Living for the Healthy Aged

● *Retirement villages, planned golden age communities, high-rise apartment complexes* for the elderly offer totally independent living in an organized setting. Their benefits are maintenance and security of the house or apartment, planned social and recreational programs, a neighborhood of peers, the option to rent or to purchase as a condominium or cooperative. These are generally privately developed and can be expensive. Check the local tax office or housing authority for property tax or rent relief for over-sixty-five residents.

- *Nonprofit retirement communities* sponsored by religious, fraternal, or labor organizations are in the same category. Costs may be high, and there's generally a long waiting list for occupancy.
- *Public housing for older persons with low, moderate, or moderate-to-high incomes* offers much the same benefits as retirement villages and their counterparts, but at lower cost.
- *Mobile home communities* abound in states with warm climates. Less costly in general, and with a peer population, they may lack organized social or recreational opportunities or programs.
- *Residential hotels and motels* offer both furnished and unfurnished apartments, usually with kitchenettes, for residents who come and go as they please. Benefits are relief from all housekeeping chores, a dining room on the premises for meals at will, companionship in communal rooms, and switchboard service.

Sheltered Living for the Not-So-Healthy

- *Senior residences* are like retirement hotels but with some additional attention paid to health and medical needs: a doctor or nurse on call, a bell near the bed to summon assistance, a staff member who checks on residents periodically. There may be a requirement to sign in and out, but no restrictions are placed on individual mobility. These may be sponsored by religious denominations or be privately operated.
- *Homes for the aged* give protective, custodial, and personal care to older people who are dependent but still functioning at a good level. They are operated by religious, ethnic, professional, or labor organizations and by private interests.
- *Health-related facilities* offer total shelter at several levels for those who require some form of nursing care determined by a physician. Depending on medical and financial qualifications, medicaid may cover the costs. Although some are nonprofit and are run by religious groups, most are operated by private corporations for profit.
- *Lifetime-care complexes* are usually operated by religious denominations. An older person can begin his life here in complete independence, living in a town house or apartment,

complete with a small kitchen. Then, later, if he has to, he can have some supervision and can take his meals in the dining room. If it's necessary at a later date, he can move on to the nursing-home level. Many places have medical and food service at all levels of living. These complexes often ask for lifetime-care contracts, requiring the person to turn over all his money and assets to the institution in return for the open-ended shelter and care he will receive. These contracts should be scrutinized carefully to see that financial terms aren't exorbitant and that they permit a refund of a reasonable portion of the money should the person decide at any point to leave the complex.

In some well-populated communities there's a new approach to housing for the elderly. A philanthropic agency or large health-oriented geriatric center may rent or buy apartments or houses where two or three older people can live together in one unit, each, generally, with his own bedroom, all sharing the other facilities of the apartment and with housekeeping services provided. An arrangement like this gives both independence and companionship. One of the best-known is in Philadelphia under the sponsorship of the Philadelphia Geriatric Center.

There's no reason that individuals can't set up this form of housing arrangement on their own. If your parent is widowed, living alone, and would like to live with another person or persons for all kinds of very good reasons, you might be able to arrange it yourself. Perhaps your parent has a friend in the same situation and with the same desire, or you may have a friend with a parent in the same situation. Or perhaps a local social service agency can steer you toward someone who's interested. The advantages to this arrangement are many: companionship, somebody else for emergency situations, and a big economy in living costs. There is, of course, a potential disadvantage—personality problems—but the advantages may be sufficiently compelling to smooth these over if they occur.

Maintaining Good Health

Good health is not a commodity that exists all by itself. It requires regular maintenance, and older people are no different in this regard from adults of all ages. Through their own recognition of important elements, their own efforts and regimens, they can improve their health or at least maintain it at an optimum level for their years and within the framework of their physical condition. Many factors go into maintaining good health; most of them are simple, derived, essentially, from common sense. Good eating and sleeping habits are basic; exercise is a vital ingredient; and climate and clothing contribute.

Nutrition

We are what we eat. Nutrition and diet are important at any age, but this is even more true of older people because an inadequate or improper diet not only can reinforce some of the infirmities and disabilities that tend to come normally with age, but can also produce unwelcome symptoms and ailments which may be wrongfully attributed to the aging process.

Your healthy parent's nutritional needs are basically no different from yours or those of your adult children. He needs a diet which gives him a daily balance from among the four basic food groups—meat, fruit and vegetables, bread and cereals, and milk. As he grows older, leads a less active existence, and experiences a decline in his metabolic rate, however, he will have a tendency to gain weight. He may find it necessary to cut back on carbohydrates and fatty foods and to cut down on his daily caloric intake if he wants to keep his weight within a healthful range. However, says Dr. Donald Watkin, "If an older person's level of activity is as high as it has always been and he's working just as hard, he has the same calorie requirements as ever."[7]

You should remember that it's more essential for an older person to have an adequate amount of protein in his diet than it is for a younger person. Protein is needed for energy, bones, and tissues. Certain specific conditions result from an insufficient protein supply: greater susceptibility to infection, mild forms of anemia, slower healing of wounds and bones. Lack of protein, along with lack of calcium, can also lead to osteoporosis. (See Chapter 7.) If an older person's diet has been inadequate over a period of time, behavioral and psychological changes can occur. Marginal malnutrition, resulting from unsatisfactory levels of protein, calcium, and vitamins, can cause weakness, irritability, and erratic or irrational behavior. After a time on a good and balanced diet, these conditions often disappear.

If your parent is in good health, no matter what his age, there's no reason for him to follow any special kind of diet. The chances are that if he has continued to be healthy, he's eating the right kinds and quantities of food already. He might feel the need each day to eat smaller meals at more frequent intervals, as his digestive processes and his body's ability to absorb food and its nutritive elements become a bit slower. It's better if he eats five small meals rather than three large ones each day. If he tells you he "can't eat such a big dinner," understand that his body is cautioning him legitimately and don't push food at him. If he suggests a small midafternoon or midmorning snack, don't tell him it will interfere with his next meal. If he prepares a light bite before bedtime, don't think it will interfere with his sleep. It may make him sleep better.

With the high cost of food today, many older people feel they simply can't afford to buy some of the foods which would be most nutritious for them. Beef and other meats are very expensive; substituting cheaper but other protein-high foods like cheese and eggs contributes to calories and cholesterol levels. If your parent's income really bars enough protein-high meats, perhaps you or a brother or sister can make a small gift of meat here and there for his weekly diet. When you invite him to your home for a meal, be sure it's a good one.

Many older people, in seemingly good health, actually don't eat intelligently and are undernourished or malnourished in terms of the necessary intake of nutrients, essential vitamins, and minerals. Older people tend to experience a lessening of appetite. Dentures may create an eating problem. Fewer taste buds, a less keen sense of smell may erode enjoyment of food. Depression or anxiety affects the appetite; so do loneliness and living alone.

Living and Eating Alone

Beware! If your parent lives alone, keep a close watch on eating habits, monitoring for regularity and content. Older people who live by themselves tend to lose interest in the mechanics of preparing and eating food. A Michigan Office of Services to the Aging survey made of three hundred over-sixty Michigan residents showed that only two-thirds of those surveyed had eaten three meals on the day before the interview and that 17 percent had had no more than three of the basic foods required for a balanced diet.[8]

Eating and all that surrounds it—selecting and preparing food, serving and sharing it—is a very complicated action. Its form and attributes are determined not only by economics but much more by one's own past, values, and associations. Eating is generally regarded and experienced as a social act; parents and children come together at mealtime, large families join for festive dinners, friends meet over lunch or afternoon tea. Sharing meals with others is a large element in the lives of most of us.

For many women, who have cooked and served countless meals to their growing families, food is surrounded by many conscious and unconscious factors. Food is often the medium through which they express love, often a vehicle for their creative energy and talent, sometimes a device for exercising authority over their children and mystifying their husbands with accomplishments which have traditionally been outside the male purview.

Many older women, robbed of this role, recollect it nostalgically and are unable to reconcile themselves to the shrunken ritual of preparing a meal for one, eating it without company.

One old grandmother, the mother of six, solved this problem neatly. She cooked regularly and superbly every day, and when no relative or friend dropped in to share with her, she left a hefty portion at the door of the elevator for the elevator operator. This had the double virtue of maintaining good nutrition for her and guaranteeing the loyalty of a long series of elevator operators.

With the self-service elevators of today, this outlet is rarely available. But just as this was an artificial device to continue the motivation for good nutrition, there are other artificial devices which can be employed as well. If your mother is living alone, you can guide her carefully, encouraging her to continue cooking and to share the results with others. In her apartment house or neighborhood there will surely be agreeable older men and women who are also living alone and who would be delighted to share both her cooking and her companionship. You can try to help her make a habit of inviting a friend or a relative in for a meal fairly often. Lunch is as good a time as dinner if her guests feel tentative about traveling in the evening. Try, if you can, to be a regular mealtime guest in your mother's home. Suggest that she prepare some dishes which were—and probably still are—among your favorites. Such a meal can be a happy time for both of you.

An older man living alone may be in worse shape. He has the same memories of family meals, of good food and conversation—and, in addition to the sense of loss these recollections may bring to him, he probably doesn't know how to cook. He may not even know how to market. An older woman alone may need a reeducation process where meals are concerned, but an older man alone generally needs a basic education.

If it's your father who's alone, he may have to start from scratch, learning the map of the supermarket and the use of kitchen equipment, learning what to buy and how to cook it. He may be susceptible to some basic cookbooks, some simple cooking classes at a YMCA or other adult education center. He might even become truly interested in cooking, and, if he does, accept his invitations to dinner gladly, bring a bottle of wine to accompany the meal, and praise the cook.

Nutritional Checklist

The U.S. Public Health Service has some pointers on proper diet for your parent:

- Fruits, vegetables, and milk in good supply will take care of most necessary vitamins and minerals.
- Fried foods, highly seasoned foods, very starchy foods, and dishes with large amounts of fat, gravies, and heavy sauces are difficult to digest.
- Boiled or baked foods and those that are low in fat content are more easily chewable and digestible.

- Fruits, vegetables, and foods with bulk prevent constipation; older people should avoid habitual use of laxatives if possible.
- Heavy meals are a mistake at any time, but especially in the evening.
- A steady fluid intake is vital. An older person should drink six to eight glasses of liquids a day, especially in warm weather when there is a tendency to dehydration.

An older person needs more calcium as he ages, not less. Older bones grow brittle, and calcium strengthens them. Physicians are now finding cases of rickets, a bone-deficiency disease, among older people whose diets aren't providing enough calcium. Encourage your parent to become a habitual milk user—plain, or in egg nogs, milk shakes, and puddings, depending on any dietary restrictions he may have. Cottage cheese and skim milk are rich in calcium but low in calories. Grains are good for energy and nourish the nervous system. Even dieters should include small quantities of bread, cereals, and rice. Potatoes and pastas also fit in this category. Try to encourage the use of fresh fruits and vegetables—they're cheaper and have more nutrients than their canned or frozen counterparts. If your parent makes a daily balanced choice from among these foods, he should not need vitamins or food additives.

If you know or sense that your parent is eating poorly and irregularly, watch him over a period of time. A few skipped meals or a few days on a meager diet won't be too damaging, but prolonging a poor diet can be. It takes about two years on an inadequate diet to produce a serious deficiency, says Dr. Watkin.

Loss of Appetite

If you notice that your parent's appetite has lagged, that he doesn't seem interested in meals or is refusing food, try to find out the reason. He may be having trouble with his gums, his teeth, or his dentures which prevents him from enjoying and chewing his food. These are conditions which a dentist can readily treat. There may be more complicated reasons. He may be depressed or emotionally upset. People who are depressed often don't care about eating, and those who are angry or who feel hurt may refuse food as a punishment to themselves or to others who are close to them. Sometimes people deny food to themselves as a symbol that they are denying life. Or there may be a physical condition which is causing appetite loss. You should not let it go unnoticed. Try to learn from your parent what the cause is, and discuss it with him and his doctor. Then you will know what you are dealing with and can try to rectify the situation.

Nutrition and Illness

Some chronic conditions of older people—arteriosclerosis, heart disease, diabetes, high blood pressure, and ulcers, for example—require special diets. Colitis and hypoglycemia, less common ailments, also demand a specific dietary routine. The presence of more than one chronic condition—which often occurs with older persons—can create a dietary conflict. High-protein cheeses are good for the hypoglycemic but unhealthy for the heart patient. The regular use of diuretics to reduce the accumulation of fluid in the body can dramatically lower the body's essential potassium level, but foods richest in potassium can be high in calories. If your parent has a chronic illness, the proper diet should be discussed thoroughly with his doctor. It would also be a good idea to consult a trained nutritionist, who can map out a diet which will contain a maximum of positive elements and a minimum of those which are negative.

When you do check out a required diet, be sure to find out just how restricted it should be. Must some foods be stringently avoided, or can they be used moderately or occasionally? Diets are very tricky vehicles and require expert guidance. They should be rigorously followed.

The national health organizations doing research on specific diseases can be of great help here. The American Heart Association and the American Diabetes Association will give nutrition counseling and suggest specific diets. Visiting and public health nurses will work with an older person to lay out special diet needs. Your city or county may have staff nutritionists who can advise your parent, and surely the home economists attached to the U.S. Department of Agriculture's Cooperative Extension Service will either give advice or suggest a qualified nutritionist who can.

There's a great deal of printed material on nutrition and diets for older people in general, and for those who have chronic conditions requiring special diets. (See the Appendix.)

Exercise

Walking is an excellent activity for older people. It's the least taxing form of exercise, requires no skills and no equipment. In addition, the passing scene often pleases the eye, always stimulates the mind. A walk a day is good for the older person's health, whether it leads to the daily newspaper, the market, another form of transportation, a social event, or whether it's just a stroll.

People of any age can swim and enjoy it. The older person doesn't have to do twenty-five laps a day in perfect form. Whatever swimming he can do comfortably will be good exercise and a good tonic for his body. Moving in water, in addition, is a recognized form of therapy—it's good for the muscles and relaxes the soul. Even if your parent doesn't live near a body of water in a warm climate, he can probably swim just as often as he likes. Many areas have community swimming pools for summer or winter enjoyment. YMCAs, their counterparts, and community recreation centers almost always have swimming pools which members can use for a small fee. These might even schedule special swimming hours for older people. If they don't, you might suggest it to them as a community service.

In one old age home near Long Island Sound, the high point of the summer for many of the over-eighty residents comes with semiweekly trips to swim in the surf.

If your parent has no physical conditions that contraindicate other kinds of exercise, they, too, will be beneficial. Golf, the sport of choice of many older persons, is in essence a more elaborate, socialized form of just plain walking. It leads to companionship for the exerciser during his pursuit of the sport and afterward, at the nineteenth hole. Its moderate physical demands are not taxing to the body, and the teasing challenge to better one's score perks up the mind.

Under the guidance of their physicians, many older people can set up an organized exercise program, beginning in a careful, circumscribed fashion and then extending the time and content of the exercise period if it's indicated. "The way to keep lively is to be lively; the way to stay active is to move," says *The Fitness Challenge in Later Years,* an exercise manual prepared by the President's Council on Physical Fitness. This pamphlet lays out a regular routine of exercises adapted specifically to the muscles and energies of the older person. (See the Appendix.)

Climate

Climate can contribute to health, but, barring chronic ailments which can be aggravated in cold climates, an older person can live anyplace you can live. Some of our coldest states—Vermont and Maine, for example—have high percentages of people over sixty-five.

The elderly, however, should avoid extreme heat, extreme cold, and extreme dampness. Too much heat upsets normal fluid and mineral balance; too much cold narrows the blood vessels and puts a greater strain on the heart; too much dampness invites upper respiratory infections.

Moving to Florida, Arizona, or Southern California does seem attractive to many older people for whom cold winters may be harsh and confining. Children often urge their parents to make this kind of move to a gentler climate. A one-season wardrobe is an undeniable boon to the budget. The absence of heating bills is tempting but can be offset by air-conditioning bills in the overhot summer months. But often a drastic move in search of a milder climate and away from the familiar and familial environment can be too great a dislocation for the older person, and adjusting to it can be difficult. It's true that your older parent will have to be especially careful in winter weather—whether he drives or walks, snowy and icy streets and roads are even more hazardous to the old than to the young. But unless a physician recommends a climate change for health reasons, your parent can adapt just as you do to the climate in which he lives.

Clothing

The choice of clothing is always an intensely personal act. Older people often tend to keep and wear clothes for a much longer time than younger ones. This is probably for economic reasons—their incomes may not allow too much money for replacements. It may also be due to a lessened awareness of "in" fashions, whose calculated aim of creating rapid obsolescence in clothing is for younger, growing pocketbooks, anyway.

This doesn't mean that most older people aren't interested in their appearance or in looking attractive. On the contrary, many older people work harder to present an attractive appearance. They may have a conscious need to stand up to the inroads of age or may use dress as one expression of their desire to hold up to their children and grandchildren an appealing role model.

If your mother likes to wear flashy jewelry and body shirts, that's good for her ego and may indicate a better sense of self-value than if she were dressed in clothes she has worn so long that they've become a uniform. You should respect this whether or not your taste is in agreement. Just caution her on the danger of high heels and of wearing tight undergarments which may cut off circulation and interfere with proper breathing. If your father is a natty dresser and continues to aspire to a certain elegance, encourage the Beau Brummell in him. People of any age who think they look better, tend to feel better. Your parents' interest in keeping up may indicate a good state of mental health, and when their mental health is at a good level, so is yours.

It's true, however, that as older people grow even older, some do lose interest in their dress and in how they look. They may say to themselves, "I'm too old to care about how I look," or, "Nobody cares about how I look." There is probably an ambivalence to this attitude, and you can get into the picture and support the positive elements. The physical, social, or economic infirmities of old age may indeed lead older people to feel that dressing well is too much of a physical or mental effort, but an older person who has always been thoughtful about his appearance still has some of the same values.

It's up to you and your family to try to understand what your parent is feeling about his appearance and then to respond appropriately. If your father always wears the same baggy sweater and your mother continues to use your father's old bathrobe—which sometimes happens—give a fresh replacement for a birthday or for Christmas. The recipient may decide to "save it for good," put it away, and not wear it, but you will have done all you can.

Although you should not criticize or nag your parent about his appearance, you should be alert to it as an indication of emotional tone. A continuing lack of interest on your parent's part may be a danger signal. Or you may find that your parent, who has always been careful in grooming and dress, begins to show disinterest and neglects his appearance. This kind of behavior could indicate some form of depression stemming from emotional or physical reasons. You should look into this seriously with your parent and his physician.

If your parent has a physical hindrance, this may require careful selection in clothing. Garments should be comfortable and fairly loose, easy to put on and take off. Zippers, buttons, and snaps should be readily accessible and preferably in the front of blouses or dresses for easy reaching. It might be difficult for the older person to see and manipulate small snappers, hooks, or buttons. Shoes and slippers should fit well, without being too loose; slippery soles lead to falls.

Safety in the Home

Older people tend to have more accidents than younger people. They have slower reaction times and weaker muscles, their balancing system becomes less efficient, and their gait is heavier, with less spring. Extra safety precautions are essential in homes where older people live. They should be careful in their actions and in the construction of their environment. Many accidents can be avoided with proper advance measures.

Floors
- Rugs can be very dangerous. Probably no rug is the best rug for an older person. A small throw rug tends to be skiddy

and, when it slides, can carry the older person to the floor. Thick pile rugs and carpets can trap an older person's slower, heavier foot, and high edges increase the danger of tripping. Watch out for high thresholds and uneven floor surfaces.

Electricity
- Electrical wall outlets should be high enough for comfortable reaching.
- Avoid extension cords and tack all long, loose wires against the floor molding.
- All lighting should be increased for older people. Good reading light is essential, as is good staircase lighting. Staircase landings are high danger points for older people who may not see the top or bottom steps.

Handrails
- Staircases should have good rails running their length, and preferably on both sides.
- Bathrooms need grab bars or rails near the toilet and for getting in and out of the bathtub. Keep a nonskid mat in the bathtub.

Temperature
- Homes should be neither too warm nor too cold. A high room temperature is dehydrating and generally unhealthy. Air conditioning can be too chilling, especially if it is blown in a draft from a window unit.
- Neither baths nor bathrooms should be too hot. Steam and heat can provoke dizziness.

Kitchens
- Equipment should be accessible, reachable without bending, stretching, or lifting. Reaching up to high shelves and standing on ladders and chairs can lead to dizziness and faintness.
- Electric stoves are safer than gas stoves.
- Older people forget that they have put a pot or pan on the stove and turned on the light beneath. They walk out into another room, go to answer the telephone or doorbell. A

timer with a bell, turned on when the stove burner is lit, will remind the cook that there's a light on the stove and will avoid possible kitchen fires.

Living Alone

An experienced public health nurse suggests a buddy system for people who live alone. Your parent should check up each day on someone in a similar position; someone should call your parent daily. Each buddy should have emergency telephone numbers for the other—a close relative and a doctor. Your parent should also keep near the phone a list of his own emergency numbers.

Drug Abuse

If your parent is taking prescription sleeping pills and you are concerned about possible addiction, speak to his doctor.

Older people may in fact develop the habit of taking pills to fall asleep if their physicians believe it is medically necessary. "So what?" you may say. "My parent is not likely to become a pusher or commit a crime to get a pill." The danger is that, anxious to ensure sufficient sleep, your parent may increase the pill intake beyond what the doctor ordered. Some sleeping pills are addictive and others aren't. The doctor may be able to reassure you about what your parent is taking.

There are other things you should guard against if your parent is taking medication. See that he doesn't keep a supply for too long a time; the chemical structure can change, and the medication loses its effectiveness. It's also not a good idea for older people to exchange medication with each other, which they sometimes do. "Try this," says one to the other. "It helps my backache." Impress upon your parent that this is a very poor practice.

If your parent needs several different pills regularly for a variety of ailments and is becoming a little forgetful, he may be taking some of the medication too frequently or not frequently enough. Real harm can follow improper dosage. You can help him by making a chart. Have him check the list and note the hour each time he takes a pill. Then you'll know whether he comes out even at the end of the day.

Even if your parent is institutionalized, you should check on medication. Don't assume that everything is as it should be. At a recent conference on drug abuse and the elderly, an official of the National Institute on Drug Abuse warned of the increasing problem in nursing homes, where medication is sometimes improperly controlled or not administered reliably. It is wise to make judicious checks and, above all, to be observant about your parent's behavior. Report any concerns directly to the physician in charge of your parent's case. Some nursing homes abuse patients with tranquilizers, oversedating them to keep them from being troublesome. If that is happening to your parent, perhaps you should investigate the possibility of transferring him to a different facility.

Safe Driving

Many adult children worry about elderly parents who are still active drivers. "He can't see well," they say. "His reflexes are slower. He shouldn't be driving anymore."

An older driver may, in fact, be more cautious on the road than a younger driver because he is aware of the fact that his reflexes may be slower. Statistics suggest that the adult child may be worrying needlessly about his parent's safety behind the wheel. A nationwide study, *Traffic Accidents and the Older Driver,* published by the Administration on Aging in Washington, D.C., showed clearly that the older driver has proportionately fewer accidents than any other segment of the driving population and is "underrepresented in the accident statistics."

If older drivers have a problem, the study says, "it would be with respect to fatal accidents, since they are involved in these accidents nearly in proportion to their percentage of the population." The study gives no explanation for this fact, other than to say that "it may be partly due to the older person's inability to withstand injury."

Of course, some older people do continue driving long after they should have stopped. If you see your parent going through red lights, making turns from the wrong lane, and really peering over the wheel because he's not sure of what he's seeing, keep watch carefully. If he starts having minor accidents, maybe you should tactfully suggest that he give up driving before there's a major one.

If your parent is a driver, he will not give up the driver's seat gladly; to him, it symbolizes competence and independence. If he has a safe driving record, you should respect his feelings. He'll probably know himself when he should no longer drive.

Safety from Crime

Fear of crime keeps many an older person imprisoned in his house or apartment as soon as the sun goes down. Daytime excursions may be frightening experiences in some big-city neighborhoods, and even in small towns there is a real and not imagined danger to the elderly—women especially. Police statistics confirm that older people are the most vulnerable segment in the population. Purse snatchers, muggers, and mailbox thieves know that an older person can be thrown into confusion more readily than a younger one, and is less capable of defending himself against a sudden approach.

For this reason, many local police departments are mounting organized education programs for older people to help them not only to avoid a possible criminal assault but to deal with one should it occur. Crime prevention seminars teach older people the tricks of pinching and kicking, how to break strangleholds and grips, even self-defense and karate. While a deputy sheriff at one seminar said that a man of a hundred and five could fight "like he's twenty-five" if his life depended on it, most of the seminar participants were skeptical of their ability to restrain panic under attack or to use force even when they were taught how. Increased civilian and police patrols, teen escort services, neighborhood visits and watch systems, and a good supply of whistles and horns to call for help were considered more realistic safety measures.

So were the safety tips given by police departments and other agencies that you are probably familiar with: cautions about purses and wallets, well-lit main streets, walking with a companion, locking doors, and other well-publicized admonitions. Try to persuade your parent to heed them faithfully.

Street crime is not the only hazard for older people, who are often easy prey for con artists and swindlers—door-to-door salesmen, promoters of get-rich-quick schemes, home renovaters, and repairmen are among them. Duping the elderly occurs so frequently that the AARP has published a pamphlet informing and alerting the older person. (See the Appendix.)

Stress

All of us are subject to stress from time to time. The teenager in his first accident with the family car, the eager college graduate looking fruitlessly for a job over a period of months, the junior executive who doesn't get the promotion he expected, the mother whose youngest child goes off to college— all of them are experiencing stress which threatens their sense of well-being and forces them to build immediate new coping mechanisms. If the person under stress can build the mechanisms, he will survive the ordeal and, often, be strengthened by the process. If he can't put together effective techniques for handling the heavy pressures, he may become physically or mentally ill.

The growing-older years can often bring stressful situations of great magnitude. The older person himself may have to cope with financial problems, retirement, the death of someone close, a change of living place. He surely will have to face up to the physical changes that aging brings. In addition, his children, who have grown into adulthood, are facing stressful situations of their own—which he is sharing with them. All too often, in later years, there is a clustering of events that create stress, plunging the older person into coincident situations that can be shattering.

Since many stress situations come up unexpectedly, there's no preparation that can be done to minimize or absorb their effects. But a person who recognizes that he is in an abnormally pressing situation can take steps to deal with its demands.

A time of stress unleashes strong emotions, and it's healthier to express than to repress them. Talking helps; so does crying. Your father may talk endlessly about his cataract operation and the difficulty of using his new eyeglasses. Let him talk because it's giving him a way of coping with the stress of surgery and the complicated new situation. If he had to bottle it all up, he might develop an ulcer. When he's made his adjustment, you probably won't hear any more about it. Or your mother may weep her way through weeks and months after your father dies. Don't tell her to stop crying. She needs to express her grief through her tears and even through her screams. If she didn't let it out, she might develop hypertension or another physical disorder.

Other cautions for your parent in times of stress:

- Be extra careful in all physical actions. People under stress tend to be accident-prone. They drop and break things, hurt themselves, dent automobile fenders.
- Try to have some small, relaxing diversions here and there: an outing with a grandchild, an hour or two at a movie, or a visit with friends. Often the person under stress pushes off the thought of even brief enjoyment, but it can be a restorative if his mind is released from anxiety and fastened on something outside his problem for a short time.
- This is not a time for making decisions. Try to postpone them. Setting a minor thing straight or making a small decision may give a feeling of accomplishment, but major ones should be shelved temporarily.

(Some of the material in this chapter on maintaining good health has come from *Working with Older People,* a four-volume publication of the U.S. Public Health Service.)

CHAPTER 4

AS DEPENDENCY GROWS:
From Care at Home to
Choosing a Nursing Home

Sometimes a family is stronger than it thinks it is. Even if you've dreaded an accident, a handicap, a severe illness, or the death of a parent, you find that you all come through with amazingly few scars when you are forced to deal directly with the needs of the person instead of the excesses of your imagination. Sometimes it's your adrenaline that comes to your assistance. Sometimes it's some advance thinking and planning that brings extra resources to your fingertips. Sometimes it's knowing when to call on someone else for help. Sometimes it's because you're getting a lot of experience dealing with gradual or sudden upsets. Usually, it's all of these plus your common sense that pull you through.

If you're coping with all the major changes in your parent's life, really managing to keep everyone and everything together, you may be having a tough time, but you're not in crisis. Any situation that upsets normal routine is capable of becoming a crisis unless the people involved draw on all the internal and external resources available to develop and maintain a practical solution. If you're not doing this, then you're not coping—and you're in crisis.

Even if the family is coping, the elderly person at the center of the stage may not be so resilient. There may be a point where his crisis and your coping just don't mesh, or vice versa. This kind of impasse frequently has to do with caretaking, not the casual kind that is satisfied by friendly visits, telephone calls, and thoughtful excursions, but rather the kind that involves a breakthrough change—having your parent live in your house, or reorganizing his own home situation dramatically, or facing the decision to move him to a supervised senior residence or a nursing home.

Stages of Dependency

Professionals agree that it's wisest not to wait to move a parent until he is old and sick. Plan ahead and move while he is still functioning normally, says Dr. Robert Butler. When the symptoms of deterioration first appear and you feel that your parent will need a more structured environment, says old-age-home administrator Harold Mawhinney, help him make the decision himself while he is still competent to do so, and go with him to visit homes.

A Virginia social worker supports this view even more strongly, drawing on her own long experience in working with older people. "Care for an older person at home is a constant upheaval. You are always changing arrangements because situations change so fast. First you need someone for the heavy cleaning, and then you have to take another step, and another. When services are fractured like that, there's anguish, waste of time, waste of everything."

She points out that there are three main stages of dependency in older people after complete independence: the relinquishing of some small portions of it as physical strength begins to ebb, a middle stage where the older person is half-independent, half-dependent on others for help, and then the complete dependence which is found among hospital and nursing-home residents who can perform almost no function unaided. "Nobody wants to rush it or jump a couple of stages to get to the final one, but fractured handling is very bad. There's a long period when people are reluctant to say to the older person, 'You're going into a home whether you like it or not.' Grandma may say, 'I'm not going. I can manage perfectly.' Then the family will discover that she leaves the gas on or that she falls. Then they have to face what can be done."

This social worker speaks for herself: "I wouldn't want to be in a never-never land where I'm not sure what is going to happen to me, and nobody else is sure, either."[1] Her firm recommendation is that the best arrangement for an older person is to go, while still totally independent, into a lifetime-care complex. Start out in an apartment with a kitchenette, progress when it's indicated to the part of the complex where there's supervision and meals in a dining room, then go directly to the nursing-home level if that's required. Every move is within a familiar environment.

On the other hand, another experienced social worker offers a somewhat different point of view, suggesting that it is not wise to plan for permanency in making arrangements for older people who are entering a dependent stage. "Any living arrangement, satisfactory as it may be at any particular time, cannot be expected to last indefinitely in most instances," she says.[2] Be prepared for change and flexibility. Meet today's needs now, tomorrow's needs later.

There's something to be said for both these viewpoints. Dealing with each step as it arises has its sensible and humane aspects: Your parent does not have to face the possible trauma of a move until circumstances are so harsh that, in their way, they command a certain acceptance from all concerned. People often adjust better to necessity than they do to a decision which is still clouded by other options which were not selected. Designing a master plan and then following it is practical and efficient, relieves the older person and his family of what could be a long, anxious period when the patchwork of caretaking must be continually put together. But the initial decision is sometimes harsh in its implications and difficult to make.

It may be helpful to realize that any decision, any plan, can be changed. Neither you nor your parent need be locked into an inflexible, irremediable solution. If, after the decision is made and carried out, living with it becomes too complicated, too agonizing, it can be changed.

The Trigger

What is it that triggers you into action? One day an event makes you realize something new has to be done about your parent's care.

A sudden stroke has resulted in a paralyzed arm and leg, with a very poor prognosis for recovery of use. You know your parent cannot return to the setting he left. He will be hospitalized for another few weeks, but you must make a decision quickly on what happens after that. Something has to be done.

Some casual questions you ask your mother reveal that she hasn't been out of her apartment for over a week. Consequently, the refrigerator and the larder are almost empty, and your mother admits that she has been living mainly on tea and instant coffee for the preceding days. She says she is afraid of falling on the street because her eyesight is not too keen and her legs feel a little shaky. She says, in addition, that since a woman was mugged the previous month in the elevator of the apartment house next door, she has been terrified of getting into her own elevator. Something has to be done.

For the fifth time in a month the homemaker who has been taking care of your chronically ill father calls at seven-thirty in the morning to say that she cannot come in to work that day. Since your father can't be left alone for more than an hour or so, this means that you can't go to your job, either. You have to be the homemaker that day. The two previous homemakers you employed—all efficient, warm people—had an equally regular history of absenteeism. As you put down the phone you know that you feel very angry. "This can't go on," you snap. Something has to be done.

One of your parents suddenly dies. You have no preplanned strategy for caring for the widowed mother or father. Something has to be done.

Something Has to Be Done

Suitable care for your parent is the central issue. Unless your mother or father is beyond rational thinking, he or she should be involved in reviewing the options and making the choice. Your parent, you, and all the members of the family who are concerned with the solution and who take responsibility for the outcome should be included in the circle of people working out the decision.

Before you decide, you should have a very clear idea of your parent's practical needs and how well each alternative can satisfy these needs. Make a list that is very specific: physical, nursing, and medical needs; social or emotional requirements; financial or other assistance. What is available, who can supply it, where can you get it? Then discuss preferences and examine why they are, or are not, acceptable alternatives. For example, if your parent's desire to remain independent, even with help in the house, simply is no longer feasible because neither you nor anyone else in the family has the physical or emotional resources to be on twenty-four-hour call when emergencies of any sort arise, then this is not an acceptable alternative. If your mother's presence in your house is sure to result in constant conflict with your spouse, then this is not an acceptable alternative. If your desire to bring your parent into your home cannot be matched with providing essential nursing service or therapy, then this is not an acceptable alternative. If you cannot find a decent and humane nursing home in your locality, then nursing-home placement is not an acceptable alternative.

In every family there will be particular circumstances which will make one or another choice a better one.

Choices

- You can bring some new or additional help into your parent's home.
- You can invite your parent to live with you.
- Someone else in the family may wish to share a home with your parent and be responsible for his care. This may be one of your brothers or sisters. It may be an uncle or aunt. Perhaps someone else in the family is elderly and needful. If your parent shares housing and caretaking services with that person, the joint household may relieve several family problems at once.
- You can arrange for your parent to live in a boarding home that specializes in caring for frail or elderly people in a homelike setting.
- You can consider whether this is the appropriate time for your parent to move to a more sheltered environment where nursing and, perhaps, medical care is available on a reliable basis. This may be a home for the aged, or a nursing home.

Your Parent in His Home

Maintaining your parent in his home when he needs a great deal of help to remain there is a mixed bag. It has advantages and drawbacks for him, advantages and drawbacks for you. There's an important virtue in allowing him to stay in his own place, in a familiar environment, and with the security-giving symbols of his life around him. Without question, many services can be brought in to help him, paid for out of his pocket and those of other family members, or paid for in part by local government social services.

According to Daphne Krause: "For the vast majority of people, their whole identity as a human being is where they've lived and what makes up their home. Their home is their way of life. It's their neighbors, their church, their grocery store. It's everything that makes them an individual. If you stay in your own home, there are all kinds of compromises you can make to help yourself. Your surroundings are familiar. You can make your surroundings help you."[3] Yet a feeble older person with a narrowed circle of friends and relatives who may not visit or telephone very often can become very lonely, especially if he can't leave his home much, or at all, for companionship.

Most older people do want to be in their own homes. If your parent remains in his, you won't have to face the guilt you might feel if he were to move into a nursing home, but managing the caretaking structure can be a large burden on you. "I spend all my time taking care of my father," says a Chicago woman who lives a twenty-minute car drive from her ailing parent. "I do his marketing and most of his cooking. Someone comes in every morning to help him get bathed and dressed, to fix his breakfast and do a little housecleaning. But I have to check to see if she's there every day, and if she isn't, I have to go over myself. A bus comes to take him to the clinic and the doctor. He can still go to sit on the park bench, but there is no bus to the part of town where his two friends live, and I have to drive him there. When I'm not with him, he's on the telephone with me all the time, wanting to know when I'll be over. He may not be ready for a nursing home, but I sure am."

Need to Be Dependent

Even the most independent person at some point in his declining life may want and need to be dependent on a child. Some psychiatrists, such as Olga Knopf, believe "the dependency of the old is a right."[4] The child must have the sensitivity to discover when the need to be dependent has been reached and to offer a proud parent the opportunity to lean without shame. This is the time when the parent is ready to be taken in to a child's home, or ready to be in the security of a nursing home where someone is always there.

A woman who traveled back and forth from coast to coast each weekend to patch up the emergencies that arose for her disabled parents finally took them West into her own home and arranged for all the services to be brought in. But at the moment when this was no longer good enough, when it was no longer safe for her parents to live out of an institution, she and they accepted the move—regretfully, but without rancor. Everyone knew she had done the best she could for as long as it was practical.

It's not that easy in many families. Duke University's Judith Altholz says, "There is a gray area between the older person who is clearly capable of making it, and the one who is incompetent. That's the time when families and parents can all be wretched, and no one seems able to make the right decision. Sometimes an outside person, the doctor, or a social worker can help. 'I,' says the expert, 'think you should move to change your life because these conditions are becoming overwhelming for you.' The older person may sometimes gladly follow the suggestion."[5]

When a doctor or social worker suggests that the elderly person be moved to a nursing home, it will be either because the patient's physical or mental condition compels it, or because the family obviously can no longer cope. If you're not coping, you probably won't need to be told; you'll know.

Your Parent in Your Home

Finances or compassion or custom often lead to the decision to move an ailing parent into a child's home. Two households may be too costly. If the parent needs supervision at almost every moment, a nursing home might cost much more money than the family can put together. Helping services in the home can be performed by the unpaid labor of family members or by part-time help brought into the home at not too great expense. Just as often, there are emotional reasons paralleling those that are monetary. Many children bring a parent into their home without any conflict. They do what they wish to do. Others bring a parent to live with them because it's their family's custom.

A parent may refuse to enter a nursing home, accusing his children of wanting to get rid of him, claiming that he will never survive the experience, clinging resolutely to the live-in support of the family. Few children can resist these approaches; emotional though they may be, they have validity. The child internalizes what the parent expresses, asks himself if he will, in fact, be abandoning his parent. The anticipated burden of guilt is too much. After all, your parent took his parent into his own home. The child confers with spouse and children, who agree to the decision that Grandma or Grandpa will come to live with them and they will all make the best possible adjustment.

Very often they do make the adjustment. Love and affection can help. Relaxed temperaments can help. Self-discipline on the part of all participants can help. Sometimes the experience is a joy. The children love listening to the grandparent, playing cards and games with a built-in companion. Grandma or Grandpa feels the same way.

"My mother lived with us for eighteen years," said the woman from Madison. "We had to take her in because she couldn't afford to live by herself. She followed me around from room to room, always asking me what I was doing. I grabbed every opportunity I could to get out of the house. But my husband was a saint with her. My eight children loved her, and, believe me, when she died, every one of them came from all over the world to her funeral."

Advance Arrangements

You will want to have the proper setting when your parent comes to live with you: privacy for him and all other family members; time to give for his physical and emotional requirements; the ability to provide him with some form of social life; the availability of good medical care. You may have some problems if your house isn't well organized and tranquil. Most older people require a predictable routine: slamming doors, groups of people in and out, meals at irregular hours are too disturbing. On the other hand, your mother or father may be unusually adaptable and really enjoy being in a lively household. It isn't fair, nor will it assure long-term tranquillity, to require younger members to restyle their lives completely to accommodate a grandparent's presence. There should be a quiet place to which Grandma can retreat and have a meal, on time, to satisfy everyone's requirements.

Try to think through in advance with your parent: How does each of you view the prospective living arrangement? What factors will be important to your parent, to you, and to other household members? Talking calmly and candidly beforehand can create a healthy climate.

Maintaining a Healthy Climate

You can only be in control of your own behavior, not your mother's or father's. If tension and conflict erode the good feeling in your household, then it is time to determine whether it is possible to reestablish good, healthy relationships by an open review of each other's irritating habits, whether an outside counselor can help, or whether it is really better for everyone to separate and make another arrangement. Some general rules may help:

- If your parent can help financially, do not discourage this. It is not only fair but good for an elderly person to maintain self-respect by knowing that he is contributing to, and not taking away from, the household resources.
- Whatever contribution your parent can make to help with family chores should be encouraged. Productive activity will maintain his ego and his feeling of independence and may relieve others in the family of some extra burdens. Don't hasten dependence and listlessness by constantly removing tasks the older person can do perfectly well.

- Privacy should be respected—and independent social life encouraged. Start out that way from the beginning, so everyone knows what to expect. Not every moment, event, or friendship needs to be shared.
- Don't give your parent any more advice than you are prepared to accept from him.

Friction Points

One clinical psychologist in Virginia reports the neurotic pattern that can emerge when a physically healthy seventy-five-year-old woman moves into her middle-aged daughter's home. "It is the accepted thing to do in this part of the country to take your widowed mother into your home," she says. "The middle-aged woman no longer has children at home to care for. Two generations of older women are living under one roof, neither with enough to do, their previous roles expired. They bicker and squabble, criticize each other, complain about one another, and develop a long battery of psychosomatic ailments. The son-in-law, oppressed by the atmosphere, finds more and more things to do away from home. Three people are joined in misery."[6]

Enduring each other's irritating mannerisms may result in periodic explosions. Because this is so frequent an occurrence, many of the mental health associations are now scheduling workshops for parents and adult children who live together in unhappy alliance. One workshop technique is to present a psychodrama that highlights typical behaviors: The setting is a kitchen. Mother and daughter are preparing supper. The audience witnesses the exasperated glances of one to the other, the sharp verbal exchanges, the tears, the withdrawal and rejection, the hurt and guilt that surround their tense encounters. A group discussion follows. Individual counseling is scheduled for those who require it.

If you and your parent are locked into an unfortunate situation, you can help each other by taking positive steps to eliminate the causes. An experienced family counselor can help.

A severe personality clash may be eliminated by changing the place where your parent lives to the home of another relative, for instance, but in general the problems of two generations or of two people living together will be similar. Any friction that arises in your home will likely be paralleled if your parent is living with someone else. Nevertheless, with goodwill on all sides, some adjustments and compromises, a parent at home may be the satisfying solution for your caretaking problems.

Care for Your Parent in a Supervised Setting

Even very loving and caring families exhaust their tolerance when they have been caring for a severely impaired parent for what seems like a long time. This kind of obligation, with its often ceaseless demands, disrupts the lives of family members, destroys harmonious family relationships, and can create great emotional problems for the caretakers. Judith Altholz advises families to rethink their arrangements if the caretaking situation becomes too draining. "If a daughter who is caring for a sick mother becomes oppressed and overwrought, she can become sick herself," she says. "Two sick people in a household are one too many."

Boarding Homes and Foster Homes

A kind of halfway measure between a family home and an institution is provided by boarding homes or foster homes which care for small groups of elderly people who do not require much regular nursing or medical care. These homes are frequently not licensed or supervised by state health departments. Sometimes they are owned or run by a registered nurse; sometimes a family trying to increase its income will take in a few older people and attempt to provide care. Such arrangements can be haphazard and unreliable. If the home is not licensed, you have no assurance that it meets minimum state standards for nursing homes, for safety, sanitation, proper diet, and professional care. Unless you know the proprietors and are satisfied that they are responsible, a boarding home is probably not a good choice. A licensed boarding home may be, but of course you will want to stay in close touch to be sure your expectations are being fulfilled.

Long-Term Care in a Nursing Home

At a critical time, when the older person's condition takes a sharp turn from better to worse, family members turn to each other and say, "Well, maybe it's time now for a nursing home."

Maybe it is and maybe it isn't. Extreme impairment, incontinence, a firm diagnosis of irreversible brain damage, physical conditions which require almost constant nursing care present situations where a nursing home is the best solution not only for the older person but for his family. But such clear situations are the rare ones. In most cases where families reach this threshold, the decision is a highly complicated one. It should be made only after thorough examination of your parent's condition, all the possible alternatives for his care, the family's financial capability, and the emotions and attitudes of your parent and each person closely involved with him.

It is surely a decision you cannot make alone or even in concert with other members of your family. First you must know your parent's wishes. Then you need an informed opinion from the physician who understands your parent's physical ailments, what their prognosis is, and how well they can be cared for in a nursing home or under other arrangements. If there's a question of your parent's mental and emotional condition, you should bring in a reliable psychiatrist for a diagnosis and prognosis. It would be helpful to consult with a social worker who often knows better than the doctor and the psychiatrist exactly what kinds of care would be available in the range of institutions in the area as compared with what kind of care could be brought into the home for your parent.

Remember, nursing-home care can be temporary if there is a sudden incapacity or illness or if your parent requires a period of convalescence and rehabilitation after a hospital stay. After suitable recovery, your parent will return to his home. Be sure the nursing home can provide the required care and that it is certified by medicare so that medicare will pay the bills.

But this is not the kind of nursing-home care that concerns most families, important as this is. Their concern is for long-term care, when the nursing home will most likely be the parent's place of residence for the rest of his life.

The term "nursing home" now has a pejorative connotation. In the last few years the distressing and often horrifying conditions which prevailed in some of the nation's nursing homes have been made public. Public figures and professionals have accused families of "dumping" their burdensome older relatives into these "warehouses for the aged" because the families were too callous to assume the caretaking load.

Some families do dump and are rightfully accused, but they are few in number and are, more often than not, other relatives of the older person and not his children. Only 5 percent of all Americans over the age of sixty-five are in institutions—and these include not only nursing homes but hospitals and mental institutions. The outstanding majority of American families do not dump—their parent is being cared for in his home or in theirs, often at great sacrifice to his children.

The glaring publicity given to the scandalous conditions in some nursing homes has resulted in better quality now; many state departments of health which regulate nursing homes are exercising tighter supervision. Nursing-home operators recognize they are dealing with families who are more aware and enlightened. There's more government money going into training programs for all kinds of nursing-home personnel. There's much more awareness that the nursing-home resident is not an object, but an individual who should be treated as a human being.

Current professional advice is to maintain older people in their homes as long as it can be managed, through the use of whatever battery of helping aids is needed. In cases where older people are supported altogether or in part by state funds—SSI, medicaid, etc.—it is less expensive for the state to maintain the person independently than in an institution. This may not be the case for families who pay the bills.

Social and emotional reasons may balance the scale for maintaining older people at home. Although many make an excellent adjustment to nursing homes, many others wither. Nursing-home mortality rates have been widely printed: about 25 percent of the inhabitants die within the first year of entering, over 50 percent within three years.[7] But one should remember that people who enter nursing homes often are in the last stages of a gripping illness, and surely the mortality rate is high also for those of advanced age, with acute illnesses, who are living outside institutions.

Children who are considering nursing homes as residences for a parent should consider carefully the parent's personality as well as his physical needs. Some older people are truly dependent—they may always have had this kind of personality, needing some help, some advice, some support to live their lives. At times a formerly independent person becomes dependent when he is older and has lost a spouse, a child, a dear brother or friend. For people who function best with a little help from others, who require assistance in managing the mechanics of their lives, who have a debilitating physical condition, a nursing home with the protection and security it offers may be the optimum environment.

Nevertheless, most caring children experience great conflict about moving a parent to a nursing home.

What Is a Nursing Home?

The average person tends to lump together under the catch phrase "nursing home" any institution or residence where old people can live and be cared for. Behind that phrase, in actuality, lie many different kinds of places offering many different levels of care and services.

Even the terms and labels that describe facilities within the overall grouping of "nursing homes" can be confusing. You should know about these labels because you will probably hear them from the doctors, hospital staffs, social workers, and other professionals who are involved with you in trying to find the best situation for your parent. The important thing is to find out exactly what kinds of services a home provides for exactly what your parent needs.

Labels

Descriptive labels have developed because nursing homes are certified to receive medicare and medicaid funds for patients who are covered by these government programs. In order to be certified, nursing homes must offer facilities and services which comply with medicare and medicaid regulations. To qualify for medicare nursing-home benefits—given only for a short time—a nursing home must be designated as a "skilled nursing facility" (formerly known as an "extended care facility"). To qualify for medicaid benefits—which apply to residents who are there for long-term and perhaps lifetime care—a nursing home must be designated as a "skilled nursing facility" or as an "intermediate care facility." Here's a short description of what's behind the labels:

- *A skilled nursing facility* (SNF) is at the level nearest hospital care. It's for those who require constant medical supervision and skilled nursing services, and professional rehabilitation therapy. There should be, in addition, a total range of other kinds of services for the physical and mental health of residents. Normally a physician has to prescribe admission. Although SNF admission is generally limited to those suffering from physical impairments, many will accept older people whose mental dysfunctioning stems from a physiological base.
- An *intermediate care facility* (ICF) cares for people who aren't well enough for independent living but are not sick enough to require constant medical and nursing attention. An ICF should give patients help with bathing, dressing, eating, walking, and other personal needs and provide a full program of social and recreational activities. Nursing and rehabilitative services are available as needed. There's no medical requirement for admission.

Institutions in each category usually have agreements with nearby hospitals and other health-related agencies in the area to provide services which the facility itself may not offer. Be sure to check this when you investigate.

These characteristics exist in many other nursing homes which do not accept medicaid patients but which give excellent care for the older person at various levels. Often a single institution will offer care at all levels. If your parent is in fact entering a nursing home at a level which requires minimal care, it might be wise to choose one where he can move along the care corridor without having to change his residence.

There are other kinds of nursing homes, known by other names and geared to caring for the older person whose medical and health needs are not demanding. The names will vary from state to state, but they can be called old-age homes, homes for the aged, or domiciliary homes. They may be operated by state agencies, by private agencies, or by special groups.

A number of homes for the aged are nonprofit; some are operated by religious groups. They care for the not-very-sick old, but more and more offer the same levels of care as the skilled and intermediate care facilities described above. The quality of life in these homes is often on a high plane, and, consequently, they normally have long waiting lists. They may not admit a person who is severely impaired mentally or physically or who is in a critical condition, although if a resident reaches these conditions they normally continue to care for him. You should try to check this possibility in advance.

Policies on caretaking institutions for the aged vary among the states, but almost everywhere in the country all institutions caring for the old at any level must be licensed by the state department of health. Boarding and foster homes, which are sometimes not licensed, are the exception. Your city or county health department can supply you with a list of licensed homes in the area.

Look Behind the Labels

Nursing homes vary enormously in their objectives, their names, their ownership and administration, according to the U.S. Public Health Service. They also vary in bed capacity, staffing, services, quality, and the cost of care. In addition, rapid changes are taking place as institutions have been adapting their services and facilities to meet national medicare standards in order to attract patients who are covered by medicare. The result has been a blurring of the distinctions which previously existed among different types of institutions and a merging of services at all levels in many single institutions.

If all this confuses you, it's probably a good thing for your parent. Your confusions should lead you to a thorough investigation of what's appropriate and available for him. Visit all the homes in your locality that seem to fit the picture, talk to their administrators and staff members, observe keenly. You cannot make a judgment until you have made a round of visits. What you find in some homes will surprise you pleasantly; in others, you may be intensely displeased.

Above all, try not to react to the impairments and the severe disabilities of some of the residents because there will be many whose state will be pitiful. Frequent visitors to nursing homes learn to overcome any initial shock they may experience and appreciate the compassionate care some institutions provide for such patients. Your judgment should be directed to the quality of life and the care and services which the home tries to give to its residents, whatever their individual condition.

Your parent should participate with you in this investigation to the limits of his ability. There is no point in his going to see every home. You can make the preliminary survey and pinpoint those which you think would be best. Then, if he can, he should visit them—several times, if possible.

Costs

If your parent's medical and financial condition warrant it, medicaid may provide financial support for nursing-home care. If medicaid doesn't take over, costs could be high.

Money is often the predominant factor in deciding how to locate a parent whose physical needs are great. Sometimes it is obvious from the start that there won't be enough money to cover the bills. Sometimes families together can put up enough money temporarily to carry a parent through a period of intensive care. But if that period appears to be open-ended, not many families have the resources to support it. If your family does, you are fortunate in spite of your woes. You will be spared what is often an overwhelming financial drain.

If your parent isn't eligible for medicaid because of the extent of his financial assets, and if family funds can provide support for a time but not forever, a sensible approach would be to start spending your parent's money on the needed services. Your parent may object strenuously to this: he doesn't want his money spent in this way, or he wants it saved for his children. This is an emotional stance and not a practical one. If you act under the spur of his emotions, you may exhaust your cash reserves and even find yourself in debt to pay for his care. The practical approach is to use up his money to a point where he will become eligible for medicaid's long-term-care benefits.

Nursing-home costs will depend on many variables: geographical location, level of care, range of services, and other considerations. Small homes located in small communities and with care that is confined to the supervisory or custodial will probably charge several hundred dollars a month. In large metropolitan communities, nursing homes providing complete care through sophisticated services may charge well over $1,000 a month. The average national cost of nursing-home care was put at $600 a month in 1975—but by the time you read this book, that will have risen. In addition, some nursing homes require a large gift or admission fee as a condition of entrance.

These figures are indeed staggering, but the economics can be parsed out. Family members can contribute portions; private health insurance policies give coverage; medicaid may come into the picture ultimately when your parent's financial resources have been reduced to the level set out by the state.

Beware

Some nursing homes require entrance agreements under which the patient pays one large lump sum on entry and then is guaranteed care for the rest of his life regardless of changes in his condition. Sometimes the entrant is asked to turn over all of his assets and assign all of his income to the home in return for lifetime care. Arrangements and contracts like these should be examined carefully by a lawyer to ascertain that they contain no loophole disadvantageous to the resident. Sometimes the fine print allows the home to ask the resident to leave if his condition worsens drastically—with no obligation on the home's part to refund any of his unused money. There have been cases where nursing homes have done just that after a patient's deteriorating physical state required more expensive care and the institution decided that it was no longer profitable to retain him. It may be best to find a home where you can pay by the month, but no matter what form the financial arrangements take, you must be very clear about them and must give your parent and yourself every possible protection for the future. Be sure you know exactly what the refunding procedures are. You should be knowledgable about state laws regulating nursing-home financial arrangements.

There are hidden costs in nursing homes. Private-duty nursing, if it's required, is usually at extra cost. Boxes of tissues purchased from the home may cost $1; shampoos and hairsets may be exorbitant, as may other special supplies and services. You should look carefully into the cost of all of these items. Many times you can supply them yourself.

To Find Out about Nursing Homes in the Area

If you're looking for a home affiliated with a religious denomination or a fraternal order, inquire of the local church, temple, or order in which you're interested. There are many, of high quality, located around the country. They may offer some spaces to people who are not members of the denomination or of the fraternal order. However, they will generally have waiting lists. They include Protestants, Catholics, Christian Scientists, Quakers, and Jews; Elks, Masons, Eagles, Kiwanis; the Salvation Army.

For an unaffiliated home, if you don't know where to start, get in touch with the local agency on aging, and the local health department. These will have lists of approved homes. Local welfare or social services departments, in addition to knowing about nursing homes, may also have a list of boarding homes. Senior citizens' centers may also have information.

The state agency on aging will tell you about a fairly new kind of expert who will be working in all the states except Wyoming, Nebraska, and Oklahoma. This is the nursing-home ombudsman, who should have firsthand knowledge of the range and quality of nursing-home facilities in the area.

The American Association of Homes for the Aged (nonproprietary homes) and the American Health Care Association (proprietary and church-related nonproprietary homes) will provide you with the names of their affiliated members. They can also make available a good checklist of things to look for when you evaluate the homes you inspect. *Choosing a Nursing Home,* by Jean Baron Nassau, is a recent book which provides additional detailed information to help you in your decisions.

In general, the recommendations suggest you pay attention to these major factors:

- Accreditation, license, and certification for medicare or medicaid should be current and in force.
- The physical premises should be well located, attractive, cheerful, clean, safe, and meet federal and state fire codes. Residents should not be in crowded quarters; attention should be given to individual needs for privacy wherever possible.
- Nursing, medical, social services, physical therapy, and rehabilitation services should be consistent with your parent's needs.
- Food should be prepared with careful attention to special diets in clean kitchens and should be served in pleasant surroundings with appropriate help if necessary.
- A full range of recreation and social activities under proper supervision should be available in activity rooms. These should be attractively furnished and supplied with materials suitable for the highest level of activity your parent can perform and enjoy.
- The staff should be professionally trained and adequate in number to provide the level of care your parent requires. You should know who is in charge of what so that you know exactly to whom to go should you have a problem.
- You and your parent, if possible, should meet and talk with the administrator and department heads before you make your final decision.[8]

After a few visits to several homes, you can tell which of them are warm, professional, and comfortable, staffed by concerned people, and which are officious, cold, and uncaring. The best advice we can offer is to visit a home without making an advance appointment, to get a feeling for the atmosphere; visit a dining room at mealtime and an activity room in session, to see yourself how patients are fed and treated; talk to residents in the social rooms and find out how they feel about the home.

You'll learn a great deal this way before you get the official tour. Then make your appointments for talks with the administrators.

When You Decide

The director of services on aging for the Federation of Protestant Welfare Agencies in New York says: "The decision to seek admission for a parent to an institution is not lightly taken in most families. But, once done, families begin to move like lightning because the whole procedure is so painful for them."[9]

Don't let speed interfere with your best instincts. Review your options. Be sure you're not pushing your parent into an institution unnecessarily. On the other hand, don't deny him the security and safety of an institution when that is really the best place for him to be. And when you make your choice you may want the further advice of professionals on how to make the move as comfortable for everyone as possible. Social workers on the nursing-home staff can certainly advise you well.[10]

Relocating

Except in emergencies where immediate placement is essential to health and safety, allow a little time for your parent to get used to the idea, to think about disposing of his possessions, for selecting the few precious things he can take with him to maintain his link with his self-identity and past life. An article called "Relocation of the Elderly" published in the professional journal of the National Association of Social Workers says, "Families should discuss the disposal of possessions with the older person before a crisis develops. In this way, the older person can maintain a central role in the process. He might derive pleasure and satisfaction from giving possessions to friends, or donating them to charities. . . . Knowing that one's former possessions will be used and appreciated is not as traumatic as not knowing what happened to them." The authors point out that "increased death rates have been linked to involuntary relocation for which no preparation has been made."[11]

The Family and the Nursing Home

Just as it's important that you have a good relationship with your ailing parent's doctor, it's important to have an equally good one with his nursing home. The arrival of a parent in a nursing home doesn't mean his departure from your life. On the contrary, you will visit, spend time there, have many dealings both pleasant and unpleasant with many people on the staff. An experienced nursing-home administrator offers these suggestions:[12]

- There must be a clear-cut understanding of what the institution has to offer—precisely what services are and are not available.
- There should be mutual confidence between you and the home administration that they will do their job and you will not interfere as long as they are doing it.
- Communication should be constant. Follow the normal pattern you had when your parent was at home: regular telephone calls and visits. Knowing that you are very much involved will give the staff a better attitude toward both your parent and you.
- If your parent complains, listen. Don't assume anything until you talk to the staff and hear their side of the story. Try to play a positive role in erasing the problem. If you are really displeased with something, talk to the administrator.
- If, over a period of time, you decide that this is not the place for your parent, you may have to make other arrangements. But this may not be disastrous if you made a good investigation before your parent entered the home and you have some attractive alternatives in the back of your head. There are more good places than bad. "This is not an irreversible decision," said one daughter after she brought her mother to a pleasant nursing home. "If it doesn't work, I know that there are three other good homes in the area."

The Best You Can Do

Your parent may react very strongly to a move from one place or kind of residence to another. Uprooting can be a psychological shock, creating new health problems or intensifying existing ones. But no solution will be perfect if your parent is ill and old and tired. Whatever you do, in or out of his home or yours, if it is done with love and compassion, with respect for your parent, for yourself, and others in your family, it will be the best you can do. That is all anyone can ask of himself.

CHAPTER 5 MONEY MATTERS: Government Benefits, Insurance, Taxes, Estates

In many families, the young child knows neither the amount of the family income nor his parent's financial condition. Sometimes this information is withheld in the early years as a matter of discretion and judgment. Most people don't share freely with their friends and neighbors, or even with other family members, the details of economic conditions. Children frequently tell—and, because of this, they aren't told.

In later years, parents have other reasons for maintaining secrecy. If they have money, they often prefer that their growing children learn to be on their own and not be influenced by how much money the family has. Parents with comparatively little money may wish their children to believe that the family finances are in better shape than they actually are. And some parents may simply believe that it isn't a child's business to know how much money there is. When the time comes, they feel, the children will find out.

When the time comes . . . Sometimes, unfortunately, that isn't until after the death of the parent. Consider the family of a ninety-two-year-old woman living in a nursing home in Ohio. Each of three daughters lives in a different state; the nursing home is in the city of the oldest daughter's residence. As inflation increases, monthly charges at the home rise. Mother is still in charge of her money and is reticent about the total amount. She wants to be sure the grandchildren remember her and plans to leave a legacy to each. She asks her daughters to help pay for the nursing home.

Daughters go to husbands and say, "Can we do it?" Husbands reply, "Of course we'll take care of Mother, but doesn't she have money of her own? After all, we have children in college and it will really hurt to send an extra hundred a month to Ohio." Daughters are caught between Mother and husbands and pressed by the needs of their own children. We feel guilty about denying her, they say, but it's silly to send her money when she has it. The trouble is, though, we don't know how much she really has.

Mother is from the old school whose members, according to psychiatrist Olga Knopf, are frugal in spending for their own needs and imbued with the idea of leaving something to their children after death. People of the not-so-old school grew older during the era of social security payments and the loosening of family ties, Dr. Knopf says, "and are quite prepared to spend all the resources they have for their own comfort."[1]

Talking About Money

If your parent is an old-schooler, like Mother, it might be difficult to talk with her about money. You may be as reluctant to probe as she is to reveal. You won't know, then, the size of the estate she hopes to leave or the steps she has or hasn't taken to minimize possible estate and inheritance taxes after her death. Nor will you know, if she remains adamant in her decision to leave an estate and not to dig into her own funds for support, how much you may have to dig into yours to maintain her properly while she lives.

But money is something that needs to be talked about. In our culture it becomes a more important and significant consideration in the later years than it was before.

One reason is that people live longer today, and their often deteriorating mental and physical conditions can require exorbitant caretaking expenses which might continue for years. Another reason is that older people tend to live alone more than they used to, partly because most can support themselves at least to some extent with their social security income, and partly because many truly feel that living in a child's home is a burden on the child. Aging parents living with children may have drawbacks, but certainly one advantage is that the arrangement saves money—the costs of a single multigeneration household are less than those of a separate household for each generation.

Money takes on increasing importance also because estate taxes are proportionately greater than they were in former years. It's possible that the expenses of your parent's last years will swallow up his savings. But if this doesn't happen and if there's an estate at his death—and just owning a home that has gone up in value may build an estate-tax liability—federal and state estate taxes may eat away a large chunk of it. Proper action during your parent's lifetime may avoid this bite.

Money Hang-Ups

Money hang-ups between generations are widespread and rest on more than economic considerations. The entire quality of a lifetime relationship is involved, and even good rapport can become strained during discussions about money— especially when questions revolve around how much who is going to spend on what, how much will come from the parent or the child, how much will be left to the child.

If you haven't talked to your parent about money before now, you may be reluctant to begin. You surely don't want him to think that "you're out after his money" or that you consider him "too far gone to take care of himself." You don't want to bruise his ego and feelings of self-respect by indicating that he's not going to have "enough to take care of himself in his old age." Neither do you want to rob him of the security he feels from knowing that "he won't have to be dependent on his children for anything" and that he has "a little nest egg of his own."

These phrases are in quotation marks because they're clichés—but they're clichés which truly reflect the attitudes many older people have about money. You may even think in some of the same clichés yourself.

Yet these are old-fashioned concepts, not relevant to the times in which you and your parent are living. The hard fact is that being old—like many other things—costs much more than it used to. It's legitimate for you and your parent to discuss together where the money will come from. Will there be enough for his living expenses in the foreseeable future? Will there be enough for expensive medical bills, perhaps for long-term care in a nursing home or some other kind of supervised setting?

If it turns out there's some doubt in these areas, you and your parent will at least have a head start in the financial planning you'll have to do, and this chapter may help you. The first part will deal with government programs which in one way or another can provide a portion of income or help with medical expenses for people over sixty-five. It will also look at income-tax benefits for you and your parent and at other areas where there may be some money-saving possibilities. Finally, there will be some easy and quite legal steps your parent can take during his lifetime to ensure a smaller tax bite on his estate.

How to Get More Money–Maybe

There are major federal government programs which can help pay for the living costs and high medical expenses of people who are sixty-five and over. These include social security, supplemental security income, food stamps, medicare, medicaid, and veterans benefits. Knowing some exact details about them may mean extra dollars for you and your parent.

Social Security

You're probably familiar with social security through the contributions taken from your own paycheck over the years, or those you have withheld from your employees' wages. The Social Security Administration's first wad of monthly benefits, paid out in January 1940, totaled $75,844. Now payments run around $5 billion a month, with checks going to some 31 million people. Social security provides the major portion of income for most people over sixty-five.

Your over-sixty-five parent is certainly among these millions.

A person who has worked at a job covered by social security will be eligible to receive monthly benefits when he retires at age sixty-five. These benefits are based on average yearly earnings for at least six years of employment and range from a little over \$90 to a little over \$300 a month. If your parent retires between the ages of sixty-two and sixty-five, he will also be eligible for social security, but his monthly check will be about 20 percent less for life. If he doesn't retire until after seventy-two, he'll receive slightly higher benefits than if he retired at sixty-five.

If your parent has continued to work after sixty-five, he can still receive regular monthly checks—as long as he doesn't earn more than \$230 in any one month. If he does earn more than that in a single month, his social security check for that month will be reduced by half of the amount he earns over the \$230 cutoff figure. After seventy-two, he can earn as much as he likes without affecting the size of his monthly check.

Income from anything else—from interest or dividends, rentals, stock profits, etc.—doesn't reduce social security benefits, and social security income isn't subject to income tax.

In order to receive social security benefits, your parent must apply for them at the local social security office. It's a good idea for him to do this two or three months before his sixty-fifth birthday or before the date set for retirement in advance of age sixty-five.

If your parent's monthly social security checks aren't being mailed directly to his checking or savings account, that can be arranged through the social security office. This saves troublesome trips to the bank and worry about mailbox thefts.

Remember that social security pays a lump sum death benefit of \$255.

Special Social Security Benefits

Some other social security benefits, less well-known, can go to older people under certain specialized conditions. These benefits don't come automatically; your parent would have to apply for them. It's well worth a call to the local social security office if you think any of these conditions apply:

- Your parent is under sixty-five and suffering from a severe mental or physical condition which prevents him from working for at least a year or which is terminal.

- One of your parents is disabled, and the other is over sixty-two.
- One of your parents, covered by social security, has died, and the other isn't covered in his or her own right.
- Your mother is divorced, but was married to your father for at least twenty years and has not remarried.
- Your parents were completely dependent financially on a child who has died.
- Your father or your mother didn't work long enough to qualify for what would be the maximum social security benefit, or is the widow or widower of such a person.

These benefits are larded with sometimes complicated requirements and conditions. The social security office can explain them to you.

The Social Security Administration in Washington and its local offices have many pamphlets discussing all aspects of benefits. The Appendix will tell you where to write for them. But it's best to start with a telephone call to the local social security office. Look in the telephone book for United States government listings. Under them, you will find the Department of Health, Education and Welfare and, under that, the Social Security Administration.

Medicare

Medicare is indeed a boon to older Americans, but it cannot be taken for granted. The benefits and coverage it promises must be examined carefully in advance for the actual value they may hold—or withhold.

Medicare is, in fact, available to virtually everybody at age sixty-five. If your parent is covered under social security, he will automatically get hospital insurance under part A of medicare, whether or not he's retired. If he isn't covered by social security, he can buy medicare hospital insurance by paying a small monthly premium. When he's sixty-five, he also becomes eligible for part B of medicare—the part that covers doctors' bills and some other medical expenses—on payment of a monthly fee of $7.20.

Remember that medicare itself is not the bill-paying entity.

When your parent, his doctor, or the hospital where he stayed sends in a bill for treatment or services, it goes to an insurance company selected by the government to process and make the medicare payments.

The Medicare Mystique

Many older people and their families are lulled into a false sense of security by the medicare promise. "If I have to go to a hospital or to a nursing home," your parent may say, "don't worry. Medicare will pay the bills."

Medicare may pay them, or it may not.

According to Dr. Gladys Ellenbogen, an economist and consultant to the Senate Special Committee on Aging, medicare is "removing less and less of the crushing burden of health costs from the aged in our nation."[2]

There are several reasons why this is happening:

- Hospital and doctors' bills and other medical charges have risen drastically across the board and across the nation in the past ten years.
- Medicare pays, at best, only a part of what the patient is billed—not all.
- Older people and their families often don't inform themselves in advance of exactly what medicare will and won't pay for.
- Hospital and medical services are always reviewed by committees before a medicare payment is made. A hospital review committee goes over the hospital services that were provided; a medical group reviews the doctor's course of treatment and charges. If the committee or group feels that the services, treatment, or charges weren't "reasonable and necessary," medicare may pay none of the bill, or only part of it. This review is made whether the bills are sent in by the hospital, the doctor, or your parent.

Inform Yourself

Familiarize yourself now with just what medicare can and cannot pay for. Don't wait until you're in the middle of an emergency or crisis situation to find out. By that time, you may already have paid the ambulance bill to an ambulance service which isn't certified by medicare, or you may already have shelled out a large sum of money to a nursing home which doesn't qualify for medicare's posthospital benefits. Medicare will not reimburse you for these outlays.

We won't list medicare's benefits here—they're numerous, varied, and tangled within a jungle of ifs, ands, and buts. The Social Security Administration, which administers medicare, has several informative pamphlets which describe the benefits thoroughly. You should read them carefully. (See the Appendix.)

Ask the Doctor

But this advance research should be only the beginning of your self-education. When your parent is actually in a situation where his doctor is suggesting treatment or surgery, where a hospital stay is indicated, where a nursing home is necessary for a short period of time, then ask the doctor how much medicare will pay for each step and service along the way. Doctors are very knowledgeable about medicare, and if they aren't, someone on their office staff will surely be. Someone on the hospital staff will also know about medicare benefits. Your rule should be always to ask in advance. Then if you find medicare won't pay for something—or will pay for only part of it—perhaps you can find a less costly alternative. If that isn't possible, at least you and your parent won't have a shock when the bills come in.

Medicare Pitfalls

Government medicare experts are well acquainted with some of the costly mistakes uninformed older people and their children make when they assume that "medicare will take care of it all." Here are some examples:

- The doctor says your parent needs certain X rays or laboratory tests. *Medicare will pay only if these are done in a laboratory certified by medicare.*
- Your parent needs someone to take care of him at home

after a hospital stay. *Medicare will pay only for a registered or skilled nurse.*

- The doctor says your parent should go to a nursing home after a hospital stay. *Medicare won't cover a nursing home at all unless your parent has been in a hospital first for at least three days, and unless he goes to the nursing home within fourteen days after he leaves the hospital. Then it will cover only a certain kind of nursing home. You must check first to be sure it's certified and gives the required type of service. Medicare will pay all the costs of the first twenty days, part of the costs of the next eighty days, and won't pay at all after the hundredth day. A person covered by medicare is allowed only 100 days of benefits in a nursing home during his lifetime. Neither you nor your parent's doctor will determine how long your parent can stay in the nursing home. A nursing-home committee will review your parent's condition periodically, and if its judgment is that your parent's condition is stabilized, he may have to leave the home.*
- Your parent has to go to a psychiatric hospital. *Medicare will pay for only 190 days in a lifetime.*

There are some things medicare won't pay for at all:

- A private room in a hospital or nursing home; it will pay only for a semiprivate room.
- A television set in the room.
- Telephone calls.
- Private-duty nurses.
- Prescription drugs after your parent leaves the hospital or nursing home.

Assignment

Medicare information specialists suggest that your parent ask the doctor if he will accept payment on "assignment." Many doctors won't, but your parent will end up ahead of the game if the doctor will.

Under the assignment method, the doctor agrees to accept the "reasonable" charges set by the medicare carrier as his total charge for his services to your parent, and sends his bill directly to the carrier. Medicare then pays him 80 percent of those reasonable charges. The doctor cannot then charge your parent any more than the remaining 20 percent of the reasonable charges.

Without using assignment, your parent will pay the doctor's bill himself and will then send the bill to the medicare carrier, which will reimburse your parent for 80 percent of the reasonable charges. If the doctor has charged more than what the carrier has determined is reasonable, your parent will have to pay that difference.

The percentage of doctors willing to accept assignment has dropped within the past few years, and with reason. Medicare is supposed to pay 80 percent of a doctor's "reasonable and necessary" charges. Doctors' fees, like all other prices, have moved steadily upward, and while medicare eventually allows for this gradual fee rise, there is often a lag—sometimes up to two years—between the time the doctor increases his fees and the time when medicare builds these increases into payments. In effect, medicare has been paying less than 80 percent, and the patient—your parent—has been paying the difference.

Doctors aren't required by law to accept assignment, but about half of the country's doctors do so.

Appealing Medicare Payments

If your parent feels that a medicare payment for a hospital or medical bill doesn't cover all the services to which he's entitled, he can ask the insurance company paying the bills to review its decision. There's a definite procedure for this and a specific time limit for doing it, which you can find out about from the local social security office. If your parent still disagrees with the decision after the claim has been reviewed, he can ask for a hearing. This appeals procedure, according to social security spokespersons, can sometimes revise medicare payments upward.

The Medigap and Private Health Insurance

A private health insurance policy can help pay for a large part of the "medigap"—the difference between what medicare pays and what your parent has to pay for health costs. There's more information about this on page 134.

Other Government Programs

You and your parent, along with most other Americans, doubtless accept social security and medicare benefits as unquestionable rights for people over sixty-five. After all, didn't they make regular contributions from their paychecks over the years for just those benefits, and aren't they therefore entitled to them? Nobody thinks of social security checks or medicare payments as government handouts to the poor.

But there are other government programs which you and your parent may not have thought about and which could possibly help him if his income is low enough to qualify. He has, in fact, contributed to these programs through many of the federal, state, and local taxes he has paid during his lifetime. Supplemental security income, food stamps, medicaid, and some veterans benefits may be open to him if his income is low enough.

When Is an Income Low Enough?

If your parent is in financial need now, with not enough income and assets to pay for his living and medical expenses, he may qualify for some of the benefits that can come from these programs. It doesn't matter how much money you have, or your brothers or sisters have. Under the law, a child isn't financially responsible for a parent. Only a spouse is responsible for a spouse.

Economists who study and advise on the financial situation of our over-sixty-five population agree that many of today's older people weren't among the low-income poor when they were young or middle-aged. They have become poor as relentlessly mounting living and health costs have battered their fixed incomes and savings. They are now too poor to pay for the goods and services they need desperately, and poor enough, perhaps, to qualify for some additional government help. If your parent fits this description, he is entitled to the help he can get from these programs, and he should have it.

Supplemental Security Income

Supplemental security income (SSI) can provide supplemental monthly income to people over sixty-five who have limited income and financial resources. Almost all states add their own money in varying degrees to the federal government support they receive for SSI payments, and consequently the amount an older person may receive differs from state to state. In all states, older people who are receiving social security can also receive SSI payments if their income is low enough.

A single person with an income of around $160 a month and assets no greater than $1,500 can qualify for supplemental security income; for couples, income should be no higher than around $240 a month and assets no more than $2,250. The exact amount is determined each year by legislation, but these figures will give you an idea of the numbers involved.

Your parent can own a home and a car and still qualify. These aren't counted among his assets, nor are his household and personal goods. In addition, certain kinds of income are excluded from the maximum income calculations. States have different eligibility requirements for SSI, so you should check the local social security office to determine what they are in your parent's state. Be prepared to answer questions about his income and resources. Even if these are higher than the stated ceiling, he might still be able to get some monthly payments, based on a sliding scale related to his income. If he has borderline eligibility, you might find that he can qualify for SSI by what the government calls "spending down"—using up some of his assets and thus reducing them to a point which makes him eligible.

If your parent is under sixty-five but disabled, he might also be able to qualify.

Food Stamps

There is a most enchanting anecdote about the over-sixty-five lady, living alone in the Colorado mountains, whose East Coast daughter told her she was eligible for food stamps. The nearest food stamps office, where she would have had to make her application for the stamps, was on the other side of the mountains. She found that the trip there and back was too long to be made in one day, and that she would have to stay overnight in a hotel.

"I can't afford the trip, dear," she told her daughter. "I'll just go out and shoot an elk and put it in the community freezer for the winter."

Your parent might not be that good a shot.

The food stamp program is dramatically underused by people over sixty-five who can qualify for it. It's undoubtedly colored by a strong welfare tinge in the minds of many older people. Then there's the fact that they have to go through a bureaucratic process to buy the stamps and, exposed to the view of other people in the checkout line, use them instead of cash at grocery stores and supermarkets. Ironically, some of their grandchildren, temporary dropouts from comfortable middle-class life, may be participating casually and with no prick of conscience in the food stamp program.

If your parent's income qualifies him for food stamps, you and he should weigh the benefits against the drawbacks. The American Association of Retired Persons, a large national organization with a membership of many millions, has suggested that members who were skimping on food "because they were having trouble making ends meet at the end of the month" might be eligible for food stamps without realizing it. More to the point, you and your parent may not want to realize it or may be too ashamed to.

Food stamps aren't free, except for people who have really low incomes. They're bought and then used like cash when food is purchased, but you pay considerably less for them than their cash value at the grocery store. In 1975 a single person could buy stamps which paid for about $45 worth of groceries a month; for a couple, the stamps would have bought about $80 worth each month. The amount paid for the stamps is based on family size and income and may change from time to time, depending on federal legislation, but food stamps should save about one-quarter of the grocery bill.

Food stamp eligibility parallels that for SSI, except that your parent can qualify for food stamps with a higher income and can be younger than sixty-five.

Application to become a food stamps user must be made in person at the food stamps office, but the Colorado sharpshooter's East Coast daughter missed up on something. If your parent can't get to the food stamp certification office, he can authorize you or someone else to go for him. This can sometimes be a cumbersome process, and you will have to provide information on your parent's income, rent, medical bills, and other expenses in order to establish eligibility. But if your parent's financial level is anywhere near the food stamp ceiling, you may find it profitable to pursue the process. Once the application is approved, stamps are bought each month at a local bank or post office. And almost any food store in the country will accept them.

Bear in mind that food stamps can be used for Meals on Wheels and for meals in communal or congregate eating centers (discussed in Chapter 2).

Telephone directories often list food stamps as such, under *F*. If this doesn't show in your directory, call the local city or county government or the local social services department. They will put you in touch with the food stamps office where you can discuss eligibility.

Veterans' Benefits

If your parent is sixty-five or over and a veteran with a low income, he will probably be able to get a small monthly pension from the Veterans Administration. If he's single, he's eligible with an income of less than $3,000 a year; if he's married, his income can't be more than $4,200. Sometimes pensions are paid on a sliding scale to veterans with slightly higher incomes. If your mother is a veteran's widow and has a similar income, she should also be eligible for a pension.

Veterans' hospitals and nursing homes will sometimes accept needy veterans, even though they may not have a service-connected disability.

To find out if your parent can qualify for any veterans' benefits, check the nearest Veterans Administration office. The VA also operates veterans' assistance centers, which can help veterans and their widows with questions about disability compensation, education benefits, medical and dental care, and other concerns.

Medicaid

Most middle- and upper-class people shudder at the thought of resorting to medicaid, but many over-sixty-five persons who are covered by medicaid now have not been on welfare all their lives, never lived in a slum, never eked out a hand-to-mouth existence. Like the former New York City schoolteacher, the widow of a Boston rabbi, the retired insurance salesman in Phoenix, they were responsible and productive people during their earlier years. Their savings were consumed by the steep costs of living in their later years, and their modest monthly incomes were not large enough to pay for their medical and health expenses. They found that if their incomes fell below required eligibility limits, medicaid would cover almost all of their medical and health expenses.

One of medicaid's purposes is to pay for a range of basic medical services for low-income older people. Even if your over-sixty-five parent is covered by medicare, he can come under medicaid if his income and assets are low enough. If he does, medicaid can pay, in most cases, for everything medicare pays for and more.

Unlike medicare, which is open to all people over sixty-five and offers the same span of benefits all over the country, medicaid eligibility requirements and benefits vary from state to state. In all states medicaid will pay for doctors', hospital, and nursing-home bills for older people who qualify. In some states it will also pay for prescription drugs, appliances, laboratory and X-ray services, home health care, and other medically related needs. Medicare does not cover long-term nursing-home costs; medicaid can.

If a person's income is no greater than the state's income eligibility requirement, the state will pay for his medical expenses. If his income is higher than the state's cutoff figure but still not large enough to pay for all his medical expenses, some states will pay for the portion of those expenses he can't afford.

"Medicaid is supported by federal, state, and local taxes," says a government medicaid expert, "and, as a taxpayer, anybody who contributed to these tax funds during his working life is entitled to medicaid and shouldn't have false pride about accepting it. Older people have arrived at times where they can't take care of themselves, and if they can't live on their social security incomes they are legitimately entitled to medicaid."

Perhaps medicaid's greatest benefit is for older people whose medical needs can no longer be met in their own or a child's home. Those who are suffering paralysis after a stroke, chronic congestive heart failure, severe brain damage, or other disabling illness need the medical and nursing care which certain nursing homes can provide—but these homes do so at a cost which few families can afford if a parent is to be a resident for a long period of time. Bills for a parent in residence at a nursing home have bankrupted many a family whose parent has not had a health insurance policy which included nursing-home care or who was not covered by medicaid. If a physician recommends nursing-home care for the medical needs of an older person with sufficiently low income and assets, then medicaid can cover the costs, and if you think your parent is approaching this circumstance, you should investigate medicaid thoroughly.

Medicaid Care at Home

Medicaid's support of older people receiving long-term care in nursing homes has been widely publicized, but medicaid can also pay for care in an older person's own home. Home health care is an area of growing attention and development, since today's thrust is to maintain older people in their own homes and out of institutions as long as possible. If you think your sick, low-income parent can remain at home with some help which he can't afford himself, you should check into medicaid.

It's true that tightening state budgets are forcing cutbacks on some medicaid services, and the adult children of older applicants for medicaid may be asked if they can help a parent financially. You certainly feel a filial and moral responsibility to help support your parent if his income isn't sufficient to meet all his needs, but there's no law that says you must. Whether or not your parent can qualify for medicaid still depends essentially on his income, not on yours. Even if you're contributing to his support, he should be able to get some medicaid help if his income alone qualifies him.

Medicaid income and assets eligibility requirements are similar to those for SSI. You will have to inquire in the state where your parent lives, and if you live in a state different from his, you might check in each state. There have been instances where a parent has been moved to the state where a child lives because the medicaid benefits were better there. But if your investigation shows that your state offers more medicaid help than your parent's, you should investigate carefully before you decide to transplant him. It's true that there is no period of state residency required for medicaid, but an older person who has just moved into a state and applies for medicaid may be asked for a statement of his intent in moving and should be prepared to explain that he moved for other reasons.

Being covered by medicaid has undeniable negatives and frustrations. The process of being investigated and of supplying the required detailed information on income, rent, and bank accounts, for example, may be very time-consuming, and there are subsequent periodic reviews of eligibility to continue the benefits. Medicaid patients are free to use the doctor, hospital, or nursing facility of their choice, provided that the doctor agrees and that the institution is participating in medicaid. Many doctors won't accept medicaid patients; some nursing homes won't at all, and others have a limited number of beds for medicaid patients. But you can find out some of these things in advance.

If you decide to apply for medicaid for your parent and you feel that he most likely will qualify, don't pay any of his medical bills until you know for sure. Benefits cover care and services furnished for three months before the application is made, and if your parent does qualify, medicaid payments will be retroactive for the period.

For information, you can call the local department of welfare, public assistance, or social services. You may find medicaid listed by itself under local government listings. In trying to pursue the ins and outs of medicaid, however, it's sometimes more productive to work through a social worker and a social service agency. (See Chapter 2.)

Dealing with Government Offices and Staff

You will have to telephone or visit government offices in your own or your parent's locality if you want information about social security, veterans' benefits, SSI, medicare, food stamps, and medicaid. Trying to deal with any bureaucratic or government agency can be time-consuming, frustrating, and sometimes infuriating. These offices are usually understaffed, with too few people facing a rising number of daily inquiries about fairly complicated material, but ultimately you will get the information you want. Here are some tips to aid you through the process:

- Always telephone before you go to any office, and get as much information as possible that way. You may find out you don't have to make a personal visit, but can get the answers you need over the phone. If you do have to go there, you will at least know beforehand what papers, documents, and information you may have to bring with you, and you will be spared the burden of a second trip.
- Make a list of the questions you need to ask and keep it in front of you at the telephone or at the office you're visiting. Check off the questions as you go to be sure you've asked everything. If answers seem complicated, take the time to write them down so that you won't forget them.
- Get the name of the person to whom you talk on the telephone or see in person, and try to talk to that person each time. This will make communication easier. You'll save time and trouble by not having to repeat your whole story, and you and the staff member will get to know and trust each other.
- Mondays, the days after holidays, and the first week of the month are heavy days in these offices. Telephone lines are busy and the queues of waiting people are long. Try to call or visit late in the week and later in the month.

- Even if you become frustrated or annoyed during your quest for information, it's best to remain courteous and calm with whomever you are talking.
- Keep all papers and correspondence that come from a government office or that relate to the subject you're negotiating. You'll need them for future reference.

Taxes

Most people want to abide by the law, and most people do. But you should know that tax laws do allow some specific deductions for special kinds of taxpayers, and that the government expects you to take full advantage of them. These taxpayers include you if you're supporting your parent, and they include your parent if he's over sixty-five.

Many over-sixty-five people may not be aware of the federal—as well as the state and local—tax benefits which can reduce their taxes. Others in this age group may know about them, but are often hindered in using them because of the labyrinthine complications of analyzing and applying them to tax forms. But there are knowledgeable interpreters waiting in the wings.

Local offices of the Internal Revenue Service usually have people on their staffs who are especially trained to provide tax help to over-sixty-five taxpayers and to work with them on their tax forms. Local communities may provide informed volunteers who will also know about special benefits for the elderly. Montgomery County in Maryland, for example, has sixty-five volunteer tax aides on call to help. Your local commission or office on aging may know of a similar service in your area. In addition, the American Association of Retired Persons (AARP) operates the Tax-Aide program for older taxpayers. Volunteers drawn from among older citizens and trained by the IRS work in more than 1,200 communities around the country and will counsel you or your parent. Check your phone book to see if there's an AARP office nearby. If not, write to AARP. (See the Appendix.) Tax-Aide is free to retired persons as a public service of the association.

If you want written material on tax breaks for your parent, the IRS has a variety of pamphlets detailing tax situations particularly relevant to over-sixty-five people. The U.S. Senate Special Committee on Aging will send out a list of tax-relief provisions and itemized deductions for older people. The AARP has available at no cost a booklet which outlines briefly the federal tax situation for older people but provides greater detail on tax regulations in all the states. (See the Appendix.)

Witnesses testifying before the Senate Committee on Aging estimate that at one time or another, 50 percent of the nation's over-sixty-five taxpayers may have overpaid their income tax—and no wonder. The special tax regulations relating to people over sixty-five are numerous and complex, and could easily lead any honest taxpayer to lose patience after he has read the fine print several times and still can't figure it out.

"There's no doubt," says Hawaii's Senator Hiram L. Fong, a committee member, "that persons over sixty-five face an individual tax return problem more complicated than that of younger taxpayers."

Perhaps your parent, fazed by the complications, is among the overpaying half of older taxpayers. Can you discuss this with him? Can you help? You should try.

Tax Breaks for You

If your parent has a gross taxable income of less than $750 a year, and you are providing more than half of his support, you can claim him as a dependent on your federal income tax return. You can therefore take a $750 deduction from your own adjusted gross income.

If you itemize your own deductions, you can then also deduct any medical or dental bills you pay for your parent over what medicare pays for him. As you know, in order to claim any medical deductions at all, the total of your medical and dental expenses and those of your dependents—including, in this case, your parent—must exceed 3 percent of your adjusted gross income. If you intend to claim a medical deduction for your parent, be sure that it is you, and not your parent, who writes the checks for his medical bills and that you keep all receipted bills.

For purposes of calculating this dependency test, your parent's gross income doesn't include social security and supplemental security payments, veterans' and railroad retirement benefits, or any other income which ordinarily would not be subject to tax.

If your parent's gross income is more than $750 annually, you cannot claim him as a dependent, even if you're paying over half of his support. Should you indeed be paying over half of his support, however, and at the same time are paying his medical and dental bills beyond what medicare covers, you can include the outlays for his medical and dental bills along with your own in taking the medical deduction—subject, of course, to the 3 percent rule.

If you and one or more of your siblings together are contributing more than half of your parent's support—with his gross income no greater than $750 a year—one of you can claim him as a dependent, provided no one of you has contributed more than half of his support. In this case, the child claiming your parent as a dependent must contribute more than 10 percent of the parent's support. If this situation exists in your family, you and your siblings can arrange to alternate or rotate the dependency claim from one year to the next, so that you each get the tax benefit in turn. If you do use this procedure, you must file a written statement—you can get the form from the IRS—signed by your siblings and saying that they are not claiming your parent as a dependent in that calendar year and that you may do so.

Most states and localities allow similar benefits.

Tax Breaks for Your Parent

If your parent is sixty-five or over, he is entitled on his federal income tax to an extra annual personal exemption of $750 in addition to the regular $750 exemption accorded every taxpayer. This means that an individual of sixty-five or over can claim a yearly exemption of $1,500; and a couple over sixty-five, a $3,000 exemption.

Your parent doesn't have to file any income tax return at all if his annual taxable income is less than $3,200 as a single person; $4,350 if both parents file a joint return and one is over sixty-five; and $5,100 if both are over sixty-five and file a joint return. Their income may even be slightly higher, because each is entitled to an additional exemption credit. It's best to check the IRS on this, however, because these income cutoff figures are always subject to change. Naturally your parent will file a return if he wants a refund on taxes withheld from part-time work or from other income.

Taxable income doesn't include social security, veterans benefits, and other types of income which the law specifically exempts from tax. The tax treatment of pension income is very complicated and depends both on the proportions which your parent and his employer contributed to the pension plan during his working years and on the time period over which the pension income is being received. It's best to check with the IRS on this. Because of the complexities, the IRS suggests that you have with you a copy of your parent's previous year's income tax return and any payment statements he has received from the organization making the pension payments.

Retirement Income Credit

Your parent may also qualify for retirement income credit on his federal income tax. This is a provision designed to help people who don't have much tax-exempt social security income but do have some other income. It provides that up to 15 percent of what the government classifies as retirement income— up to $1,524 for an individual or $2,286 for a couple filing jointly—can be subtracted from his final income tax bill. The IRS defines retirement income as coming specifically from these sources: taxable interest, dividends, pensions, and annuities. Retirement income does not include wages, salaries, and certain business income. The ultimate amount of retirement credit your parent may be allowed has to be balanced off by his earnings, social security, and other nontaxable income sources. Retirement credit benefits aren't as broad before age sixty-five as they are afterward, and they're broadest after age seventy-two when earnings no longer count to reduce them.

The complexities of computing retirement credit are indeed astounding, and if it's too much for your parent to calculate, the IRS will do it for him when he sends in his filled-out income tax form or if he takes it to an IRS office. He should simply complete the form without indicating the amount of his income tax liability and send it on to the IRS with the request that they compute his retirement credit. The IRS will do that and send back a note with the amount of income tax your parent owes. Your parent can then send a check in return. If the completed form and request come into the IRS enough in advance of the April 15 tax-filing deadline, there will be time for the process to be completed before the deadline date. Otherwise, the IRS will extend the April 15 deadline for ten days.*

In addition, there are allowable itemized income tax deductions for all taxpayers, with which your parent is probably familiar: sales and local taxes, contributions, interest on loans, a portion of medical insurance premium payments, medical and other expenses. If he claims any of these deductions, he must itemize them on his tax form.

Pay Attention to Medical and Drug Expenses

You and he should pay particular attention to allowable deductions for drugs, medications, and medical expenses. These may expand into new areas as your parent grows older and requires more medical treatment; he may not be aware that many are deductible. Transportation for medical expenses is deductible, for instance, as are health insurance premiums, special telephone equipment for the deaf, the cost of liquor prescribed by a physician for medicinal purposes, home health services, and many other medically related services and items.

Itemized Deductions Can Help

Older people who haven't been able to take advantage of itemized deductions before may find that their increasing

*At press time, Congress was considering proposals for substantial liberalization of retirement income credit. Check IRS.

health expenses may now allow them to do so. The law allows deductions of only those medical expenses which are more than 3 percent of adjusted gross income. When your parent was younger and working, he probably had smaller medical expenses and a larger income than he has now, and the total medical expenses might not have reached above the 3 percent level. Now, though, his medical expenses are probably larger and his income smaller, so outstripping the 3 percent figure is far more likely.

Remember, too, that there's still another possible tax break for your parent: under certain conditions, he can exclude from his taxable income all or part of the gain that comes from selling his home.

Your parent may not know about these tax benefits available to him after age sixty-five, and whether he's past this age or approaching it, you might ask if he's familiar with them. If he isn't, you or he should begin to talk to your local IRS office. As a matter of fact, it's a good idea to talk to the IRS, anyway. The regulations are very complicated, and there are interlocking conditions which can be baffling. Also, the government is now in a period of constant reexamination of existing tax regulations, and there's often change from year to year. For dependable tax guidance, therefore, it's best to turn to an IRS office or to a reliable lawyer or accountant whose business it is to follow and understand current tax regulations.

The IRS is listed in your local telephone directory under U.S. Government. To find a tax attorney, ask trusted friends to recommend one or call your local bar association. These often have a referral service which will supply you with the names of several attorneys specializing in tax law. You might also call your county courthouse and inquire there. There's no established way of finding an accountant, but perhaps your friends who operate businesses might be able to recommend one. Or you can look in the classified telephone directory under Accountants, talk to several, and then make a choice.

State and Local Tax Breaks

Don't overlook state and local tax breaks for your parent. Many states offer special tax exemptions and deductions to older residents, generally giving relief in the areas of income and property taxes.

About half the states allow extra personal income tax exemptions for over-sixty-five taxpayers. About two-thirds give special tax treatment to retirement income, although sometimes the relief applies only to pension or retirement income coming from past employment by a state department or agency. Some states include federal civil service retirement pay in this provision. In addition, states often allow special medical deductions for older people.

Almost all states give older residents some property tax relief, often called circuit-breakers or homestead exemptions. Sometimes there's an outright exemption from property tax payments, sometimes a credit or refund of part. Generally, this help is allowed to people over sixty-five; in some states it starts at age sixty or sixty-two, and, in a few, not until seventy-two. These property tax exemptions usually require a period of prior residency, and usually apply only if income is below a specified level, or the value of the property is below a specified amount.

A few states—Minnesota, Connecticut, and North Dakota, to name three—give some relief to over-sixty-five renters.

Since tax relief provisions vary enormously from state to state and since they are frequently reexamined and revised, it's best to check the specific situation with the state department of finance or taxation where your parent pays his taxes.

Don't forget that your parent's local city or county government may also offer special tax relief in common or uncommon ways. You should check the local department of finance to see just what benefits there are for over-sixty-five residents.

Money-Savers

More than others, older people need to save money. A monthly investment in a health insurance policy can save a great deal of money during a period of critical illness or disability. Buying generic drugs can save money routinely. And the fact that they are, indeed, older citizens of their communities, can give them special discounts on many of their regular purchases and expenses.

Extra Health Insurance

Older people require frequent and varied health services, for which medicare will pay only specified or limited amounts. If your over-sixty-five parent doesn't have a private health insurance policy already, he should get one with broad coverage. Generally, when people retire at sixty-five, they're offered the opportunity to extend at a relatively low cost the hospital and medical insurance coverage they may have had from their employer. Insurance advisers suggest that the most practical step is to arrange for this by age sixty-four, but there's no problem about coverage after that age.

The reason for buying a private health insurance policy is what's called the "medigap." This is the name for expenses medicare doesn't cover at all—long-term nursing care, dental care, out-of-hospital prescriptions. Medigap also describes the awesome difference between what medicare pays for someone's hospital and medical costs and what he pays himself. In times of major medical need—and even in the course of the normal medical requirements of older people—this financial gap can create huge bills which you or your parent would have to pay.

Because of the medigap, more than half of the nation's over-sixty-five population has some kind of private health insurance policy to bolster medicare coverage. Premiums for individuals range from about $4 a month for a policy with relatively minimum benefits to around $16 for one with comprehensive coverage. These figures also vary from region to region as they reflect local medical and hospital charges.

Most policies for over-sixty-five people don't cover home health care. They will cover the cost of a registered nurse, but generally not the costs of a homemaker or home health aide who helps with bathing, dressing, and housekeeping for the invalid or convalescent. There's a beginning trend toward this, however, among some insurance companies. If you think this is a service your parent may need at some time, you may find coverage if you investigate among several insurance companies.

It's a good idea, anyway, to look into policies offered by more than one company. Although all give benefits for hospital and posthospital nursing-home stays, not all will cover special nursing and out-of-hospital medications. Most reliable insurance companies offer a special policy to over-sixty-five people that complements medicare benefits.

Here are some things to remember if you or your parent investigates private health insurance:

- A service benefit policy is better than an indemnity policy. The service benefit policy will pay the entire cost of a covered service—the 20 percent of the doctor's bill and the hospital costs not covered by medicare, for example. The indemnity policy will pay only a fixed amount toward any of these covered items.

- Don't buy a mail-order policy, one which is purchased by mail after it has been advertised in newspapers and magazines, on radio and television. These are often deceptive in the benefits they purport to give. It's best to buy from a reputable insurance company or agent.

- It's a good idea to have a policy with nursing-home coverage.

- Carefully read the limitations on preexisting conditions. Compare policies and try to get one where coverage on preexisting conditions begins as soon as possible after the effective date of the policy. For people over sixty-five, the time limit for preexisting conditions is generally twelve months, although some companies have a shorter limit, some have none at all, and some may go up to two years. You should also find out exactly what the company's definition of a preexisting condition is, and how far back it will inquire into your parent's medical history to determine if one exists.

- Be careful about canceling policies and buying a new one, even though it may appear that the new one has better benefits. Remember that with a new policy the limitation on preexisting conditions begins all over again.

- Be familiar with medicare benefits before buying a policy, and with benefits from any other policy your parent may hold. If a policy duplicates benefits your parent already has, he will be paying part of the premiums for something he doesn't need.

- Check the date when the policy becomes effective, to be sure there isn't an inordinate waiting period.

- Check to see if there's a cancellation clause which will allow the company to cancel the policy if certain conditions occur.

- Find an insurance policy with open enrollment, where your
parent can buy a policy at any time and doesn't have to wait
for a specific period during the year.

You can get guidance from your state department of insurance, which is actively concerned with protecting the
insurance-buying public. Most departments publish booklets
which instruct consumers in what to look for and what to avoid
in buying insurance policies. Some have material relating directly to health insurance policies for older people.

Saving on Drugs and Medications

If your parent can buy medications by their generic names
rather than by their trade or brand names, he will save up to 50
percent on his drug bill. You, too, can purchase prescription
and nonprescription medications by their generic names—but
since older people generally require more medications than
other segments of the population, the saving to them is considerable.

The generic name of a medication is its official or established
name, not exactly its chemical name but close to it. The trade or
brand name is that under which different pharmaceutical companies distribute the medication. Some widely used examples
are Valium, whose generic name is diazepam; Diuril, whose
generic name is chlorothiazide; and Serpasil, Reserpoid, and
other antihypertensive drugs, whose generic name is reserpine.
Senator Gaylord A. Nelson of Wisconsin, who has held extensive hearings on this subject, points out that there is no significant difference in quality between generic and brand-name
drugs. "In fact," he says, "there have been many cases of generic drugs meeting higher standards than their brand-name
counterparts.... The latest official findings of the Food and
Drug Administration confirm that we do not have to pay outra-
geously high prices for many drugs we use. In some instances
we can buy a drug for one-twentieth of the heavily advertised
brand-name price."[3]

Benjamin Gordon, an expert in the field and an economist
on the staff of the Senate Small Business Committee, suggests
that your parent ask three questions if his doctor prescribes a
medication:

- Do I really need this drug? Sometimes, says Gordon, a doctor feels that a patient wants medication, even though the doctor himself may not think it necessary. Sometimes the doctor reaches for the prescription pad as an automatic way of ending the consultation. If the doctor answers no to the question, there's no further problem. If he answers yes, ask the next question.
- Can I get this drug on a generic basis? If the doctor then prescribes it by its generic name, you've saved some money. If he says the drug isn't available on a generic basis, ask the third question.
- Can you give me a different drug which will do the same thing for me but which can be prescribed on a generic basis?

Following this procedure regularly is bound to save at least some money. Mr. Gordon asks, "Why shouldn't the doctor prescribe the drug on a generic basis if it's available?"

Small Money-Savers

- Your parent probably knows about discounts available to the over-sixty-five (and sometimes the over-sixty) for public transportation, theater tickets, courses at colleges and universities, and other educational programs. Older people qualify for discounts regardless of their income.
- In some communities, many local merchants will give discounts to older people on purchases ranging from clothing to automobile repairs, from orthopedic appliances to permanent waves. Often this is arranged by the local commission on aging, which issues identification cards for this purpose to eligible persons.
- Banks in many areas offer free checking accounts to older people.
- Members of organizations of older people (see Chapter 2) can use a variety of travel services at lower-than-commercial prices.

Estates

We've talked a lot about money in this chapter—the money required to take care of your parent's needs and how you can add to it or conserve it. This section will talk about the money your parent expects to leave to his heirs and how he can protect it as much as possible, through perfectly legal means, from the taxes the government might levy on it upon his death.

You may know roughly the amount of your parent's estate and just what it consists of. You may be familiar with the terms of his will and how he plans to dispose of his possessions. Or, perhaps, you don't know very much about the extent of his assets and worth and don't even know whether he has made a will. You may think he doesn't have very much of an estate at all to leave to any heir.

If you're informed at all, you're ahead to the extent that you know to what degree your parent has protected his heirs from potential tax inroads on the estate he leaves. If you think your parent could arrange for better future protection, you might decide to talk to him about it soon. But if you're ignorant of your parent's worth and plans, you could be in trouble.

All estates with a net value of over $60,000 after deductions are subject to federal estate taxes.* Many individual bequests, in addition, are subject to state inheritance taxes. If your well-meaning parent, who planned for you and your children to inherit all his worldly goods after him, didn't take some steps to shift some of his money or assets to his heirs during his lifetime, his estate may come to them in much smaller amounts than he planned because of the tax bite. These cautions apply also to protect a spouse who will survive; with a properly worded will, a marital deduction of up to half of the estate can go to a surviving spouse free of federal estate tax.

Many adult children don't want to confront a parent with questions about wills and estates. Verbalization seems too painful for both sides, reminding parent and child that the parent is getting on in years and could die soon. If you have a loving and practical parent who wants to sit down and talk with you about his will or his estate, don't brush the overture aside. Many adult children, feeling flustered and uncomfortable, answer with, "Don't be silly. You're not going to die anytime soon," and

---

*At press time, Congress was considering varying proposals to increase the estate tax exemption. Check IRS.

repeatedly postpone such a discussion. This attitude is part of our death-denying culture, it's true, but it is an attitude which can create great problems for the child after the inevitable does, in fact, occur, and the parent dies.

Also, the adult child may not want to appear pushy and presumptuous by bringing up the subject. To do so may appear to indicate lack of concern about the parent's continued health and life and only an interest in how much the child will inherit after the parent's death. It does seem a bit sticky, if you haven't been informed at all about your parent's plans to distribute his assets, to sit down and ask outright, "Are your affairs in order? Do you have a will? How have you handled your estate?"

If both of your parents are living, it may be easier to approach your father on this sensitive subject by asking legitimately what he has done to inform your mother about how to handle her financial affairs when she is alone and to what degree he has protected her from possible legal and tax problems should he predecease her. It may also be simple to approach your mother if she's a widow; she may be uncertain herself as to what steps to take—if any—to give both herself and you the greatest possible protection, and she may be relieved to have your interest and general advice.

A parent who is closemouthed about his assets and their disposition may be a little suspicious and hostile to begin with, and you will have to tread carefully. But sometimes, as a parent grows older, he will himself voluntarily bring up the subject of his estate, his will, and where his heirs can find papers, documents, and valuables after his death.

If your parent does this, consider yourself fortunate and sit down and listen. If it involves, as it does with one grandmother who lives alone in an urban apartment, hiding jewelry in a bag of onions, cash in a can of mothballs, bankbooks in bookshelves, and documents tucked into drawers, take notes so you will remember it all. Some older people need to have peace of mind about what will happen to their goods and belongings after death, to know that their children and grandchildren will have everything that is coming to them. This knowledge may represent continuity and security to an older parent. Don't toss the subject off lightly; pay attention.

Does Your Parent Have an Estate?

Your parent doesn't have to be J. Paul Getty or the president of General Motors to leave an estate. If he owns a house or a condominium, a car, a couple of thousand dollars in stocks or savings accounts, an insurance policy, he probably has a taxable estate. Maybe he's been a sporadic collector of stamps, coins, prints, or other small items. The Internal Revenue Service can come in after his death and value his collection at an amount which might astonish and pain you when the bill for estate tax deficiencies appears. Whatever estate he leaves over $60,000 should be protected as much as possible. Later in this chapter there will be some suggestions about how to do so.

Estate taxes, like income taxes, are progressive; the greater the value of the estate, the higher the tax is, proportionately. If you know the total value of your parent's taxable estate, you can figure out roughly what the federal taxes will be.

States will also levy inheritance taxes—the taxes to be paid on each separate beneficiary's share of the estate. Inheritance taxes vary among the states, but they're usually smaller for lineal relatives and the surviving spouse of the deceased than for other persons named in a will. In some states, the inheritance tax has been replaced by a federal-type estate tax, and in others it has been supplemented by an estate tax. These state taxes, however, are usually levied at much more modest rates than the federal estate tax and generally are credited against the federal tax liability.

In addition, the estate will be docked for the lawyers' fees and administrative costs, such as commissions paid to executors and administrators involved in settling it. These could run from about 4 to 7 or more percent of the gross estate.

Wills

Your parent should have a will, whether or not he thinks he has an estate. The will, moreover, should be drawn by a competent lawyer. It should be up-to-date, based on the current ages, situations, and needs of his heirs. A twenty-five-year-old will is almost certain to be out-of-date, and even a ten-year-old will might not reflect family relationships and requirements at the time a parent dies. It might also be difficult to locate the witnesses to a will executed many years earlier, and this might result in unpredictable delays. Wills should be revised periodically, and almost automatically after major family changes—births, deaths, marriages, divorces, remarriages. They should also be gone over when tax regulations and other applicable laws are changed. In addition, if your parent moves from one state to another, he should check out his will with a lawyer. State laws differ, and often a will that complies with one state's requirements flouts those of another.

If your parent leaves no will, you may be subject to some nasty events:

- His estate may not go where he would have wanted it to go; intestacy statutes will decide its disposition.
- Estate taxes may be higher, and certain deductions may be lost.
- Administration costs and legal fees may be higher.
- Since your parent has no executor of his estate, a court will appoint an administrator, who will probably be required to file a surety bond. Not only might the surety company then supervise him continually, but he will have to go to the court for orders to act on many of the matters connected with the estate. An executor who is named in a will may serve without bond.
- Distribution of the estate will probably take longer, and family tempers will grow shorter. Brother and sister, parent and child with histories of harmonious relationships have been known to engage in sharp infighting when faced with the sour plum of an undirected estate.

If you can discuss no other aspect of money with your parent, you must at least ascertain whether there's an up-to-date will. If you don't already know, one way of approaching him might be to peg it on the subject of your own will. Tell him you're just getting around to making one and want his advice based on what he has done. He might discuss his own situation, and you might be a lot better off.

Tax-Saving Devices

Suppose you know the total extent of your single parent's estate and the terms of his will. He leaves everything to you without realizing, as you calculate it, that you are going to have to pay out more than one-fifth of the estate in estate and inheritance taxes. Is this really what he would want for you?

One forty-five-year-old man pondered this thoroughly and then went to talk to a competent estate attorney. Armed with information as to what could be done legally during a lifetime to minimize possible estate taxes, he proceeded to have a calm, thoughtful discussion with his parent—in this case, his seventy-one-year-old widowed mother. He told her he loved her and that he knew she loved him and that he hoped and expected she would live for many years. He said he was grateful for the care she had taken in conducting her affairs so that there would be a small but comfortable sum of money willed for his benefit and that of his wife and children. He wasn't interested in the amount of her estate, he said, but he was concerned that the taxes to be paid from it would eat up a good bit of the money she had worked for and practiced economies to save. He said he thought she wouldn't want that to happen, either, if it could be avoided by steps taken in her lifetime.

In her case, because she wasn't rich and because—like many older people—she was "saving for her old age," she had to move slowly and carefully. Even on her limited income she was a good money manager, and over a period of many years she gave each of her four grandchildren $500 a year. The money was deposited in a separate savings account for each one, and Grandma, in this fashion, knocked off a reasonable amount from her estate tax liability. The only taxes paid on the money have been the grandchildren's low income taxes on the interest from their accounts.

Making gifts during a lifetime is one approach that can cut down on potential estate taxes. The law allows an individual to make untaxed gifts to any donee of $3,000 a year. If your parent is well-fixed financially, he can give up to this amount each year to any number of his children, grandchildren, and other relatives with no gift tax payment. If you have two parents, they can give up to $6,000 a year untaxed to an unlimited number of people.

In addition, each donor has a $30,000 lifetime exemption, and a married couple has a $60,000 lifetime exemption. Should a donor exceed the $3,000 annual tax-free gift to a donee, the excess is applied against his $30,000 lifetime exemption, or a couple's $60,000. Only when the latter is exhausted will there be a tax on the excess.

It is the donor, not the recipient, who pays the gift tax on a gift he makes—but what should be borne in mind is that gift taxes are lower than estate taxes. In effect, the person who leaves the estate pays the estate taxes, because they are taken from the body of the estate before it is distributed. If your parent's financial position indicates that he will leave a substantial taxable estate, he will have to make the decision as to whether he wants to pay the lower gift taxes on gifts he may make in his lifetime which are in excess of the yearly exclusions and lifetime exemption, or if he wishes a much larger tax to come from his estate after his death. Gift taxes are payable in a number of states, so your parent should check state regulations.

Trusts

Grandfather was a sharp businessman of comfortable means who looked ahead a bit. He knew that there would be substantial taxes on the estate his daughter and sons would inherit after his death. He also knew that his children's children would pay taxes on much of the same money once again when they, in turn, inherited from their own parents. Grandfather decided to skip one generation of taxpayers by putting part of his assets in trust for his grandchildren during his lifetime. He was indeed a man of property, and he took six pieces of real estate he owned in the San Francisco Bay area and set each one up in trust for each of his six grandchildren. A trustee manages these properties for the grandchildren. The income they produce goes to the grandchildren. Since they won't be part of his estate, no estate taxes will have to be paid on them. The grandchildren will continue paying income taxes on the income, and if at any time the trust sells the properties, they will pay a capital gains tax on the profits.

Grandfather could have established the trust using cash, stocks or bonds, or some other income-producing asset. If he held patents or copyrights, he could have entrusted them to his children or grandchildren. He could have established a trust fund for each of his children, with the proviso that they receive the income during their lifetimes and the principal when they reach a specified age. Trusts offer a very flexible and varied device for passing property from one generation to the next without having to pay estate taxes, or for skipping an entire generation of estate taxpayers.

Watch Out

This kind of living trust, created by the donor during his lifetime, is one acceptable means of handling assets before death in a way which avoids estate taxes after death. If your parent is interested, he can choose from a variety of trust situations, but the only type which will take potentially taxable assets out of his estate and remove them from later taxes is one which—during his lifetime—denies him control over, or income from, the money, property, or other asset that has been put in trust. This is a large step for your parent to take, and he can do so only if he feels he can live comfortably on his remaining money after he has turned some over irrevocably to you or his grandchildren. Your parent must think through this move very carefully with a lawyer who is thoroughly familiar with state and federal estate tax laws.

Gifts in trust and outright gifts can take many forms—cash, property, stocks and bonds, and other assets. Although it is always wise to consult a lawyer who knows the ins and outs of federal and state regulations concerning gifts, they can often be made in a simple fashion. This is surely true of gifts of property that don't produce any income, such as jewelry and paintings or other art objects.

Trusts and gifts are not techniques to be used solely by Rockefellers, Vanderbilts, and Kennedys. There is nothing wrong with a trust fund or gift under the Uniform Gifts to Minors Act of $1,000, $3,000, or $5,000 in cash, especially if the trustee or custodian is a friend or relative who receives no fee for his role and need give no accounting. And there's nothing wrong with a gift of $500 or $1,500. Whatever the amount of the trust or gift, it takes money out of the estate and removes it from tax levies later on.

Attitudes

Whether or not there will be a surviving spouse will make a difference in how a parent approaches actions during his lifetime, as will the number of heirs. The extent of his means will obviously determine to a large degree what steps he could and would want to take, as will his age at the time he decides to take any steps. At eighty, his outlook will be different from at sixty.

His attitude will, of course, shape all his actions and might not have anything to do with his actual wealth. The grandmother who gave annual gifts to her grandchildren was far from wealthy, and she was truly anxious to have the money to care for herself if she should live for a long time and come to need expensive care. But she was sensitive to her son and respected his thoughts. Many wealthy parents, sharing Grandma's legitimate worry about taking care of their own, possibly draining future needs, can't respond as she did. They may say to themselves, I have to take care of myself and my spouse first; there'll be plenty of money left, anyhow, for my children, even after taxes.

This is obviously their privilege, no matter how much money they may have, and if they feel this way, you may not be able to pursue the topic with them. The kinds of conversation and arrangements we've been talking about imply a mutual trust between parent and adult child. If it isn't there, the conversation may never get started at all. But if the confidence is there, and you think your parent will leave an estate after deductions of over $60,000, you should suggest he spend some time talking to an estate attorney. Wills, estates, gifts, and transfers involving the passage of property are governed by intricate federal laws and by differing state laws.

An Estate Attorney

An estate attorney knows exactly what you and your parents can do to comply with relevant tax requirements and still save potential estate tax payments. He knows what estate taxes will be. He knows about gifts, gift taxes, and gifts to minors. He knows about the range and advantages of trusts and how they not only can help the beneficiary of the trust but can insulate the donor from adverse tax consequences. He knows about transfers of property and business interests. He can write a will which assures what your parent wants and which will protect the heirs.

If your parent will go with you to an estate attorney, it will be a sound investment of time and money for both of you. If you don't think your parent would go with you, go on your own for an exploratory talk; your own family will benefit ultimately. You will pay a fee for it, but you will get a solid return on your money.

In Contemplation of Death

Talking about wills and estates should take place while a parent is in good health. A sickbed, particularly at a time of terminal or catastrophic illness, is an irrational and unproductive background for this kind of discussion and can also limit severely what a parent can do to avoid estate taxes. Government tax collectors will almost automatically challenge gifts made in a person's last years. There is, in fact, a statutory presumption that any gift or transfer made within three years of a person's death has been made "in contemplation of death" and is therefore subject to estate taxes.

Consider the fifty-five-year-old man whose eighty-two-year-old mother is now, suddenly, very sick with what may or may not be a terminal illness. Other than the awareness that his mother had sold some pieces of property in Chicago, is living in a comfortable condominium in Southern California, and has had enough money for an annual trip to Europe, he has no precise knowledge of her assets or the terms of her will. She has never made a gift of money, stock, property, or any other asset to him, his wife, his children, or his sister's family. He assumes that he and his sister will be her sole heirs, and he suddenly realizes that there might be a fat tax on the estate.

Can he talk to her tactfully and reasonably about disposing of her assets when she is hospitalized and both are sensing the impending possibility of her death? He may bring himself to the discussion, and his mother may agree to make some immediate arrangements for transferring some of her worth to her children or grandchildren. But if she dies within three years after she has acted, it may be difficult to overcome the contemplation-of-death presumption, in which event everything which was transferred to her children or grandchildren will be subject to the estate tax.

But nothing will have been lost by trying. Estate attorneys say that even under circumstances which appear close to death, the transfer of property is still a sensible action from which the heirs stand only to gain and not to lose.

If the IRS does not question the gift or transfer as having been made "in contemplation of death," your parent will have avoided the estate tax on that amount. But even if the IRS does challenge the transaction and makes the challenge stick, you will have to pay only the estate taxes you would have paid anyway had the transfer never been made; there is no penalty tax on gifts and transfers made in contemplation of death. If enough property was transferred to have warranted payment of a gift tax, this payment will be credited against the new estate tax liability. The final estate tax amount may even be lower because the estate itself will have been reduced—for estate tax purposes—by the amount of the gift tax previously paid. It is all terribly complicated, but one thing is clear: Although it's not a bad idea for a well-off parent to make a gift at any time of his life, the time to talk to your parent is now, and not during an illness or a crisis situation.

Common Sense Can Mean Dollars

There are some mechanical arrangements you can make now that will make life—and death—easier. You will be able to act expeditiously if your parent suddenly becomes ill or is incapacitated by a lingering illness.

You should know:

- Where your parent keeps his will, his bankbooks, his insurance policies, his stock certificates and bonds, and any other important papers.
- His social security and medicare numbers.
- The name of his lawyer, his insurance agent, and his accountant.
- The location and numbers of checking and savings accounts and of his safe-deposit box.
- The companies with which he has life, health, and other insurance policies and the numbers of the policies.
- With whom he has a pension plan, a Keogh or other retirement plan.

Then, if your relationship with your parent makes it possible, you and he should go beyond this in sharing essential monetary facts. To do so will ensure easier mechanics in emergency and crisis situations.

- You or a sibling should have power of attorney, specifying how you can act for your parent in financial matters should the need arise. You can buy a printed form for a power of attorney in a stationery store; or for banking purposes, you can obtain one from the bank where your parent has an account which he will empower you to use. Your most intelligent approach, however, would be to ask a lawyer to draw up a form in which your parent will designate exactly what powers he gives you.
- You should have access to a safe-deposit box with him so that you can reach important papers and documents if he is hospitalized or bedridden and can't get to them. You should know exactly where others are kept in his home.
- If possible, he should have a joint bank account with you or a sibling so you will have ready access to cash for his emergency needs.
- You should know when his insurance premiums are due. Then you can pay them if he is unable to. The policies won't lapse, and you will know exactly which will be in effect when he dies.

Assuming a Watchful Role

These things should be done while your parent is in good health and on top of his life. It's too onerous and complicated to arrange them if he is mentally or physically incapacitated. But suppose his health begins to fail and you see signs that his mind and his judgment aren't as keen as they were. Then you must be vigilant without being overbearing, and you should set up some precautionary tactics.

- You must see to it that he doesn't enter into any kind of contract without having a lawyer go over it—a contract for sale, rental, or purchase of a home; for buying an automobile or other major article; for purchasing an insurance policy; for a course of instruction or recreation, from yoga lessons to a Caribbean cruise.
- You must check on dates when payments are due—for utilities, rent, or mortgage—to be sure that they continue to be made on time. Utilities have been turned off and other services halted because ill or absentminded older people forgot to pay their bills.
- You must be sure that social security and all other income checks are actually deposited in your parent's account as they come to him. Your parent may overlook them or put them away and forget them. Perhaps the most effective and simple method of handling social security checks is to have your parent execute Form SF-1199, which authorizes the Social Security Administration to send his check directly to his bank account.

Alternatively, you can have yourself appointed as the recipient of your parent's social security checks. The local social security office can arrange this for you if you provide medical and other documentation testifying that your parent can no longer handle his own funds. The checks will then come to you, and must be used only for your parent's expenses.

You must assume a watchful role, trying to keep a balance between protecting your parent and, at the same time, maintaining his independence. Perhaps he will only need some reminders as to dates for paying bills, money that is coming in or going out. You may need to prepare a checklist for him or for yourself, to keep on top of his financial affairs. Perhaps you should offer to help by paying the bills with him and, together, keeping his checking account in order.

Protective Action

What if your parent becomes more forgetful, more confused in his daily activities, or if an incapacitating mental or physical illness prevents him from managing his affairs at all? If a developing condition affects the way he handles money matters, you may have to think about taking some legal steps to protect him and his assets.

There are some things you can do. You can use the power of attorney he has given you—assuming it is broad enough, and depending on what rights it allows you—to pay bills, deposit and withdraw money from bank accounts, perhaps to sell stock or other assets if your parent needs cash.

But the power of attorney your parent has given you doesn't deprive him of the power to handle his money himself if he wants to. He can still withdraw money, make business deals, and sell his assets just as you can. If his sense of judgment and his ability to conduct his affairs properly are impaired—for whatever reason—he may be doing unwise things with his money, spending large amounts of it foolishly. He may be draining funds which might be needed for his continuing support or cutting into the estate he planned to leave to his heirs. And remember that in certain states a power of attorney is no longer valid if the person conferring it becomes mentally incompetent.

"Behavior like this is a very sensitive and often painful matter," says Geneva Mathiasen, former executive director of the National Council on the Aging. "Families are afraid of losing their inheritance as mother or father buys useless oil wells or falls prey to confidence men, and they approach gingerly or in anger." Parents, convinced that they know what they're doing, will often resent any suggestion that they're behaving in an irrational manner and will "resist any incursion on their independence."[4]

Or the older person, far from behaving aggressively about spending large amounts of money, may be too damaged mentally to handle any at all, unable to manage money mechanics in any way.

A Revocable Trust

Perhaps the most flexible and useful device for handling the financial affairs of a parent who is beginning to show signs of abnormal behavior is a revocable or "living" trust. Even parents who are functioning well might wish to establish this kind of trust because it relieves them from having to pay any attention to bills, checks, and bank accounts and removes any concern about handling money. Under this increasingly common arrangement, your parent transfers his assets to a revocable trust, which he can change at will. You and your siblings can be the trustees, or, if this is not feasible, a local bank might be used as a trustee or cotrustee. The trust agreement would authorize the trustee to use the trust income—and principal if necessary—to pay your parent's bills and otherwise provide for his care, maintenance, and support. It would contain the same powers to handle property that are usually contained in a power of attorney. In this way, all of your parent's financial affairs can be attended to privately, without the intervention of any cumbersome and potentially embarrassing legal proceedings. This kind of trust, unlike a power of attorney, will remain in full force and effect even if your parent subsequently becomes incompetent.

In many states it's possible for your parent to specify in the trust agreement where the remaining trust property is to go after his death. In other words, he can write his will into the trust document. If this is done, the remaining trust property will pass after his death directly to his beneficiaries, in the manner outlined in the trust and without the necessity of subjecting the trust property to the delays and administrative expenses of probate.

When You Should Take Charge

Certainly you will be alarmed when you first observe your parent behaving erratically with money, whether it's losing or not depositing checks, writing large bank overdrafts, making

bizarre purchases, not paying utility bills. "This kind of behavior comes and goes when it first emerges, but don't get
scared and think that your parent needs to be in a mental
hospital," says Mathiasen. "You are probably more frightened
by this than your parent because the parent usually believes he's
fine and isn't apprehensive." When you begin to see your parent acting in this manner, however—regardless of his own ap-
praisal of his behavior—you will obviously have to start watching very closely, doing whatever you can to supervise both the
income and outgo of his money. You need to do this both for
his sake and for your own.

It is acutely painful to watch a parent who is unreasonably
prodigal with money, who cannot muster the necessary practical intellect to dispense it, and whose behavior is generally irrational. But if your parent persists in this kind of behavior, you
will have to face up to some solution. You will need professional
and legal help to do so. (For medical information and advice,
see Chapter 8.)

Protective Services

"Protective services" is the term applied to legal services given
to older people who can no longer manage their own lives.
Usually these services are given by a state agency to older
people who are without family and relatives, first judging
whether, in fact, the older person needs them, and then deciding what the extent of the services will be. This is a simplified
description of protective services, but it defines the kind of
action you may have to initiate yourself.

How can you judge when you will have to intervene for your
parent? Intervention is a sensitive, philosophical problem now,
when courts are more and more cautious in taking away the
civil rights of any human being. Surely, it's a sensitive problem
for you; almost no child chooses willingly to strip a parent of
dignity and self-determination.

Lawyers and social workers in protective services agencies
have certain criteria for determining the need for protective
services. Broad though they are, they might serve you well in

your own situation. Your parent may be in need of protection if:

- He is unwilling or unable to take action to protect his interests.
- He is mentally confused.
- His behavior shows mental, physical, or emotional incapacity which may lead him to harm himself or others.
- He cannot do properly what he needs to do to maintain his life.
- He is incapable of managing his money.

Some states offer geriatric evaluation services which can help you. (See Chapter 2.) A team, consisting usually of a doctor, a psychiatrist, and perhaps a nurse or social worker, will examine an older person thoroughly, make an evaluation, and then recommend whether and to what degree the person is able to take care of himself and his affairs. The commission on aging or the department of health or social services in your parent's locality should be able to tell you whether such a service is available for you.

These diagnoses, whether they come from private physicians or from an evaluation team—preferably, perhaps, from both—will give you the experts' judgment on your parent's ability to manage his own life. Depending on the circumstances, a court can appoint a temporary guardian or conservator or a permanent one.

A Conservator

Should you see an extended pattern of irrational behavior and you feel that there is a substantial sum of money involved, you may want to think about having a conservator appointed to manage your parent's finances. This is not a step to be taken lightly, and, although state regulations differ, it always involves a legal procedure. You must have medical and psychiatric testimony to present to a court and, on the basis of this evidence, the court will decide whether or not the appointment of a conservator is warranted.

If the court appoints a conservator, your parent will no

longer have control over his financial affairs. The conservator will manage them, supplying your parent with the money he needs to live on and making regular reports on your parent's finances. He will be awarded a fee for his services. You might be appointed conservator yourself, in which case you can spend your parent's money only on his needs and will be responsible to the court which appointed you. Sometimes the conservator will be a disinterested third party. Counties and cities are establishing such services for older people who can no longer direct their own money matters or their own well-being—but these are mainly for low-income people without families of their own to take responsibility. The common assumption is that a person who has been declared incompetent to manage his own affairs is doomed forever to incompetence. This isn't necessarily accurate. Bear in mind that, with certain illnesses, treatment and changed conditions can sometimes ameliorate even a seemingly acute condition, and the need for a conservator, in those cases, may be temporary.

Going to court to ask for a conservator is an extreme step in trying to guard your parent from the financial consequences of his erratic behavior. You should try everything else before that to help him manage his own money. It is too painful in every way to bring the cold authority of the judicial system into family relationships. But should your earlier actions not be enough to restrain your parent's abnormal behavior, then this is a step you can take properly and in good conscience.

You can protect your parent in this way whether or not you live near him. Perhaps he lives at a distance and there's no compelling reason to move his residence near you. In this case, if there's a relative in the vicinity, the court may appoint him conservator. Or you can turn to a county or city agency in your parent's area for advice and help in dealing with the legal process. Most local commissions on aging will have a legal office attached.

Laws governing guardians and conservators differ among the states, so be sure you know the law in the state where your parent lives.

CHAPTER 6

YOUR PARENT AND HIS DOCTOR

One of the most encouraging advances in medicine in recent years is the increasing knowledge about old age. Good doctors are beginning to understand better the bodily changes that occur as we go through the life cycle. They are more able to retard or reverse some of the destructive processes that rob so many of a healthy old age. Many myths are being exploded, not the least of which is that people die of old age per se. True, the body and brain slow down, some of the processes that regulate the various functions alter, the tissues change, cells change or die, the muscles weaken, and the pace diminishes. It may not mean that the quality of thought diminishes, but it is true that it may take an older person a longer time to deal with information and act on it. People do not seem to die of this aging process, however; rather, it is now believed by many researchers that the aging human, like all living things coming to the end of the life cycle, is vulnerable finally to the stress of disease, or pathology, or the accident that kills.

Rather more is now known about the diseases that afflict the elderly and finally overcome them; more is known about the possibilities of treatment, cure, and of rehabilitation when handicaps appear. More is known about the possibilities of medication, surgery, and psychiatry. Despite these advances in knowledge, countless older people continue to be sick and miserable, and countless families are dealing with the everyday consequences of the chronic or catastrophic illnesses of their

155

parents. Many older people are abandoned needlessly to suffering or to their dotage. While new social policy is evolving and we all may look forward eventually to a more humane system of health care for our elderly, we are plagued by today's frustrations.

Finding the right doctor at the right time can be a real problem. Protecting an elderly parent in a big hospital is a real responsibility. Talking to a doctor so that each of you is contributing to the success of your parent's medical care is a real talent. Not being overawed or cowed by the mystique of medicine is a real necessity. Finding out enough about your parent's illness so that you can be alert to danger signals is a wise precaution.

The outstanding practitioners in the field of geriatric medicine are the first to tell you that things are not what they ought to be. "Neglect is the treatment of choice, with medicine failing to care for their physical needs, mental health personnel ignoring their emotional problems, communities neglecting to fill their social expectations," says Dr. Robert Butler.[1]

The challenge, then, if you are the caring child of an ailing parent, is to overcome your awe of the doctors, to help find a good one who cares about what happens to your parent, and to inform yourself about the particulars of whatever illness your parent may have so you can cooperate intelligently with the doctor in the prescribed treatment, or be an ombudsman if required.

We said earlier that old people don't die of old age. What do they die of? Heart disease, stroke, cancer, diabetes, and accidents are the most common causes of death in people over sixty-five. Heart disease usually stems from arteriosclerosis or hypertension. Strokes are likewise related to closures in the vascular system and to high blood pressure. The chance of having these diseases increases with age. The same is true of cancer. Diabetes is increasing as a disease of the elderly, as the life span lengthens and treatment for younger diabetics is more successful, permitting more of them to reach maturity and reproduce and live longer. Accidents seem to be related to worsening vision, hearing, diminution in the other senses such as smell and taste, and degeneration of the central nervous system. Reflexes are slower, bones more brittle, and healing processes slower. Dizziness sometimes comes with sudden motion.

What doesn't kill old people can disable them, put them in pain and misery. Arthritis and rheumatism are high on the list of offenders in this category, as are pulmonary disease with resultant difficulties in breathing, various circulatory diseases, paralysis, amputation, and gastrointestinal disorders that can limit the activity of chronic sufferers. Older men are especially vulnerable to diseases of the urinary tract.

There is a close correlation between physical impairment and mental disorder. Depression is the frequent companion of the elderly who are ill. But depression also appears without physical cause, with sudden bereavement, retirement, loss of income or social status; it sometimes comes without any apparent cause at all.

Doctors who deal with the elderly know that they are frequently victims of several diseases simultaneously, and treatment depends on carefully orchestrating the routines and medications so that they do not interfere with one another.

Seriously ill, handicapped, or frail people have special needs, and their families have special problems. We asked a number of outstanding doctors what families need to know about some typical diseases and afflictions of elderly people. For you who are among the children of such parents, the following information should help.

We caution you to remember that each is an individual case and that the generalizations included here can only be regarded as guidelines. The specifics are illustrative, not comprehensive. The intention is to alert you to some of the common problems that appear and to help you find some of the solutions that may be eluding you. First, it is important for an older person to have a good doctor.

If Your Parent Needs a New Doctor: How to Find One

"The secret of the care of the patient," said a respected teacher of medicine a generation ago, "is in caring for the patient."[2]

If your mother or father is unhappy with a present physician, or has moved to a new community, or the old family doctor has retired or died, in your search for a new doctor be especially careful in the choice. While many doctors are good doctors, some of them are not necessarily suitable for elderly people. So you will want to find someone who is professionally competent, personally compatible, and, preferably, attached to a good hospital. Here we will highlight the important factors you and your parents should keep in mind.

- If a family member or a friend has confidence in a physician, start by asking that doctor for a recommendation for a new doctor for your parent. Geography is not a problem. Doctors have medical school friends, professional society colleagues, and detailed directories to consult for references in other parts of the country.
- If you're consulting friends and neighbors, ask only people whose judgment you respect. Gossipy tales won't help much, but should alert you to potential personality conflicts.
- A university medical school or hospital or any large general public or voluntary hospital is an excellent source of referrals. Usually you're given several names and expected to choose from a list.
- Double-check with the national health organizations for medical specialists, for example, the local Heart Association for cardiologists, the American Cancer Society for cancer specialists, the Arthritis Foundation for specialists in arthritis.
- You can inquire of a county medical society or privately owned hospital, though recommendations from these sources are usually limited to their own membership and may not necessarily be of the quality you would prefer.
- If you're entirely on your own, you can find the state medical directory in the library. Each licensed physician in the state will be listed. It really isn't a good idea to go by the book alone; a good education and hospital affiliation are usually assurances of technical competence, but give you no clue to personality or style or current professional development.
- Be careful about hospital affiliation. When you check a doctor, check the hospital with which he is associated. Inspect the hospital personally, if you can, to see how elderly patients are treated and to get your own sense of the atmosphere.

A final word of advice: It is not a good idea to go searching for a specialist before you have a good internist in general charge of your parent's medical care. The internist today is the closest counterpart of yesterday's family doctor. Most good internists are equipped to deal with the chronic illnesses of the elderly, and, if they are really good, know when to call on specialists for additional consultation or treatment. The danger in your going directly for a specialist is that you may misread the symptoms entirely, and look for a dermatologist to treat a skin rash when the rash is only the symptom of a much different, and possibly very serious, condition.

How to Judge and Evaluate a Doctor Attending Elderly People

If your parent has selected a doctor with good hospital connections, who is well recommended as being professionally competent, and is "nice," what next?

The first appointment will give you a great deal of information about this new doctor, and you and your parents can then decide whether the choice is suitable. It is a good idea for some family member to participate in a first visit. Then ask yourselves these questions:

- Has there been sufficient time made available for this initial visit? *An hour is reasonable. Elderly people need time and compassion from their physicians, as well as technical competence. There should be time to take a good history, learn family medical idiosyncrasies, unusual incidents, common complaints, and to perform standard tests. The doctor should take the time to chat with your parent, get a real feeling for personality and anxieties, and allow time for questions. The doctor should know about your parent's social and economic circumstances and should be interested in talking with you, as well, to get your perspective. It is up to the doctor to put the pieces together; often the medical problem is not what the patient thinks it is. If the visit is too mechanized, too abrupt, then this doctor is not desirable for your elderly parent—unless his competence is essential as a specialist or surgeon, or it is an emergency—and finding a new doctor is better than starting a relationship of frustration and unhappiness.*
- During subsequent visits, does the doctor continue to give

your parent the attention his condition requires? *After the initial diagnosis, a doctor should be reasonable about answering questions and explaining procedures so that you and your parent continue to understand clearly what is happening, what to do, and what to expect. (See pages 161 to 165, responsibilities of patients.)*

- Are you confident that this doctor is sensitive to the limits of his own knowledge? *A good doctor should know when to call another doctor for a consultation for help in diagnosis for unusual care. Lay people are sometimes shaken when the physician suggests calling in another doctor, and wonder if this physician is any good after all. It is good, not bad, when a doctor is willing to admit he doesn't know, and is willing to ask for help.*

- Does this doctor object if you or your parent wants another opinion? *It is especially desirable to seek another opinion if radical treatment or surgery is suggested. You should feel free in the relationship to request this.*

- Has the doctor told you how to reach him in emergencies, late at night, or over weekends? *You should know what alternative arrangements are available in emergencies.*

A case in point will illustrate how a physician can affect a patient: One doctor told an over-sixty-five patient with viral pneumonia that her heart was affected. He ordered her to take digitalis and put her on a salt-free diet. This would be a permanent regimen, he said. Following his diagnosis and prescription, she seemed to age ten years overnight. Concerned about the dramatic difference in her mother's behavior, her daughter insisted she consult another physician. The second doctor explained that unusually rapid heart action sometimes does accompany a pneumonia, that she had now recovered completely and there was no residual side effect. "I hope I look as good as you when I'm your age," said this new doctor. The parent left the office, smiling, a new spring in her step, the extra ten years shed. This took place fourteen years ago. She is today a vigorous eighty-year-old, healthy and active—on a normal diet.

So pay attention to this most important person in your parent's life. It can make all the difference.

How You Can Help Insure the Best Results: Be Open

There should be no hesitancy on your part, or your parent's, to mention anything bizarre or unusual about health or anxieties. The doctor may see you separately for part of a visit to get all sides of the story. Since the doctor must know everything in order to help, he should encourage this and give you confidence that the privacy of the information divulged will be respected. It is important to establish an open kind of relationship.

Appoint a Spokesperson

In times of both chronic and acute illness, appoint one member of the family, preferably one who is comfortable talking to doctors and is not shy about asking questions, to be in touch with the doctor. You cannot expect a doctor to repeat over and over to different people what is happening.

Cooperate with the Doctor

Just as you expect the doctor to be responsible and responsive, so must you cooperate with him. The doctor has many patients and families who are owed time, skill, patience, compassion, understanding, and information. Respect the time you take. Don't be a pest, calling needlessly to prove you are attentive to your parent, more responsible than your sister, more caring than your brother. Don't telephone without a specific question to ask, or information to give. If you want to have a long discussion, make an appointment and inform the doctor ahead of time of your purpose. If you want advice on how to handle a problem, let him know that. If you don't understand a technicality of language, tell him so. Ask him to explain; don't wander in a blizzard of confusion and blame it on him. And help your parent to understand and carry out the doctor's directions.

Be Vigilant

If you notice something unusual and inform the doctor, this should not be regarded as interference. Don't wait for the next scheduled appointment to report bad side effects to medications or extreme pain. If a timid patient doesn't want to "bother him," the doctor is often not ever aware of undesirable events. Some people are uncomfortable raising questions with the "experts," but a good doctor is not offended by the intercession of a concerned family. He appreciates information from a responsible person, which would not otherwise be available, so that he can take appropriate action. Suppose your parent has been given new medication, for example, and has been told to take it until the next visit. If unpleasant side reactions develop and your parent becomes dizzy, vomits, can't sleep, gets a skin rash, inform the doctor even if the specified time isn't up. Let him decide whether to continue or change.

Be Realistic

Doctors are people. They are subject to the same drives and ego needs as everyone else. They like approval and try to avoid pain. They like success and don't like failure. That is why some doctors avoid taking on the care of old people: people who are sure to die don't make good records. Some doctors have emotional problems about death and dying themselves, and see in the elderly patient a constant reminder of unpleasant things to come. Other doctors are prima donnas, expecting patients to put up with really rude or unconscionable behavior in exchange for their technical knowledge or skill. A few doctors are simply unpleasant, and neither you nor your parents should feel so overawed that you tolerate behavior in a doctor you would not find acceptable in anyone else.

But suppose the doctor is really a nice person, dedicated and attentive and obviously doing the best that can be done? Then don't invest him with superhuman qualities. It is best to be comfortable in the doctor–patient relationship. Have confidence, ask questions, appreciate the truly skilled hands to which you entrust your parent's life, but don't expect miracles where none can exist.

Long-Distance Communication

Here you are in your home. Your mother is across the country, hospitalized. An aunt has seen to the emergency and tells you there is no need for you to travel now; it would be better to come later when your mother will need you at home. But you are restless, unsure. Should you talk to the doctor yourself, or leave it up to Aunt Alice?

Of course you should call the physician yourself to reassure yourself that everything is OK and that Aunt Alice has made a good judgment. But be judicious.

When you telephone, call person-to-person. Introduce yourself and quickly explain your relationship to the patient. Unless there is an urgent emergency, don't insist on speaking with the doctor at that precise time if it is interfering with his office hours or rounds. Ask that the call be returned "collect" at the doctor's convenience during a time period when you are also available. If there is an emergency, explain what it is so that the nurse or answering service can take appropriate action. You may suggest that the doctor telephone you directly, collect, if he would like you to come at a later time, or if he thinks you should be informed of a new development.

Questions People Sometimes Forget to Ask

- How much will this cost? It is not unusual for people worried about the immediate medical emergency to forget to ask the doctor how much the treatment or surgery or hospitalization will cost, and then be upset when the bill arrives.
- If surgery is planned, is special nursing available? This should be arranged ahead of time, if possible, to assure the patient's comfort and security, and is especially valuable the first night or first few days after surgery unless the patient is in the intensive care or special recovery units. If you call at the last minute and in times of shortages of private nurses, you may be the one to sit up all night. Are you prepared to do this?
- Does the doctor expect that a visiting nurse or companion will be necessary at home following surgery or any other hospitalization? Again, it is wise to prepare for this in good time, not during the last few days of a hospital stay.

Doctors and Money

Different doctors charge different fees for their services.

Frequently these charges vary from the allowances that are provided by medicare, medicaid, Blue Cross, Blue Shield, or the many medical plans in which people are enrolled. (See Chapter 5.) You or your parent can easily determine the doctor's fees by asking. You'll know ahead of time what to expect and therefore should be able to decide whether or not your family can afford that physician's fees. You need not be surprised by the bills.

Elderly people, frequently lonely, often worried about their symptoms, afraid and sometimes forgetful, can take up a great deal of a doctor's time without realizing that time does cost money. It takes a diplomatic and caring physician to offer advice or comfort quickly, without seeming to be abrupt. You should know your parent's habits and some of his failings before you make harsh judgments about the doctor's attitude. It is a delicate matter to find an absolute definition of "reasonable" attention. Just take a little time and think about it before you decide what is or isn't reasonable.

Another characteristic of the elderly is to compare current fees with those they remember from their younger days, and to complain. This is no different from remarks about the price of steak or tomatoes or the price of a movie. Remember—filling out insurance forms is a nuisance to you; doing it for hundreds of patients is a time-consuming and expensive task.

These comments are not included to diminish the complaints or real grievances of patients who are paying exorbitant fees, who are unable to afford necessary care, and who are wondering how soon some form of national health insurance will relieve them of the fears and consequences of catastrophic illness and economic disaster. Patients with the means to pay, however, should remember that the physician is also a consumer whose costs are escalating with inflation, and that his time costs money.

Many doctors are aware that extended-care costs can bankrupt a family. You should not be shy in discussing financial matters with a doctor and bringing his attention to the potential economic consequences for your family of certain courses of action. Particular attention needs to be paid to medicare reimbursement if your parent goes to a nursing facility without first being hospitalized. Thousands of dollars may be involved. (See Chapter 5.)

Everyone Needs an Ombudsman in Today's Medical Centers

Once upon a time, when the doctor and the nurse were among the few educated members of the community, their authority was unquestioned and their practice assumed to be correct. Today, these assumptions are not necessarily supported by experience. It is not that their education or training is less; it is that attitudes, complex hospital organizations, understaffing, social and racial complications, urban decay, and a host of other factors have eroded the simple aura of confidence that once accompanied the doctor–patient–hospital relationship.

"The last place to be if you're sick is a hospital" is a common cliché of the seventies. Frequently the hospital is not a place for tender loving care, especially if you are old and not suffering from a dramatic, exotic, "interesting" disease. Pain and discomfort, if routine, may be severe to your parent but not much to get excited about if you are the professional caretaker. Sloppiness, filth, wrong medication, unanswered calls for attention or assistance are not all that unusual. If you love the family member who is hospitalized, it is a good idea to stick around and find out what is happening in the hospital. Is someone paying attention? Maybe it should be you! Don't assume anything.

Here's What to Look For

- *A clean room.* A well-ventilated and -heated room, clean water pitchers, clean glasses, and a drinking tube are every patient's right.
- *A way to call for help.* An easily reachable button or light that gets a response is every patient's necessity.
- *Professional attention on a regular basis.* The nurse, doctor, intern, resident, aide—someone should be checking at regular intervals each day on vital signs, effect of medication, progress or regression, bowel movements and urination. There should be a timely response to unusual symptoms.

- *Diet trays.* If your parent is on a salt-free, sugar-free, low-cholesterol, soft diet or other specially prescribed diet, is that what is delivered? You really have to check the trays. Not everyone in the kitchen is necessarily literate or careful. Supervision may be lax, and it may be your diabetic mother or father who is getting regular ice cream for dessert, sauerbraten for dinner the day after an intestinal operation, or prunes for breakfast after a bout of diarrhea. It happens.

- *Medication.* Is the pill the right one, for the right patient, in the right room? You may be embarrassed to ask, but that is better than finding your father comatose after taking someone else's knockout drops. If the medication is making your parent feel rotten instead of better, causing vomiting, sleeplessness, dizziness or palpitations, depression, anxiety, or manic exaltation, don't ignore it. Be sure to call it to the doctor's attention; no one else may do so.

- *New orders.* Perhaps the doctor makes a change in medication or diet. Days pass, and nothing is different. You'd better start asking questions.

- *Ill-treatment.* Old people are vulnerable. Some staff members think they're cute, like babies; others are repelled by gnarled fingers, lax muscles, untidy habits, forgetfulness. Exploited low-level employees frequently victimize the elderly. They can be cruel, mean, even physically rough with them, taking out their hostilities to society. You don't need to suspect everyone who comes in contact with your parent. But if your parent complains to you and is afraid to speak up to responsible hospital staff, don't ignore the complaint and dismiss it as aged paranoia without investigation and without assuring yourself that everything is as it should be.

The director of a large city hospital has said, "Someone has to follow up on what is happening. Be protective of the patient. It is not necessary to be offensive to the professionals in order to make your presence known. If the patient is scheduled for surgery, it is entirely appropriate for the family to ask the physician ahead of time to arrange for information and not to be kept in the dark. Families are entitled to be 'stroked' in times of great anxiety and stress.

"If someone is hospitalized for a long stay, a family may have to raise hell if things are not 'reasonably right.'

"Don't assume excellent care or that attention to all the important details is actually happening.

"It is a good idea for a family to keep track of urine, eating, bowels, and sleep ... someone really has to check up on this. Neglect can be dangerous and serious secondary complications can arise because of this neglect."

Says one experienced physician, "I am amazed at how little people do really intrude with requests for information. They wait for a real flak before they ask for information to which they are entitled. Especially when they have doubts, they are entitled to some explanations."[3]

So strike a balance and do what is reasonable; don't monopolize a doctor's time with unnecessary and unreasonable requests, but don't hesitate to ask for information or to give information that is critical to the patient's well-being.

One final word of advice: bring cookies to the nurses; fruit if they are on diets. Doctors like good things to eat also. They appreciate the attention as individuals and respond to your relative in kind. This may sound like payola, but sometimes it's the only guarantee against callous bureaucracy.

The Patient's Bill of Rights

In 1972 the American Hospital Association (AHA) issued a statement on patients' rights. These rights have been incorporated into some state health codes. Member hospitals of the AHA are expected to honor the guidelines. In general, the patient is to be assured of considerate and respectful care; the confidentiality of his case; the right to information about his case, including possible risks; and the right to refuse treatment under certain circumstances. The patient is also protected from unwanted experimentation; is given the right to information about the professional people assigned to his care and about any alternate facilities to which he might be transferred; and is given the right to explanations of his bill. (See Appendix.)

CHAPTER 7 DISEASES OF THE ELDERLY

Heart Disease

Knowing that your parent has "heart trouble" is not enough. Heart trouble is a loose description of various kinds of heart disease, congenital or acquired. You need to know the name and characteristics of the particular kind of heart disease afflicting your parent if you are to deal intelligently and sympathetically with it. Diets, exercise, and routines are different for different kinds of heart disease. A supervised, reasonably intensive exercise program may be just what the doctor ordered for a person with a good recovery from a heart attack. A similar program could harm a patient with congestive heart failure. So before you give your own advice about what is or isn't a good idea, it is better to discuss with the doctor the precise nature of your parent's cardiac problem.

Most heart disease in older people results from hypertension (high blood pressure) or from arteriosclerosis. Resultant changes in the walls of the arteries, including thickening, can cause closure, clots, and heart attacks. Some people suffer from both hypertension and arteriosclerosis. Congenital heart disease, or malformation, is, of course, something people are born with. People have enlarged hearts, hearts with a great deal of dead muscle (necrosis), damaged valves, and a variety of pathological conditions that affect the normal function of the heart—which is to pump blood through the arteries and nourish the system. When these functions are impaired, for whatever reason, people have some kind of heart trouble. Cardiac arrest can result from any of these causes. The heart stops. If emergency treatment is undertaken quickly, the heart can sometimes be made to function again. If too long a time has elapsed before heart action is started again, brain damage occurs. If the heart is not started at all, the patient dies. Prompt attention to people having heart attacks (coronary thrombosis, or coronary occlusion, or myocardial infarction) and to people in acute heart failure (pumping action is faulty, and fluid accumulates in the lungs to a point where breathing is impaired) can save lives. Routine use of nitroglycerine can relieve the temporary pain of those cardiacs who suffer with angina pectoris, a suffocating pain in the chest that results when the heart muscle itself is not getting enough oxygen because the blood supply is impaired. Routine use of pacemakers can regulate erratic heart rhythm and abnormally slow heart action.

It is up to the doctor to determine the ability of the patient to function and to help the family understand what the patient should or should not do. Again, this is not a simple matter, since some patients with minor heart damage are so psychologically damaged and frightened by heart disease that they are afraid of any physical activity and resist doing things they really can do. Other patients, with enormous damage, so "deny" their disease that they overperform at real peril to their lives. It is important for the doctor to know the patient in order to evaluate the condition and prescribe a realistic, appropriate, and beneficial course of action. Many cardiac patients are in the sole care of their internists or family physicians, where these still exist. It is a good idea, nevertheless, to have the additional advice of an experienced cardiologist from time to time because there may be subtleties of diagnosis and treatment which are better known to the specialist. It is not at all unusual for a good internist to ask a cardiologist to check a reading on an electrocardiogram (EKG) for more precise interpretation, and it is to your parent's advantage if this happens.

If you are observant, you can help both the cardiac parent and the doctor. Discuss with the doctor the diagnosis, treatment, activity, and the clinical picture as it worsens so you know what to look for.

Emergency: Call the Doctor

The most general rule to follow is this: If you see a dramatic difference in behavior, looks, eating habits, bowel habits, sleeping habits, or if you note increasing fatigue, shortness of breath, intensity or frequency of pain, increased coughing, cold sweat, *call the doctor.*

- *Chest Pains.* Anything unusual is significant. Pay particular attention if your parent suffers from angina pectoris and has "learned to live with the pain." If there are changes in character or increases in frequency and duration, notify the doctor. This pain typically is relieved by nitroglycerine and usually doesn't last more than about fifteen minutes. If the pain lasts longer than that, call the doctor. If chest pain radiates out to the arms, and your parent seems unusually quiet and is breaking out in a cold sweat, waste no time. *Call the doctor.*

- *Suffocation sensation, shortness of breath.* These are symptoms which may even awaken people from their sleep with the feeling they can't breathe. They may be signs of acute heart failure. An open window or door may seem to give temporary relief, but the person may start coughing, break out into a cold sweat, or even foam at the mouth. *Call the doctor.*

- *Indigestion, nausea, cold sweat.* These symptoms, also accompanied by diffuse pain, may frequently disguise the presence of an ongoing heart attack. Sometimes people think they're having "gas" or a gallbladder attack. *Call the doctor.*

- *Loss of appetite, nausea, dizziness, diarrhea, profound weakness, palpitations, ringing in the ears, headaches, seeing spots.* These signs may signify drug toxicity. They can result from overdosage of drugs, conflict of drugs, or individual sensitivities. Since many patients are on diuretics, digitalis, quinidine, or other medication that must be carefully monitored for required changes of dosage, be observant. When there are sudden changes in habits and feelings, *call the doctor.*

- *Swelling of feet, abdomen, unaccountable weight increase, lightheadedness, shortness of breath.* These signs in a known cardiac signify the patient needs treatment. These symptoms of congestive heart failure, accompanied by a cold sweat and difficulty in breathing, can mean the patient is in acute failure. *Call the doctor.*

- *Change in heart action: rapid or slow or irregular.* It is an emergency if the pulse goes over 100 or below 60. If the patient reports that his heart is "racing" or "bumping," that it is going very slowly or that he feels faint, remember that sudden changes in pulse rate can reflect heart damage or drug intoxication. If you can't take a pulse, don't experiment. *Call the doctor.*

Living with Chest Pain

Many cardiacs learn to live with chest pain. Nitroglycerine is the tiny wonder drug that gives quick relief for chronic sufferers. Treating angina with nitros may cause headaches initially, but these usually go away. And unless the pain lasts unusually long, as specified above, there is no reason for persons with angina not to go about their business, provided they take reasonable precautions to avoid physical or emotional stress.

For example, they should not eat too much in general, or at any given meal. They should avoid cold and windy weather or take extra care to dress warmly, covering noses and mouths with a scarf. (Some doctors believe they should not walk outdoors at all on cold, windy, raw days. Extreme cold or wind can bring on angina.) They should avoid the excessive emotions of pleasure or of pain, the excitement of a political argument or a sports event, or sexual intercourse; with an elderly patient, all these can bring on angina. Sufferers cannot afford the luxury of violent emotions, so families are cautioned to "take it easy" with them.

Some patients use angina, this recurrent pain, to manipulate those around them. It makes it very difficult for you if your mother complains of chest pains every time you go out for the evening, or when you are planning a vacation, or when your daughter dates a boy your mother doesn't like. It is certainly true that at times serious symptoms may erupt that require emergency attention. But you will have to be observant and know that the doctor can help you to evaluate the reality of the case. Organic symptoms do take precedence over personality, but they should be judged within the context of the personality. Knowing the emergency signs listed above should help. When in doubt, call the doctor.

It is very important that people understand the nature of their disease, the importance of pain, of medication, of diet, of routines that are prescribed for them. It helps if the family understands these things, too. Dr. Robert Stivelman, a noted California cardiologist, says, "The hardest part of taking care of patients with heart disease is getting them to follow diets and live emotionally with their disease." Those who are disabled emotionally by their disease are frequently very difficult to treat. In their concern and frustration, families may counter the doctor's advice. "It won't hurt," they say, "if you have a little piece of candy now and then, or a rich dessert, or a piece of salty, spicy fish or meat." "True," says Dr. Stivelman, "an occasional high-cholesterol goody may not have serious consequences for those on low-cholesterol diets, but for patients on low-sodium diets, those with pulmonary edema, hypertension, or congestive heart failure, it is essential to be rigorous. It is not true that a little won't hurt." People on controlled-sodium diets absolutely cannot eat a treat. Don't seduce them with treats. Says Dr. Joseph Ney of Washington, D.C., "Once they start cheating, there is no limit."

Telling People About Their Disease

Telling people with heart disease how ill they are is a touchy thing. Depending on their ego strength and emotional needs, they will react differently. Some can take a realistic assessment of their condition. Some con the doctor into telling them and then go to pieces if they find they are seriously ill. Others deny everything, cannot really accept their illness. These are the people who persist in asking the doctors the same questions over and over. "What does he mean," your elderly mother asks, "when he tells me I have a very bad heart? I'll ask another doctor." She really wants to be told her heart will improve, that she will get over this disease, that she will not die of it. Her doctor has told her what medication will ameliorate her symptoms, what routines will increase her comfort, what cannot be relieved or predicted. "But this is no life," she says, complaining at the dullness or restrictions, terrified of every new pain.

It is, indeed, "no life" for some patients, says Dr. Stivelman, particularly those in congestive heart failure, who cannot take any exercise, find it is taxing to walk to the next room, let alone out for diversion.

For the families of these patients, there is an extra burden to "bring the world to them," to relieve the tedium, and provide some of the small pleasures that make it worthwhile to get up in the morning. Watching a parent become weaker and weaker, more and more frail, just peter out, is in some ways more difficult and painful than accepting sudden catastrophic illness or sudden death. If it is a time that is used preciously to enrich each other's lives and relationships, some families call this a beautiful time. But if the relationships are poor to begin with and the extra time to be spent becomes a nagging burden, or if the economic or other needs of the family preclude their spending this extra time, then the guilt problems begin to accumulate and everyone feels destroyed. If you cannot deal with this yourself, a psychiatric social worker can help. Dr. Ney says, "All the seriously ill want is to be with their families."

Should Cardiacs Live Alone?

No one can predict a sudden emergency. But, in general, unless a patient has become too weak to take care of his daily needs, or unless he is too terrified, a patient with minimal heart damage can live alone, work, shop, socialize, take exercise according to the physician's direction, and lead a relatively normal life.

Dr. Raymond Harris writes in a U.S. Public Health Service manual for physicians on the clinical practice of geriatrics: "After a heart attack, the elderly patient should be encouraged to return to physical activity and social participation normally enjoyed by people of his age. Senior cardiacs can perform many sedentary jobs. Most elderly cardiac patients, especially those above 75 years of age, will not seek employment. The physician should encourage them to engage in social intercourse and community group activities. The senior cardiac has more to fear from sedation, social segregation and senility than from cardiac disease. Social intercourse and participation often benefit him more than digitalis."[1]

This should be a warning to families as well not to wrap a cardiac parent in cotton wool and remove him or her from the mainstream of life.

But be observant. When your mother begins to have palpitations after shopping for herself and carrying heavy groceries, or your father regularly comes back from some hard exercise gray in complexion and with blue lips, it may be time to reevaluate the situation, consult the doctor, and make new plans. Perhaps the elderly person has gone almost imperceptibly from a status of having had minimal heart disease to a more serious state. If suitable household care is neither available nor financially possible in the home, then it is time to look into the health-related facilities that provide the attention and security that are required.

Pacemakers, Surgery, and Other Matters

These few words are not a comprehensive discourse on heart disease. They are not intended to make you a substitute physician. There are many varieties of heart disease not even mentioned here that require wise counsel, close attention, and careful treatment. We have touched only on the more common problems associated with "heart trouble." Recent advances in technology and surgery have opened wide new vistas of hope for cardiac patients. Pacemakers, for example, effectively control heart rate and avert the faintness or even sudden death that can come with irregular heart action. Pacemakers need to be checked on a regular basis, usually are replaced in about two years or longer. The procedure for checking and replacement is benign. It is a good idea, if your parent has a pacemaker, to keep track of the dates and remind an aging parent that it is time to go to the doctor or the clinic for the necessary checks.

Open-heart surgery, valve replacement, and other new developments in chest surgery are available options for many people, including the elderly. Whether it is suitable or not is a completely individual matter. Age per se is not the criterion for this surgery. The doctor in charge should be in a good position to spell out the advantages and dangers for any given patient. You will not want your parent to be a guinea pig for experimental surgery without knowing all the possible risks. On the other hand, you will not want to deprive him or her of longer years of comfortable living if the risk is minimal. If your parent's doctor suggests such surgery and you are not sure, don't be embarrassed to get another opinion. The final decision has to be made by your parent, not you.

Should You Tell a Person with Heart Trouble Bad News?

"Families take a big chance," says Dr. Ira Gelb, a New York cardiologist, "when they keep things from their ailing parents." There is a growing body of professional opinion, psychiatric and medical, that stresses the individual dignity and rights of all people, including the right of ill persons to hear bad news or good news and react accordingly. The right to grieve for a departed relative or to visit a fatally ill child or grandchild is a right that should not be taken away without considerable thought. Perhaps there is a way to lessen the shock of bad news, to introduce the problem gently. "Your son is in the hospital having some tests made. He'll probably be OK, but perhaps you'd like to visit."

If there is really bad news to share, it is best to present it, carefully, in very protected circumstances. You, the doctor, a clergyman if your parent is close to one, will want to be there. Do follow the doctor's advice as to whether the news is too stressful and dangerous for the cardiac parent to hear. Perhaps some medication will be wanted. For some very ill individuals, the doctor may well advise you not to share the bad news immediately, but most doctors believe there are always ways to be found to present bad news early. There are many families who hide bad news altogether from an aging parent, and especially an ill one with a bad heart. Problems arise. By sheer coincidence a stranger will inform the parent, or assume he already knows and offer condolences. This emotional shock may well be worse than the one you were trying to avoid in the first place. So think hard and carefully when you decide what to do, and remember that each case is individual.[2]

Hypertension: High Blood Pressure

A massive public education campaign has only recently exposed this silent killer, high blood pressure, as the most prevalent chronic disease in America. You can now have your blood pressure taken at a van outside the supermarket, at the nearest public health station, in your office, on a street corner, or at a senior citizens' center. Attention to blood pressure is intended to reveal the presence of abnormality so that prompt and appropriate treatment can begin.

Hypertension is the most common cause of death in the United States. It is more prevalent among the black than the white population and accounts in part for the shorter life span of blacks. But, according to the U.S. Public Health Service, "Hypertension is so prevalent in the aged that many physicians consider it a normal, even inevitable aspect of aging that does not require treatment. This view is untrue. Hypertension impairs circulation in the brain, heart and kidneys, increases cardiac work, precipitates congestive failure and aggravates arteriosclerosis. The elderly—who can least afford such effects—may benefit from antihypertensive treatment."[3]

Strokes, heart attacks, or kidney failure—any of which might have been avoided, lessened, or postponed by early diagnosis and treatment—are sometimes the first indications people have that they are suffering from serious hypertension.

Anyone can get high blood pressure, but if it runs in your family, you are more likely to develop it. More women than men suffer from high blood pressure in old age, while it is more prevalent in younger men than in younger women. Fat people are more vulnerable, but all kinds of people can and do get it.

Once hypertension is diagnosed, rigorous treatment, change in diet, and medication can usually control it. For the elderly, however, it is imperative that dosages of drugs be carefully monitored so that required changes can be instituted quickly if necessary. Low-salt diets, diuretics to remove the salt and excess fluids which accumulate because of hypertension, and certain other drugs are usually prescribed to control its effects.

But the chemical balance is so critical and elderly patients are so sensitive to certain drugs (which can cause depression, for example, or dangerously deplete their potassium) that it is not good enough to go once for treatment and prescription and then forget about it. This disease requires lifelong treatment, but at the beginning of treatment, particularly, doctors will try a variety of combinations of drugs and therapy to find the one most appropriate to the individual. That is why any side effects, such as dizziness, fatigue, or diarrhea, should be promptly reported if these occur after a new drug has been prescribed.

Hypertension in itself describes an abnormality in the regulation of the blood pressure while the blood is being pumped through the system. When the pressure of the blood against the walls of the vessels is too high and stays up longer than it should, the vessels themselves are damaged. If the vessels are too thin, they can bubble or burst; if too hardened from sclerosis, they can block in the heart, causing heart attack, and in the brain, causing stroke. As pressure increases, the heart has to work harder. Overworked, it enlarges. Overtaxed, its pumping action falters. Congestive heart failure is a frequent result. Similarly, high blood pressure can damage the kidneys, with subsequent kidney failure and a buildup of waste, causing uremic poisoning. Death can be the result.

The problem with hypertension is that so many people have it and don't know it. That is why regular physical examinations and blood pressure readings are so important for everyone, and imperative for older people. Once hypertension is diagnosed, treatment really works if too much damage has not already been done. If your parent has neglected this preventive routine previously, and the symptoms appear, damage is likely to have taken place—but treatment can control or postpone further problems.

Hypertension Danger Signals[4]

- Light-headedness.
- Dizziness.

- Sleeplessness.
- Shortness of breath.
- Vision problems.
- Palpitations of the heart.
- Swelling of the ankles.

Says Dr. Raymond Harris, "For mild hypertension it is best to prescribe the least treatment that produces results. Mild hypertension often responds to weight reduction and restricted salt intake of no more than 3 to 4 grams of sodium per day (1 gram for patients with congestive heart failure). Walking and other mild activity and recreation should be encouraged and reassurance should be provided frequently." If these measures don't work, then, of course, drugs are used. But watch for toxicity and report effects to the doctor.

Such clichés as "He got so angry he looked like he'd have apoplexy" or "She's so upset she'll have a stroke" are the layman's way of recognizing that emotional stress can indeed elevate blood pressure. For the person with hypertensive disease, this can be quite serious. So, again, the prudent course for the family of an elderly person is to avoid confrontations and highly charged emotional scenes.

Stroke

While it is true that the brain can be damaged by a stroke, the nature of the damage is different from that caused by brain disease, and so are the results. (See Chapter 8.) A stroke—the popular term for a rupture or blocking of a blood vessel in the brain—usually causes part of the brain tissue to be destroyed. But damage is focused in a particular place. This place may be small, as in a small stroke, or very large, as in a massive stroke. Which tissue has been damaged, and how much of it, determines the function or lack of function remaining. The brain has "control centers" which regulate whatever else happens in our bodies, including, for example, our ability to move, feel, read or write, see or hear. With strokes, the damage does not spread as it does when there is brain disease. It is focused on whatever tissue was involved in the cardiovascular event. Once the condition is stabilized, the surrounding tissues, which may have been swollen by the trauma, can begin to heal. Then it is possible to determine exactly what permanent damage has occurred. This is why a doctor needs to observe and test a patient following a stroke before he can inform you of what really to expect. Some people, of course, go into coma and never recover. Some are partially or totally paralyzed. Some are unable to read or speak or write. Some can do one and not the others. Sometimes a clot following a stroke will impinge on some part of the brain; surgical removal can restore some lost function.

But, once he has stabilized, if you find that your parent has had some partial loss, you can really help by encouraging any rehabilitation suggested by the doctor. Rehabilitation therapy is marvelous to see; it teaches people to make the most of what they have, not emphasize what they have lost.

Cancer

Cancer takes more lives than any other disease except diseases of the heart and vascular system. People dread it because most have been witness to the devastation it can cause. Some cancers, caught early, are curable. Some cancers can be treated with chemotherapy or radiation, and can be arrested. Some cancers can be excised by surgery. Some cancers resist all treatment and kill. Some kill quickly; some kill slowly.

Cancers are of enormous variety and range. Any tissue of the body is susceptible to cancer—the process of uncontrolled growth of abnormal cells. We hear doctors speak of metastasis. This means that cancer cells travel through the lymph channels and bloodstream and settle in new places, causing new tumors to grow in the new locations.

When this happens, the prognosis is usually bad. When the cancer is contained in a particular place where treatment can be focused or surgery used to eliminate it, then there is greater chance of successful treatment. There are different patterns that characterize the different forms of cancers that have been identified.

As people survive other diseases, courtesy of new drugs and surgical techniques, they become candidates for cancer as they age. This is what the American Cancer Society recommends to families on the alert: have regular checkups and help your parents to know that many cancers caught early can be successfully treated. The danger signals which should send one to a doctor quickly have been well publicized by the American Cancer Society, but it can do no harm to remind you, and through you, your parents.[5]

Cancer Warning Signals

- Change in bowel or bladder habits.
- A sore that does not heal.
- Unusual bleeding or discharge.
- Thickening or lump in the breast or elsewhere.
- Indigestion or difficulty in swallowing.
- Obvious change in a wart or mole.
- Nagging cough or hoarseness.

Diabetes

Diabetics live in dread of blindness and amputation. Families of diabetics live in dread of the appearance of diabetic symptoms among their young. The familial links of this disease are strong, but a new phenomenon is appearing. As the life span increases, persons without knowledge of previous family history of diabetes are showing diabetic symptoms in their middle and old age. Some say if you live long enough you are bound to get diabetes. This may be a loose description of the fact that the aging body does not process sugars and starches (carbohydrates) as efficiently as before. Of the more than four million diabetics in the United States, it is believed that about one-fourth remain undiagnosed.[6]

Dr. Harold Rifkin, chief, Division of Diabetes, New York's Montefiore Hospital and former president of the New York Diabetes Association, told us, "Diabetes in older people may manifest itself in ways that are similar to symptoms in younger people, but not always: with excessive thirst, excessive urination, and sudden weight loss. However, older people may show very different symptoms: a sudden increase in weight, for example. They commonly report itching of the skin, particularly in the genital area; this is associated with the increasing presence of sugar in the urine. But, frequently, mature diabetes is picked up only by the complications it presents: cataracts, glaucoma, high blood pressure, kidney disease, retinal pathology, or neurological disease. It may appear suddenly after an acute emotional upset or a catastrophic illness such as a stroke or coronary attack, or with the onset of gangrene of the legs. Sometimes there is an unexplained numbness in the extremities or a tingling feeling in the toes or an ulcerated sore on the feet that doesn't go away.

"Sometimes the very first manifestation of diabetes in old people is coma brought on by dehydration. We are now seeing this more frequently with people who never knew that they were diabetics. Frequently such situations are mistakenly diagnosed as a massive stroke. If this happens, it becomes a real medical emergency. Perhaps they've had diarrhea, or vomiting, or a small infection, and they haven't been drinking enough water to compensate for the fluid they've lost. These latent diabetics can go quickly into coma, a condition which is reversible with appropriate fluids. But quick diagnosis and treatment is of the utmost importance."

If your parent has been diagnosed for diabetes and is under treatment, there are other problems you might anticipate and want to avoid. Elderly diabetics frequently run into trouble because their previously stable diabetes goes out of control. Control is usually achieved by diet, and/or medication, and/or injection of insulin. These new problems may arise, for example, because previously active people may become sedentary as they grow older, and then "have nothing to do but eat."

Or, as inflation squeezes budgets tighter and tighter, their fixed income may be too small to pay for the appropriate diet they require. Their diabetes may become unmanageable if they fill up on foods which produce increasing obesity. Or, if they are victims of "gastropathy," their digestion is impaired, their food absorption poor. They may complain of diarrhea, or bellyache, have no appetite, and avoid eating at all. Again, their diabetes may become unmanageable since their stability depends on eating specified groups of food at specified intervals.

Further complications result even for diabetics long accustomed to injecting insulin, when they are no longer administering the lifesaving drug properly. Their eyesight may be failing, and they can't see the syringe; their hands may tremble, and they don't draw up the insulin properly or inject it properly. Consequently they haven't taken the proper dose, spill sugar, and may go into coma.

If your parent is diabetic and has been for a long time, you may be taking the treatment for granted. It would be wise to check with the doctor to be sure that diet and medication are being properly followed. If deteriorating symptoms appear, don't assume they can't be reversed. The doctor may suggest that the time has come for someone to assist with the insulin injection, or to monitor the diet and mealtimes carefully.

If your parent has not previously been known as a diabetic and exhibits any of the symptoms described, be sure a doctor gives a prompt examination and that he considers diabetes as a possible cause. It is not inappropriate for you to raise the question.

And, finally, be sensitive to the psychological stress this disease imposes. Because of poorer eyesight, pains in the limbs, rigid meal schedules, some diabetics may find it difficult to socialize, sit through a movie, eat in a restaurant, or enjoy a party where none of the food is for them. They then are additionally vulnerable to the deterioration that comes with loss of social stimulation.

Or they may seem anxious—the threat of blindness is real for diabetics, especially for those who have developed visual problems. Fear of amputation haunts them as memories linger of diabetics in their youth on crutches or in wheelchairs. Dr. Rifkin points out that laser-beam therapy is saving sight for diabetics these days. With newer surgical techniques available for bypass vascular surgery, there is also greater hope than ever before that diabetics can be spared amputation. And if, in fact, amputation is unavoidable, there are more sophisticated prosthetic devices available so that real mobility can be more assured.

You can help your diabetic parent to understand all this, and also to know that surgery of any kind is not the menace it once was. Some people believe that diabetics can't handle infection, that they can't heal after surgery. "Not true," says Dr. Rifkin.

"They can handle infection quite well with quick action by the doctor, and they can heal with proper care."

More difficult to treat, says Dr. Rifkin, is the guilt that older people feel when their children and grandchildren show diabetic symptoms. "They blame themselves for transmitting the disease and get a renewed flare-up of their own symptoms. Because people are more familiar with the tendency in families to develop diabetes than the tendency to acquire cancer or heart disease, there seems to be a greater guilt syndrome attached to diabetes, which interferes with conventional treatment. These people require a great deal of tender, loving care, and reassurance that they are not to blame."[7]

Lungs, Breathing, and Respiratory Disease

Pneumonia used to be known as the old man's friend. When everything else in his life was falling apart, the pneumonia came and carried him off. Now many pneumonias succumb to antibiotics, leaving the elderly to wrestle with other diseases. Lung cancer and emphysema are the major respiratory killers these days, far outdistancing the once-prevalent tuberculosis. Pneumonia can still cause trouble for an elderly person, particularly the viral pneumonias which antibiotics cannot help. That is why elderly patients are encouraged to get out of bed following surgery, to move around in bed rather than to stay absolutely still. Even if it is painful to move, as with arthritis, the danger of lung congestion and consequent pneumonia is reduced when a person continues to be mobile.

These diseases attack breathing capacity. When a person really cannot breathe, death follows. But everyone who ages, even without pathology and disease, loses some breathing capacity. As muscle strength diminishes, the act of breathing becomes more difficult. This loss of muscle and breathing capacity combines to reduce the ability of people to work and exercise. It is a process that begins quite early in life. Note the champion athletes who retire in their thirties because they can no longer compete with prime athletes in their twenties.

This slowly diminishing strength, while normal, should not be confused with the chronic symptoms which may imply a need for treatment. Shortness of breath, wheezing, and coughing among the elderly are not just chronic conditions to be tolerated, but medical conditions to be investigated. What may be passed off as a chronic bronchitis may indeed be a case of emphysema, a killing disease now on the rise.

Emphysema accounts for more deaths now than lung cancer. People with a great number of recurrent respiratory infections, with barrel chests (expanded by the greater effort required to breathe), should check with their physicians. Elderly people may require oxygen at home to help, and some people can be helped with rehabilitative techniques such as those available at the New York University Institute of Rehabilitation.

Emphysema and lung cancer seem to be related to tobacco smoking and the assault from polluted air on the lungs. Industrial fumes, dust, and smoke are the enemies of all people, but particularly the elderly. In times of pollution alerts, deaths among the elderly rise.

Deaths among the elderly also rise during flu epidemics, and it is for this reason that doctors recommend that elderly people take flu shots each year as protection.

Older people are not hypochondriacs when they complain that they are chilly when others are warm, or that they feel drafts and are afraid to "take cold." Older people do feel colder and are sensitive to drafts and chills because they tend to be less well-insulated. The loss of some of their subcutaneous fat makes them more acutely aware of temperature changes. Grandma may really need a shawl, and Grandpa a lap robe, to keep comfortable while others are sitting around in their shirtsleeves.[8]

Arthritis

Arthritis hurts. It can cripple people, immobilize them, and cause intense pain. Among the elderly it accounts for knobby knuckles, stiff knees, bent backs, and aches and pains to plague the staunchest. Arthritis can be a serious disease. It is true that it can't be cured, but much can be done to control pain and stiffness. There are different kinds of arthritis, requiring different treatments. Most importantly, if the condition is diagnosed in time, much crippling can be prevented. That is why people with the following warning signals should see a doctor for diagnosis and treatment:

Arthritis Warning Signs

- Persistent pain and stiffness on arising.
- Pain or tenderness in one or more joints.
- Swelling in one or more joints.
- Recurrence of these symptoms, especially when they involve more than one joint.
- Pain and stiffness in the neck, lower back, knees, and other joints.
- Tingling sensations in the fingertips, hands, and feet.
- Unexplained weight loss, fever, weakness, or fatigue.[9]

Most feared is rheumatoid arthritis. Here joints become inflamed; they swell, are tender, ache, and become stiff. This disease is systemic. Its cause is still unknown, but it is chronic and progressive. It can cause great deformity if not treated early, and can make people feel sick "all over." But rheumatoid arthritis accounts for only about 2 percent of the miseries of old age.

There are other variations, including gout, but most common among the elderly is osteoarthritis. This affliction touches about 15 percent of the men and 25 percent of the women over sixty. With osteoarthritis the joints are not inflamed; instead, the connecting cartilage is abraded and deteriorated, and new bone tissue may be attached at the surface of the joints. Sometimes excessive use of an arthritic joint can speed the process, or an accidental injury, or excessive weight. Sometimes the enlarged joint can press on nearby nerves in the neck, spine, or ribs, and pain radiates out to other places beyond the point of origin.

Usually only one or two sets of joints are involved in osteoarthritis, so doctors feel comfortable in assuring most patients that the disease is not likely to spread to other joints, but it can nevertheless cause serious disability and substantial pain and discomfort. Obese people seem more inclined than others to suffer this disease, and there is some thought that the joints have been taxed by the extra weight.

It is true that arthritics can feel a change in the weather, but it is not necessarily true that a change of climate will accomplish any miracle relief. People have arthritis in warm, dry climates as well as in damp and chilly climates. So try to persuade your parents to think twice about moving, or at least to spend some trial time at different times of the year in any new location to which they might move to help the arthritic.

Whatever measures of relief are applied, they should be undertaken with the consultation of a reputable doctor. Stiffness and discomfort can usually be eased with heat or a warm bath. Gentle motion or massage sometimes helps. Better posture to prevent further irritation of joints, better diets to reduce weight, bed boards for too-soft beds, shoes that fit and provide adequate support and balance, and prescribed exercise to avoid gelling and atrophy of cartilage, joint, or muscle can provide some relief. Aspirin is still the preferred drug with the most benefit and fewest complications, and can relieve much arthritic pain. For those sensitive to aspirin, doctors can prescribe other mild medication. There are other medications used as well: gold salts for rheumatoid arthritis; or some of the steroids, like cortisone. But these last are used only under strictly controlled conditions, with a careful watch maintained for side effects. In the most severe cases, surgery is sometimes employed, and new prosthetic devices promise some people renewed motion. Modern technology can provide new hip joints, even knee joints and finger joints to replace these moving parts if they become immobilized.

While you are compassionate and understanding, be cautious. People who are in continuous pain are often ready to "do anything" to get rid of it. They are vulnerable to quack remedies and will even endure radical or worthless medication in the hope of obtaining relief. Responsible practitioners caution families that there have as yet been no miracle cures found for arthritis.

Pain is a miserable companion. As it comes and goes, your parent may be limber one part of the day and unable to move the next. Arthritis acts that way, so don't think you're being manipulated. According to the Arthritis Foundation, "Some people think the arthritis patient gets cantankerous and uses his disease to gain sympathy. Sympathy he needs, but not the overbearing kind. He needs quiet understanding and help in 'getting out of himself.' He needs to be involved in doing interesting things. Don't exclude him from your affairs. His knees may be stiff, his fingers crooked, but his mind and emotions are active and sensitive. Help him use them . . . and it will help his arthritis."[10]

Osteoporosis, Fractures, Nutrition

Falling down and breaking a hip is a common fear of older people, and well it might be. Fractures may result from accidents; they also are the frequent consequence of a degeneration of the bone tissue, a condition called osteoporosis. Even minor stress can break a weak or porous bone.

Women seem to be more prone than men to osteoporosis as they age, but both sexes can be prey to the process, which usually first affects the spine and pelvis. Sometimes it signals its arrival with chronic midback pain. Sometimes it progresses without discomfort but can be observed as the back seems to hump, the person "shrinks" in height, and physical activity becomes more and more burdensome. Sometimes a spontaneous fracture occurring in the spine or hip is the first sign of the damage already done. This thinning out of the bones can be diagnosed by X-ray and blood tests.

While hormones seem to have great influence on the bonemaking functions of the body, and the majority of women who do get osteoporosis do so after menopause, nutrition is now recognized as a contributing culprit. Osteoporosis can be treated with a diet rich in calcium and protein, sometimes with medication. Walking and activity may be best for some. Braces and bed rest may be required by others.

Once other bone disease is ruled out, the proper treatment for osteoporosis should be initiated and continued. This is a lifetime problem, which may or may not improve, may or may not get worse. Because it can be a serious and severe disease, painful, incapacitating, it is obviously a good idea to prevent it if you can. The National Institute of Arthritis and Metabolic Diseases therefore urges people over forty to continue the high-calcium, high-protein diets we all know are so important for the growing child. Milk can be fat-free, low in cholesterol if your parent has other dietary concerns. But do yourself and your parent a favor by sharing this information and explaining why a glass of milk at three o'clock is just as important for Grandma as it is for Johnny when he comes home from school.[11]

Bellyaches, Gastrointestinal Illness, Constipation

The gastrointestinal system is particularly responsive to emotional stress, and elderly people often complain of real discomfort for which doctors cannot find any organic cause. Death from gastrointestinal disease is usually a result of malignancies, and occurs only about one-third as often as death from cardiovascular disease. Nevertheless, the complaints of older people about stomach pains, gas, constipation, feeling "bilious," belching, and nausea are common. Families are never sure whether poor eating habits, insufficient exercise, and self-preoccupation and worry are the root causes of distress.

As in all other cases, a good examination by a good internist is the first necessary procedure to rule out the presence of organic disease. Following this, some understanding of the normal processes of aging on the gastrointestinal tract will help you to live with the continuing complaints. The complicated digestive processes that govern our use of food do change somewhat with aging, and of course with the presence of other diseases—arteriosclerosis, heart disease, liver or kidney disease, diabetes—bellyaches and other distress occur. If your father has lost his teeth and sticks to a soft diet, avoiding hard-to-chew foods, there will be an effect on bowel movement. And if your mother is tense and depressed, she may also become constipated or have an attack of colitis. The body is a sensitively tuned instrument, its various systems interdependent.

The greatest advances in psychosomatic medicine have occurred in recent years. Very few of the current generation of elderly people are conversant with or satisfied with psychosomatic explanations of physical discomfort. So, when their digestive systems go awry because they are grieving or lonely or sexually frustrated, or are feeling useless or poor or worried, or are afraid of cancer or of death, they frequently disbelieve the doctor who tells them there is nothing "organically" wrong with them. The fact is they do have physical pain, and many signs mimic the symptoms of organic diseases, so that doctors and families alike need to deal with the symptoms and provide the continuing reassurances or the security to overcome the tenseness that triggers off the whole syndrome. Psychotherapy, mild sedation, a bland diet, reasonable exercise, and new interests often help.

An impatient or unsympathetic doctor can just prolong the disturbance. Too heavy a reliance on cathartics can disrupt normal bowel function. A spicy, excessively rough, or irritating meal can cause distress. And unrelieved emotional distress and tension can continuously provoke colitis, constipation, and dyspepsia.

You can't teach an old dog new tricks, according to folklore. The fact is that cardiac patients have learned, with the new techniques of biofeedback, to regulate their heart rhythm; ulcer patients have learned to control the amount of hydrochloric acid they empty into their digestive systems. Perhaps you can help your parents to understand some of the new knowledge so that they, too, will have the opportunity to help themselves.

Having accepted a possible psychosomatic explanation, however, don't go overboard. Acute gastrointestinal symptoms are frequently a sign of heart attack. They should be checked by a doctor promptly. If a coronary problem is ruled out and distress continues, reexamination, careful observation, and tests by a doctor should follow to detect organic changes if these have occurred or have escaped earlier examination. If the problems are organic, then of course these must be dealt with promptly and appropriately. Surgery is much less risky than it used to be, and age alone is not the factor to determine whether or not it should be undertaken. Cancer, acute gallbladder, acute diverticulitis, bleeding peptic ulcer, and rectal polyps are some of the organic conditions for which surgery is indicated.

The decision to operate, if other problems are present, should be made by the internist in consultation with the doctors who are responsible for the heart, lung, vascular, or other disease which might complicate the procedures.

Hearing Problems

It's not unusual for older persons to suffer some hearing loss, to be able to hear sound without being able to distinguish the words. Hearing aids are increasingly used to give the extra assist required to help elderly people maintain a conversation, listen to the radio, watch television, go to the movies, and otherwise lead normal lives. For some reason, vanity seems to be more involved with hearing aids than with eyeglasses. Gone are the days when it was assumed that if a girl wore glasses she was doomed to spinsterhood. Quite the opposite, the TV commercials say. Hearing aids, however, seem to be shunned by older people who really need them, either as a matter of vanity or because they are afraid of the mechanical adjustments and difficulties that sometimes arise.

If you're shouting at your parent, think about it. Your parent may have a hearing impairment, and shouting won't help. Remember that people with hearing loss may hear low-pitched voices better than high ones, or vice versa, which will account for their understanding some people better than others. Speaking slowly and enunciating your words clearly, looking directly at the person when you speak, may help some but not others. Find out just what is causing your parent's hearing loss and direct your attention to that. Sometimes hearing loss is caused by impacted earwax that needs to be removed by a physician. Some serious hearing disabilities can be relieved by hearing aids, others by newly developed surgical techniques. If arteriosclerosis or other disease is causing the loss, controlling the disease may help. Whatever the cause of diminished hearing, it is a good idea to check with a reputable specialist (otologist) for diagnosis and treatment before assuming that nothing will help.

People who really cannot hear what is happening around them or who have been accustomed to normal conversation and begin to experience hearing difficulty become anxious, depressed, and frequently angry. So tread carefully if you become involved.

The following are some steps you can take:

- Check with a physician for diagnosis and suggested treatment.
- If your parent is willing to try a hearing aid, provide the encouragement and patience his adjustment requires. This is not an item to buy casually off the shelf or from a salesman at the door, but should be bought after consultation with an expert. Some instruments work better for some people than others. Individual compatibility is essential, even though you can't expect the precise correction you get from eyeglasses. Tonal quality is distorted; outside sounds are picked up and magnified. Compromises must be made, and sometimes there is a long period of adjustment to a new hearing aid. Your parent will have to decide whether it is better to hear "funny" rather than not at all.
- The telephone company can make special arrangements for people with hearing problems. (See Chapter 2.)
- Television stations in many cities provide text with news programs so that deafened people can watch the news events and read the commentary at the same time. Check out your local stations.[12]

Vision

If you can help your parent preserve his eyesight, you will have made an enormous contribution to his later years. With other activities limited, elderly people rely on their eyesight for entertainment, for reading, handwork, and crafts, for television, to watch a grandchild, or to enjoy a sunset. Regular checkups by qualified eye doctors are the best way to detect incipient trouble and assure the prompt treatment that may stave off limited vision or blindness.

People who have been wearing glasses most of their lives are not surprised when they need some change in prescription as they grow older. And many older people who never before required glasses seem to regard it as normal when they need glasses in their later years in order to read comfortably or see things at great distances.

Focusing problems for close reading or distant detail usually develop between the ages of forty and sixty and then begin to level off. "My arms aren't long enough," is the common refrain of the middle-aged before they concede the time has come for bifocals. If no real eye problem develops, they continue to enjoy the pleasures of the sighted world, and they are fortunate.

Not so fortunate are those whose vision is suddenly or gradually diminished by specific eye disorders or the impact of systemic disease. Cataract, glaucoma, and macular disease are the disorders most frequently associated with the aging eye. Diabetes, hypertension, arteriosclerosis, kidney disease, and neurological pathology often present themselves first as eye problems.

If your parent suddenly suffers a vision loss, pain in the eye, hemorrhage in the eye, blurred or double vision, surely he'll lose no time in seeing a doctor. But if symptoms develop gradually and he is not under a physician's care, great damage to sight can be avoided with early diagnosis and treatment.

Cataract, the clouding of the eye lens, is a leading cause of blindness in the United States. Yet it can in most cases be treated successfully by surgery. Age is not a factor in cataract surgery, and in 95 out of 100 cases vision is restored. Once it is diagnosed, the ophthalmologist can watch the development of a cataract and recommend surgery at the appropriate time.

Glaucoma is known as the sneak thief of sight. Acute glaucoma usually comes on suddenly, with great pain, and the patient knows he's been stricken. But chronic glaucoma can rob a person of his sight quite painlessly over a long period of time. If your parent is so afflicted, he may realize only very gradually that he's having trouble with his eyes. Medical treatment, if it's begun early, can control the progress of glaucoma in most instances, but any sight that is destroyed cannot be restored.

Macular disease, or macular degeneration, is a major cause among older people of what is now known as "Low Vision." The American Society for the Prevention of Blindness describes the macula as "the small area of the retina which is responsible for fine or distinct vision." If your parent is suffering from macular disease, he will find it difficult to read fine print, such as the letters in an ordinary book or newspaper. This disease can also come on gradually or suddenly; it is progressive and can't be stopped. Some cases are reported to benefit from early treatment.

If your parent can benefit from the aids and devices available for Low Vision people, you should encourage him to obtain and use them. He may abandon reading because it's troublesome to hold a book very close. Using magnifying glasses, putting on telescopic glasses, reading only under a high-intensity lamp, holding a book close to the eyes are mechanical devices or techniques which can help. These will be different from his accustomed ways of reading, but once he gets used to them they can make all the difference in keeping him in touch with the world.

Because diabetes, which can lead to blindness, has now jumped to third place as a major cause of death in the United States, there is greater prospect that the increasing incidence of the disease will create growing numbers of visual problems. If your parent has frequent need for a change of glasses, this may be the tip-off that blood sugars are abnormal and that he should see a physician for a general checkup. Until the disease is stabilized, your parent may continue to complain that his glasses are never right, so be patient and be sure that he carefully follows the prescribed diet and medication schedule.

Retinopathy can result from diabetes; the longer a person has diabetes, the more likely it is that this condition will develop. The American Foundation for the Blind describes diabetic retinopathy this way: "As the disease progresses, vision may be blurred or distorted and hemorrhages may cause a reddish tint over the visual field. . . . By no means do all persons with retinopathy become blind." Early diagnosis increases the chances of controlling this disease. Its potential danger is reason enough for your diabetic parent to be seen regularly by an ophthalmologist.

If your parent is restricted by poor vision, we refer you to the many organizations which have developed programs for the near and legally blind. (See the Appendix.) Additionally, you will want to know that large-print books and newspapers are available; recordings of good books can help pass the time. You can even get *Playboy* in Braille. And those who are separated by long distances can try using tapes and cassettes instead of depending on letters for family communication.

What You Can Do

- Be sure that your parent is examined regularly—about every eighteen months—by a qualified eye doctor. An optician who fills eyeglass prescriptions is not a doctor.
- Any change in vision, pain, or unusual symptoms should be reported quickly to a physician for diagnosis and treatment.
- If cataract surgery is recommended, encourage your parent to accept it. While cataracts are developing, there may be frequent needs for eyeglass change. Be patient.
- If your parent has Low Vision, help him to get special assistance at a Low Vision clinic in your locality or state.
- If your parent is legally blind (20/200 vision), make sure he knows he is entitled to a special income tax exemption.[13]

Rehabilitation

The most exciting work is being done for handicapped people in the great rehabilitation centers throughout the country. Physical and occupational therapy, speech therapy, prosthetic devices to replace lost organs or limbs are available to the elderly as well as to the young. Among the best-known centers are Rusk Rehabilitation Institute at New York University Medical School, Rancho Los Amigos in Downey, California, Texas Institute of Rehabilitation and Research of Baylor University, The Rehabilitation Institute of Chicago, and Cornell University's Burke Institute of Rehabilitation.

Pioneering leaders have renewed physical power for thousands of disabled people. At Warm Springs, Georgia, at smaller facilities like the Goodwill–Easter Seal Rehabilitation Center in New Haven, Connecticut, at county and regional rehabilitation centers in hospitals and nursing homes throughout the country, elderly people are taught to walk again, to speak again, to use their hands again, "to make the most of what they have." If your parent has been recommended for physical therapy, you should make every effort to help get him or her to the place where this therapy can be given. For further information write to the Association of Rehabilitation Facilities listed under National Health Organizations in Appendix B.

Mother M. Bernadette de Lourdes, administrator of St. Joseph's Manor in Connecticut, says, "Families give up too quickly. If an elderly person has had a stroke or is handicapped visually or orally or in any other way, don't assume that because he is old nothing can be done. Not so. At the least, a real effort should be made."

In a Westchester County YWCA swimming pool, stroke-paralyzed patients are helped out of their wheelchairs and into the water for special exercises with the physical therapist. Patients with mastectomies regain muscle tone and control in their arms at a dance exercise class.

Whether the program is modest or extensive, the right prescription for rehabilitation procedures may give your parent and the entire family a zesty new feeling about life.[14]

CHAPTER 8 BEHAVIORAL CHANGES[1]

When a parent's behavior begins to change with age, families are understandably troubled and bewildered. It can be a time of great stress and fear, a time when it is necessary for adult children to take charge and acknowledge that a parent is no longer capable of controlling his own life. Sometimes the implied role change is never completed because even with some handicaps and loss of control the parent continues to hang onto independence and fights to retain his own sense of being. Sometimes the fight succeeds. Sometimes it fails. Whatever happens at such moments in a family's life, it is bound to be a difficult time.

Looking to professionals for help is a wise course, but one that needs to be pursued with caution. For when you deal with your parent's behavioral changes, you need to be sure that the doctors you consult are not only trained to evaluate and diagnose geriatric behavioral problems, but are willing to carry out suitable treatment. It has been the sad experience of many families to be told that what is causing a parent to act in a bizarre fashion is "just old age," to be expected, and there's not much anyone can do about it. The fact is that there are very many different causes for erratic behavior among the elderly and for the seeming deterioration of intellectual function. Effective treatment depends on detecting the causes properly.

Behavior is affected by physical illness, by mental illness, by physical and emotional trauma, and, on a less dramatic but just as important a scale, by all the events and relationships of one's life. We expect an adult of normal intelligence and in reasonably good physical and mental health to be in touch with reality, exercise good judgment, and be able to take care of himself.

As we age, each of us loses some of our eight to ten billions of neurons (brain cells) that constitute in aggregate the mechanisms by which we handle information in the brain. The brain controls all our functions, physical and mental. No one can yet explain exactly how or why we lose neurons, but most of us end up with enough neurons to keep us functioning independently until we become otherwise handicapped or die of some other disease or accident.

Benign Forgetfulness

Can't remember a name? Where you put your glasses? Your mother forgot to tell you that your husband telephoned to say he isn't coming home for dinner?

It happens to all of us as we lose some of the equipment we started out with. People do not generate new brain cells, but normally lose the ones they have at a relatively stable rate. As a result of this normal loss, we may become forgetful, take longer to process information, be less creative in thinking up novel solutions to problems, and rely more and more on old ways of doing things. This may be why some people regard the old as "rigid" in their thinking and in their ways. But there is an enormous range of difference among old people; it is not safe to make any categorical statements about them as a group. Very bright people start out with more resources; even when they lose some neurons they may still be way ahead of those people who started out with fewer intellectual resources. The relatively benign attributes of old age may sometimes be annoying to live with, but should not be mistaken for the really serious symptoms of senility that call for special treatment or special caretaking.

When the loss process is speeded up by disease, or brain

tissue is destroyed by disease or accident, then you are dealing with serious matters requiring careful attention. If mental illness interferes with normal use of available cell and neuron resources, then there are additional complications. And the serious symptoms, whatever they may be, are sometimes misleading. Should you be tolerant because your parent is just forgetful, just depressed, your mother "losing her marbles," your father getting "dotty"? Should you shrug off a parent as just nasty, just unreasonable, just argumentative, just obstinate, just senile? Or is something else happening?

To find out, you'd better ask a doctor, and, when you do, you should be prepared to ask some questions. A doctor may give you the catchall diagnosis that your parent is suffering from senility, the natural consequence of "hardening of the arteries of the brain" or some "brain damage." While organic changes in the brain may account for the troubling symptoms, many physicians may overlook other possible causes for what is generally described as senile behavior.

A distinguished psychiatrist, Dr. Robert Butler, says, "The failure to diagnose and treat reversible brain syndrome is so unnecessary and yet so widespread that I would caution families of older persons to question doctors involved in [their] care about this."[2]

Reversible Brain Syndrome

Dr. Butler explains, "Reversible brain syndromes are characterized by fluctuating levels of awareness which may vary from mild confusion to stupor or active delirium. Hallucinations may be present, usually of the visual rather than the auditory type. The patient is typically disoriented, mistaking one person for another, and other intellectual functions can also be impaired. Restlessness, unusual aggressiveness or a dazed expression may be noticed."[3]

Malnutrition, toxicity from medication, surgical or emotional trauma, social isolation, a treatable mental illness, a serious viral infection, congestive heart failure, coma from diabetes, alcoholism, or dehydration from diarrhea or vomiting—all are possible causes of this kind of behavior, and to the extent that the conditions are correctible, the bizarre behavior can be modified or reversed.

The diagnoses and opinions of many physicians today may be based on quite honest beliefs, but we caution you now to remember that new information in this field is being developed very rapidly by researchers. The more you know about all this, the better able you are to ask the important questions. The following information should be helpful in this connection.

Organic Brain Syndrome: Chronic Brain Disease

Neurologists tell us that senility has the greatest and most profound impact on families because of the enormous psychological strain and unrelieved burden imposed when a child watches a parent who has nurtured and cared for him lose judgment, authority, and control. Dr. Elliot Weitzman, researcher and chief of neurology at New York's Montefiore Hospital, says that "real coping comes when others have to deal with someone's mind, with the changes in the central nervous system that affect emotional, cognitive, and intellectual capacity. All the relationships in the family structure are altered when someone loses the judgment to make decisions, the ability for self-care, the ability to communicate. It is as if the afflicted parent has lost his 'humanness,' and the child of that person is profoundly affected."

What is it that can so damage the mind and bring you and your parent to such a wretched state? It could be arteriosclerosis that narrows the blood vessels in the brain and reduces the oxygen supply, but it now appears that this condition accounts for only a small fraction of the cases. Most of the senile are suffering from chronic brain disease, a destructive disease of the brain that robs them of their intellectual capacities, their emotional and physical control, their judgment, and their orientation to reality. Some physicians now refer to this as chronic brain disease (CBD), others as senile dementia. Some call it Alzheimer's disease, which is more properly identified with pre-senile dementia, the similar symptoms and behavior that overcome young-to-middle-aged people. It is estimated by Dr. Robert Terry, chairman of pathology, New

York's Albert Einstein College of Medicine, that about 11 percent of the over-sixty-five population in the United States is suffering symptoms of this disease.

Mild to moderate symptoms can become severe if the patient lives long enough for the disease to run its relentless course; about 4.4 percent of the 11 percent, or about 100,000 Americans, is suffering severe symptoms in any given year. Chronic brain disease is progressive, insidious, and irreversible. In the early stages, it can be managed. As it advances, however, patients increasingly lose the ability to care for themselves; the most severely affected are usually institutionalized. These are some of the people you see in wings of the nursing homes, curled up in fetal positions, or bent over in wheelchairs, or screaming and strapped to their beds—a prospect that horrifies and terrifies young and old alike.

Although medical science does not as yet know what causes this disease, there seems to be some genetic base to it. Yet even if they do not fully understand it, doctors can now identify chronic brain disease by advanced radiographic techniques. The brain picture it presents is distinct from other kinds of damage. That is why expert medical and psychological and radiographic tests should be administered to be sure that patients suffering other treatable diseases are not incorrectly consigned to a doomed existence.

Patients with organic brain damage resulting from chronic disease or sclerosis present similar severe alterations in behavior. These include loss of memory for remote as well as recent events (no detailed stories about "when I was a boy on the farm and Aunt Martha brought me a green lollipop"), disorientation in relation to "time, place, and person" (your mother may believe you are her mother and she is a baby, not know where she is, and not recognize people or relationships), and a loss of intellectual capacity. Such a person may be incontinent, may become delusional, may claim that his money or possessions are being stolen, that he is being poisoned, or, in a religious fervor, may claim direct conversation with God. Extremely agitated, a sufferer may scream, be easily irritated and enraged, have temper tantrums, attack people physically, walk into company nude, call out obscenities, or fire off lewd comments to anyone around.[4] These symptoms may come and go at first, and be interspersed with normal or rational adequacy, but increasingly, as the disease progresses, irrational and uncontrolled behavior dominates. Sometimes drug therapy calms such a patient; sometimes it can work in reverse to excite and stimulate adverse behavior. Medication obviously needs to be carefully administered and monitored.

What You Can Do: Maintaining a Routine[5]

When symptoms first appear, the elderly person may be living alone, with a spouse, or with some member of the family. Those afflicted can manage, or be managed, by maintaining a very routinized life. Small changes can so disrupt them, however, that they are unable to cope, and the resulting disorganization may be the first symptom anyone observes. Perhaps Grandpa walks to the corner newsstand each morning to buy the newspaper and then returns home to read it. But one day the vendor is ill and doesn't open his stand. There are no colorful magazines on display, no protruding shelf of newspapers, nothing that is familiar to clue Grandpa to his whereabouts. He may walk right past the closed newsstand, which now looks like a big green box, and keep on wandering down the street, lost and unable to find his way. The open newsstand was his clue to turn around and walk home. Or, if Grandma suddenly needs surgery, she is hospitalized and left alone in a strange dark room at night. She doesn't know where she is, why she's there, becomes terrified, obstreperous, and hard to manage. Quite rational when she arrived, she seems now to have taken leave of her senses. Yet, with understanding from professionals and with patience from her family, she can recover from this disorganization brought on by the strange environment.

Says Dr. Steven Mattis, chief clinical neuropsychologist at Montefiore Hospital, who works with senile patients and their families, "Don't be so frightened when you first discover your parent's problems that you rush him off to an institution. Even if the long-term prognosis is not good, the patient will not slip right away. It is important to know exactly what the diagnosis is so that you can plan for the future. Different people regress at different rates. While your parent can live independently for some time, you should monitor this ability to be alone. The more routine the activity, the better; this way your parent will not have to adapt to new situations which are disorganizing to him. If he always has tea and toast for breakfast, that's fine; he won't have to decide what to have each morning.

"When a person with only moderate symptoms is put into a strange environment," Dr. Mattis continues, "it may seem that the symptoms get worse. Everything is new and it may seem he is terribly disorganized, but he can recover once a new routine is established. A person with this kind of disease can sometimes learn a new routine, if it is kept simple and unvaried, even if he can't recall an old one."

Reality Orientation

Reality orientation is standard procedure in many institutions caring for the senile. "Today is Tuesday," says the nurse at the Beth Sholom Home. "You are in Richmond, Virginia. It is ten o'clock in the morning, and the sun in shining. Mrs. Peters is sitting next to you. She wants you to help her hold this book. It shows pictures of her grandchildren and yours." This approach will not cure anything, but it helps root a senile person to his surroundings.

If your mother is beginning to show signs of deterioration and you don't know whether to "go along with it" when she forgets you telephoned, or visited, or deposited the check, or went together for a ride, it is reassuring to know that the professionals find some good results when they insist on reality. You need not be aggressive, but you should be gently insistent about the reality. Mother Bernadette suggests that you remind your mother that you telephoned yesterday or came to visit. When you telephone you can say, "Please make a note that I called you at two P.M. today. I will call you again tomorrow at two P.M." Then, perhaps later if she chides you on your neglect and this becomes an issue between you, you can say gently, "Look at the pad." Repetitive insistence seems to help positively in some cases. In others, insisting on the reality may make the person sad or hostile. If you do try this technique, it is not to prove that you are right, but rather to help your parent keep in contact. If you find the tactic useless, abandon it. Perhaps then you are in need of further professional help in deciding what to do next.

Watch out for:

- Poor nutrition. Lack of proteins can trigger psychotic episodes. Caught early, the damage can be halted.
- Toxicity to medication. Some standard medication given to the elderly can effect behavioral changes: Digitalis can produce the appearance of senility in some patients. If you notice a sudden change in your parent's behavior, such as becoming exceedingly quiet or noisy, investigate. Perhaps the dosage needs to be corrected, or a substitute medicine ordered.
- Changes in dress. If your previously neat and fastidious parent suddenly becomes sloppy and disheveled and no longer seems concerned about the kind or condition of his clothing, the doctor should be informed and the situation investigated.
- Unexplained falls. These should not be ignored. They should be explained. Inform the doctor and be sure he checks for cardiovascular problems, diabetes, visual problems, or degeneration of the central nervous system.
- Depressions and withdrawal. May signal mental illness or the onset of chronic brain disease.

Some Problems When You're Far Away

If you are lucky, you, some member of your family, a friend, or a neighbor will be the first to notice that your parent is acting strangely. Sometimes elderly people, living in places distant from their children and seemingly in good shape, can be deteriorating gradually without the family's being aware. The first the family knows about trouble may be when that parent is found wandering in the street, confused and unable to find the way home. The police may take him to the station house, even mistake him for an alcoholic. Usually the police will attempt to find someone in the family to come and take charge; other times they will take him to a hospital for diagnosis.

Diagnosis

The truth is that in the early stages of chronic brain disease it is very hard to distinguish between it and benign forgetfulness, between it and depression, between it and a "reversible brain syndrome." Your father may be facing retirement, for example. He looks healthy and continues to play golf. But he's having trouble making decisions. It is easy to assume that concerns about the approaching departure from his business and anxiety about his future are stirring him up. Perhaps that is the cause—akin to an adolescent identity crisis. But perhaps it isn't. A definitive diagnosis based on contrast studies can be made by new radiographic techniques over a six-month period. If there are clear signs of brain damage, you know you're in for trouble, but you will have time to plan for the altered family life-style that is sure to follow.

If the diagnosis is negative, however, you can quickly dissipate the fear everyone has of impending senility and treat the situation in whatever manner is appropriate.

Depression

Depression is an affliction now recognized as affecting up to 15 percent of the adult American population at any given time. Among the elderly, the proportions may be higher. Every older person is depressed at some time, says psychiatrist Olga Knopf. New psychotherapeutic techniques and new drugs have clearly eased the anguish of many depressives who have sought treatment. The reluctance to treat the elderly with mental illness is recognized among physicians themselves as a neglect by the profession. For whatever reason, the older person may be left to his own agonies, unattended. If that person is your parent, you should know that people over sixty-five have been successfully treated for depressions. You should also know that if the physician prescribes drug therapy it takes several weeks to take hold. Don't abandon medication quickly because it doesn't work immediately. Give it a fair chance. On the other hand, of course, if side effects appear with medication, this should be reported immediately to the physician; your parent may be sensitive to the drug, and other treatment should be substituted. If the cause of the depression is senile dementia, then of course the drug therapy may alleviate some discomfort temporarily, but you should not expect at all that the course of the disease will be altered.

What is depression? How can you tell if your parent needs psychiatric help, is suffering from undetected organic disease, or whether he or she is just unhappy about life and will soon snap out of the doldrums?

Depression, as a mental illness, is defined by its characteristic symptoms. When a person is just sad, the therapists may describe him as having a "depressive affect." But if he is really mentally ill, he will exhibit what is known as a depressive syndrome. Dr. Steven Mattis describes the syndrome this way: "feelings of helplessness, feelings of hopelessness, loss of mirth ... no humor present, loss of appetite leading to noticeable weight loss, may become constipated; sleep pattern is unusual: may fall asleep without difficulty, but awakens many times during night, and by three or four A.M. may not return to sleep at all. The result is that he is really sleep-deprived, and therefore will be fatigued at the early part of the day and then perhaps get a lift during the day. This is different from the pattern for the 'anxious' person, who may start out OK in the morning, but becomes increasingly more anxious throughout the day and 'flakes out' toward late afternoon or evening. He may get suspicious. To the extent that guilt is expressed and delusions are reported, a distinction is made between neurotic and psychotic depressions."

Neurotic and Psychotic Depressions

The neurotic person will react to external events: widowhood, for example, retirement, a decaying financial status. Moods will go up and down according to the course of these external events. The professionals call this "exogenous" (outside) or reactive depression.

A psychotic depression, on the other hand, according to Dr. Mattis, is usually triggered by internal events in the individual. It is "endogenous" (inside), and believed now to have organic causes such as hormonal abnormalities. No precipitating external event is necessarily required to bring on a psychotic depression. It follows it own course. Drug therapy or electroshock treatment are the treatments of choice for psychotic depression. People who are neurotically depressed may say, "I feel empty." Psychotic depressives may believe they actually are empty, that they have no internal organs. Thus, the delusional aspects are one clue to diagnosing such patients.

You should know that if your parent is diagnosed as having a neurotic depression, he should by all means seek treatment, which is usually drugs or psychotherapy and not electroshock. A person who is neurotically depressed can become psychotic if there's no treatment given and if the external events become so overwhelming that the individual really cannot cope. Most often this occurs with what the psychologists call a "loss of the significant other"—the death of a spouse or a child or someone very close and psychologically important. If such an overwhelming event occurs to a person who is very dependent, has severe financial pressures, and engages in mourning that is never completed, then there can be real deterioration and movement into psychosis.

Brain Tumors

Brain tumors can also cause depressed or irrational behavior as the growths impinge on the control centers. Some tumors are benign, can be surgically excised, and the patient returned to normal function. If other brain tissue is destroyed by the necessities of surgery, then there can be residual damage that impedes function, causing much the same kind of condition that results from a stroke or accident. Here again the damage is focused and is not diffuse as it is in brain disease. If the tumors are malignant, with luck they can be excised; if they cannot, like other cancers, the disease can spread to other parts of the brain or other parts of the body.

Sad? Depressed? Senile? What to Do

At what point, you may ask, does a caring child change from "understanding that life is really sad and tough" for a parent to knowing that he'd better get into action? Says Dr. Mattis, "When you notice a weight loss, when you notice a real withdrawal from social contact, even with what at first may appear rational excuses: 'I don't feel like seeing anybody, I'm not in the mood for company. So and so annoys me.' A loner may go unnoticed for a long time before a child becomes aware that his parent is never jocular, that he never calls any friends and rebuffs the ones who call him."

Such people may then seek a physician's advice because they don't "feel good," and look for physical causes for their plight. Once again the quality of the physician is paramount. If there is no good physical cause for the depression, it won't help for a doctor to say, "You're OK, stop worrying." A really depressed person needs more than that. If you do not wish to intrude on your parent's intimate feelings, that is understandable, but if you begin to hear, "What is life all about? It isn't worth living," then perhaps it is time to discuss this with a physician and get some help. Suicide is the ultimate threat. The decision to intervene in a parent's life at such a juncture once again brings up the matter of role change. It means taking on the responsibility for the parent to get treatment for an illness less tangible, perhaps, than appendicitis, but just as real in how it affects his being.

There is a great deal of depression among the elderly. The external events of their lives would be enough to make them sad, and their illnesses are surely reason enough to make them weary. But even if a person cannot change the real events of his existence, he can be helped to deal with them. There should be no sense of stigma attached to getting help; rather, it is a sign of a caring family to suggest it and arrange for it. Furthermore, if it should turn out that the depression has an organic base, either because of individual chemistry or because of chronic brain disease, or even if it is caused by such brain trauma as an accident or stroke, it is important to get treatment and help the patient to use the resources that remain available. "The patient needs to use all the neurons he's got," says Dr. Mattis, and depression inhibits this.

Some nursing-home administrators will tell you that a senile patient feels neither pleasure nor pain, that you should not be concerned that the patient who is "out of it" is unhappy. Says Dr. Mattis, "It is quite true that pleasure and pain can be defective in demented people, that they will laugh or cry inappropriately. There is a point at which the quality of humanness seems to be lost. But it is hard to say where that is. Some behavior seems to be reflexive; there is a primitive system operating and a pinprick will bring a withdrawal, and stroking may seem to give some pleasure. It is very difficult for their children to deal with this."

So difficult, in fact, that professional workers in many hospitals complain that children abandon such parents. "They just don't show up; they may sign the papers but leave it to us in the hospitals to do all the work, including moving a patient from a hospital to which he may have been brought by the police, to a nursing home to which he may be assigned by a medical review board."

This abandonment is explained by the psychologists in this way. "There must be a psychological point when the child's guilt becomes mourning and the parent becomes psychologically dead."

CHAPTER 9 THE HEALTHY AGED

Old age is not a door that opens into another room and then closes, locking the entrant into a fixed situation. It's a continuum, a developmental and growth process, as all of life is. And, like all of life, while there are elements which can make older years less rewarding and more monotonous, there are other elements which can make them full and enjoyable.

Your participation in the decisions of your parents' lives is likely to be minimal while they enjoy good health unless their economic circumstances deteriorate. Nevertheless, it might be helpful for you to understand the elements that might prolong their sound and admirable state and to know what it is that provides satisfaction to the men and women who are just as they've always been—only older, and not quite so fast-stepping.

Each Older Person Is Unique

People who age successfully do things that make them feel good. It isn't just a matter of physical health and economic security. The eighty-year-old lady limping with her cane along the sidewalk to take her low-cost daily noon meal at the local communal eating center might enjoy her life much more than the eighty-year-old lady who is eating alone in the restaurant of her expensive apartment hotel. The key factor is how the older person feels about himself, how he uses his time, and how he feels about the way he uses his time. There are as many different uses and feelings, almost, as there are older people.

Older people are just as diverse as young teenagers. The tinge of their youth may still be within them. "I've never been able to shed the mental image I have of myself as a lad of about nineteen," said writer E. B. White late in life. There is no one old person. Your parent is uniquely different from others of the same chronological age, growing older in varying ways with a different time clock. Overall physical condition is a large contributing factor, as is the presence or absence of illness or disease. Attitude and good mental health are overwhelming factors, assuring that your parent will either be a full participant in his life until death or that, at some point as he ages, he will begin merely to wait for it.

The Successful Aged

"You won't put me to sit by the fire," an Irish mother told her daughter. Hearty and healthy at seventy-five, she was putting her family on notice that she would not follow the old country ways. In Irish villages, when a son marries and brings home a wife, the mother continues to live in the cottage but turns over her charge to the young daughter-in-law. Mother is left "to sit by the fire," to be an observer, not a participant.

The successful aged do not complain and feel sorry for themselves. They emerge relatively whole from the grief and mourning that follow life's crises and losses; they are sad about what they have lost, but happy about what they have. Their world is now and not yesterday, and they do not continually impose their sorrows on others. They give their emotional strength, their experience, and their support to their families and friends, without counting their generosity and with no demand for reciprocity. People enjoy them, learn from them, and seek them out. They may be rich or poor, healthy or not. They don't just survive; they live.

The Positive Equation: Mental Health

What kind of people age successfully? Researchers who have been raising this question for years can now define some common characteristics.

The successful older person seems to accept the natural processes of the life cycle and appears to be more tolerant of the physical changes taking place within his own body. He recognizes their effects on his physical capacities and energies, and organizes his life to accommodate those changes by forgoing activities that are too difficult or stressful to accomplish. Having limited the structure and conditions under which he expects to operate, he can function smoothly and without constant frustration. He learns how to substitute new satisfactions for old ones now impossible to achieve. Making this accommodation is not simple—it is a discipline which requires great effort—but the enlightened ager succeeds in the effort.

The integrated older person judges himself according to criteria which reflect his current life realistically and are not relics of a more energetic, more ambitious past. His values and goals relate to his personal and physical resources at any given time. He learns new roles for himself and unlearns old ones, says Dr. Robert J. Havighurst; he integrates new values and goals into his personality, says Erik Erikson. However you describe him, he is performing some kind of useful function and is involved with other people, maintains his self-esteem at a high level, and wins the approval of those around him.[1] If you are lucky enough to have such a parent, the experience will enrich you and you will have a glowing model to follow.

Specifically, according to Dr. Bernice L. Neugarten, professor of human development at the University of Chicago, the older person who finds life good:

- Takes pleasure from his daily activities.
- Regards his life as meaningful and takes responsibility for it.
- Feels he has reached his major goals.
- Has a positive self-image and feels like a worthwhile person.
- Is optimistic in attitude and moods.[2]

These are broad precepts, but perhaps they apply to your parent. If they do, you're most fortunate. If they do not, you might be able to use them as guidelines. Perhaps your parent is a chronic complainer who derives little enjoyment from any part of life. Your mother may feel frustrated that the potentials of her youth were never realized, or your father is angry that the choice of a lifelong profession was wrong. If so, knowledge of these attitudes might help you look at your parent objectively and see where you can help him make the changes that would bring him to a more positive approach to his problem. This chapter suggests avenues to help build your parent's morale and mental tone.

The Positive Equation: Physical Health

If your parent maintains good physical health, growing older will be easier for him and for you. When he has no distressing chronic conditions, no serious physical handicaps, he will continue to function as he has done through his adult life. He will sleep well, but probably sleep for fewer hours each day. He will eat well, but probably eat less than he did in the decades before. He will continue physical activity and exercise, although less strenuously.

Even if he suffers from a moderate impediment, he will still move forward on a relatively even keel if he has good education in learning how to live with his illness or handicaps, energetic support from you and the rest of his family, and a positive attitude that aids him in making the necessary accommodations to the changes which will occur in his life-style. Heart patients, diabetics, and others coping with chronic illness can live reasonably normal lives nonetheless. Arthritics and people with physical handicaps can arrange the mechanics of their lives so as to function independently and well.

Basic good health is a cushion against many of the intrusions of age. If your parent eats a nutritious diet, he won't be so susceptible to infections, colds, and other minor ailments as he would otherwise be. If he gets enough sleep, he won't fatigue easily and will be able to continue the activity patterns of earlier days. You should encourage him to take a nap as a restorative if his energy tends to flag at some point during the day. Drinking liquor in moderation—unless a special condition rules out alcohol—can be good for the psyche and circulation. Keeping good muscle tone through nontaxing exercise also contributes to general good health. (See Chapter 3 for more details on maintaining good health.)

Balancing the Equation

One of the things we say repeatedly in this book is that the essential needs of older people are not very different from those of adults of any age. They need comfortable and appealing shelter, nourishing food, companionship, the sense of being useful and productive. What adult doesn't have these needs? And what normal adult doesn't need stimulation for the intellect, refreshment for the spirit?

In order to maintain a good feeling about life, your parent needs to have what you need to have: interesting and rewarding activities, interesting and rewarding interchanges with others. Volunteer work, travel, recreation, and other interests pursued at home and in company with others are some of the activities that nourish the mind and sustain the sense of well-being.

New Careers

Sometimes growing older heralds a new career. Enforced retirement, economic necessity, or just plain boredom may lead your healthy parent into a search for a new job opportunity. Breaking in is a tough business at any stage of life, and especially tough when the older person bucks up against the business world's preference for young comers who have "new ideas" and command a lower salary. It's even rougher during the recession-unemployment period we've been going through in the past several years.

The classic retiree in the mind's eye is a man, but women are entering the picture in growing numbers. Although a Harris poll showed that retired single women, as a group, are more satisfied with retirement than any other group of retirees, recent census figures tell us that the percentage of over-sixty-five men who continue to work decreases, while that for over-sixty-five women is rising. Married women, particularly, can be expected to develop new careers, perhaps first careers, in their middle and late years as they prepare for the reality of a longer life expectancy than their husbands.

The woman's liberation movement has opened the door for women in the business and professional world to extents never dreamed possible by your parents. If your mother was the "power behind the throne" for years in your father's business career, there is every reason now for her to build on that experience and venture out for herself. Many a business has been run by a widow taking over after her husband's death, but starting out from scratch is more unusual. Women's counseling services springing up all over the country in cities and in colleges will welcome your mother for a consultation if she has the vitality, courage, and interest to venture out on her own.

Whether it is your mother or your father who is considering a second career, there are guideposts and bodies of knowledge which can help them in searching, planning, and preparing.

Some years ago a small paperback book, *Not Quite Ready to Retire,* listed 351 job descriptions and business possibilities for older workers. Such a list is bound to change as the needs of our society change, or as entirely new fields of economic enterprise are opened up by expanding technology and social needs. Environmental control, energy conservation, health and day-care services are but a few new areas of job opportunity.

A practical help for your parent is a free pamphlet offered by the Catholic University of America in Washington, D.C., called *Self-Marketing Tips for Unemployed Professionals.* Tips include how to find out what you are suited for—whether, for example, you should own your own business or be a salesperson; whether you need further education or training; how to write a résumé; where to find listings of trends in unemployment and employment in specific locations.

The U.S. Department of Labor also sponsors programs to retrain older workers for available jobs, and although funds have been severely cut in recent years, information on past experience and current programs can be obtained from the Department of Labor or from the National Council on the Aging, in Washington. (See Appendix for addresses.)

Finding a New Job

Certain employment organizations across the country specialize in putting together jobs and older people. Many cities, like Washington, D.C., with its Over 60 Counseling and

Employment Services, and New York City, with its 40 Plus, have agencies which maintain a bank of full- and part-time job openings for older people and may offer service at no fee. The U.S. Department of Labor supports 2,400 local state employment service offices throughout the country, and each of these has on its staff either a full- or a part-time older workers specialist who is familiar with job opportunities in the area and can give your parent tailor-made counseling. A private firm specializing in older employees is Mature Temps, Inc., with offices in over a dozen cities. This employment agency places older people in temporary jobs on a contract basis, paying their salary, social security, and insurance. Retirement Jobs, Inc., through its five California offices, has successfully placed thousands of older people in rewarding jobs. The Senior Personnel Placement Bureau in Norwalk, Connecticut, pioneered ten years ago in setting up a job clearinghouse for older people, and is still going strong. Surely in your parent's area there will be an employment service geared to help him in his search; many city and county governments have established just such agencies.

Some business and industrial firms are now beginning to rehire retired employees for jobs different from those they held during their earlier working periods. The John Deere Tractor Company in Iowa employs a group of its former workers as guides to lead tours of visitors through the plant. The Texas Refinery Corporation hires over-sixty workers to augment its sales force. "Our customers are people who own property, and many of them are elderly and retired," says TRC's board chairman. "We've found from experience that senior citizen property owners relate better to older salespeople." Perhaps your retiring parent can carve out a new job with the old firm.

Starting a New Business

Many couples dream of starting a small new business together after retirement—a bookshop, a motel, an art gallery, or a restaurant. But there are bound to be problems in entering a new field of activity. Caution commands that thorough investigation precede any capital investment, and risks for the older person are more serious if the required investment is taken from their security fund. Investigation of potential partners who paint glowing pictures of quick profits is especially important. Your mother or father may have good business experience and sound judgment and not require these cautions; but many people retiring from long-held professional jobs have not had entrepreneurial experience and do not realize fully the effort required or the risks involved in taking on what looks from the outside like an "easy business."

Careful analyses of the economic climate of a community, the choice of a location even in a flourishing community, required capital, ability to obtain credit, likely costs, and potential income are only the beginning of the kind of evaluation that should precede any decision to open a little business. Your parent's lawyer and accountant can help with some advice about potential problems. One should seek the advice of people who have been in a similar business and know the pitfalls. The Small Business Administration (SBA) in Washington, D.C., and its regional offices have a great deal of useful information available for the asking; they will also answer questions in personal interviews and can even supply some financing if your parents qualify. Your parent should seek out the SBA regional office closest to him. (See the Appendix.)

Volunteer Work: A Two-way Street

About four and a half million Americans over sixty-five are currently volunteering their services for a wide span of community needs. They bolster the paid staffs of hospitals and clinics, staff thrift shops, and drive the old, the ill, or the handicapped who require transportation. Many are active in civic affairs. Others provide psychological and social support services to other elderly people not able to get around: They visit the homebound, set up or participate in telephone reassurance programs and hot-line counseling. Others volunteer their services for schools or day-care centers, trying to add an extra dimension of personal caring for children who are deprived or in trouble. Some retired businessmen offer guidance on business problems, accountants help out with tax forms, lawyers contribute legal services to a poverty law center, and doctors give free clinic services to a community health center. When the mature person, free of job commitments, volunteers his time on a regular and sustained basis, he is making an enormous contribution to the quality of life for others.

While more volunteers come from the ranks of employed people over sixty-five than from those who are no longer working, there are indications that many elderly people would be happy to participate as volunteers if only someone would show them the way. If your mother is too shy and your father too reluctant to be among the active volunteers in the community, you might be helpful in introducing them to an enthusiastic volunteer or to a volunteer group where they can make a welcome contribution and derive a renewed sense of self-worth. After the first step, it may become part of your parent's routine.

Older people, retired from their jobs, often feel an overpowering sense of alienation from the mainstream. The elderly poor who exist through long, lonely days staring out of windows at the passing sights, and the middle-class widows who sit alone waiting, often with rancor, for a busy relative or child to visit or telephone, share the same plight.

Some of the elderly poor have been recruited into the Foster Grandparents programs. Lured by the prospect of a small stipend to augment their social security check, this corps of volunteers has made dramatic contributions toward meeting the extraordinary needs of millions of children who need extra help in schools, day-care centers, or hospitals. In New Rochelle, New York, where an especially active Foster Grandparents program flourishes, a drop-in visit quickly shows what a boon this is to the surrogate grandparents. Regarded selfishly, without even considering the value of their services to the children whom they serve, the program gives a new lease on life to the foster grandparents themselves. Meeting as a group to be trained for their work, they extend their social ties. They have developed an esprit de corps that would be hard to duplicate elsewhere in today's cynical society. A middle-class grandparent could do the same kind of work on his own without being paid.

Thousands of "Volunteers with Vision" across the country

are learning to transcribe into Braille books and articles which the Library of Congress provides to the blind through its Division for the Blind and Physically Handicapped. The Library of Congress itself teaches Braille transcription in a free correspondence course, and many local social clubs and religious groups conduct classes for volunteers. Some volunteers transcribe books printed in small type to large type, so that the partially sighted can continue to read. Others with good enunciation and well-pitched voices record books on tape. Musicians can help by transcribing musical notation, by lending a talented voice, or by giving technical advice.

There's almost no service agency of any kind that doesn't need some volunteer help. The Red Cross, schools, public libraries, institutions caring for people who live with handicaps —all can use bright faces and helping hands. Museums train docents—volunteer lecturers who give visitors guided tours— and historical sites use volunteer guides. Surely the political process is a fertile area for interested volunteer workers. During campaign years, there's no candidate who won't bless the volunteer who comes to campaign headquarters to offer assistance, and the field for year-round work for political and social causes is open-ended. Local Democratic and Republican clubs need to keep their files and mailing lists in order; groups working on civil liberties, human rights, environmental protection, and other basic issues could not exist without solid phalanxes of volunteers. A vast corps of volunteer workers, for example, has contributed heavily to Common Cause's success in getting citizen-oriented legislation passed on both national and state levels.

There are offbeat and highly productive volunteer jobs for older, experienced persons. Tell your parent to walk wherever his interests and talents lead him, as one just-retired sixty-five-year-old man did some years ago. A former bank vice-president, he came to the office of WGBH, Boston's educational television station, said he was retired and wanted a volunteer job. Was there anything he could do at the station? The station management, with neither enough staff nor money, was in the act of trying to mount its annual fund-raising drive, and gladly turned the project over to the gentleman. So far, he has finished his eighth annual fund-raising auction and may even now be organizing the ninth. Working eleven months out of each year, he has made the station's week-long auctions into a great event, attracting hundreds of auction items, thousands of bidders, and enormous publicity in the large area the station serves. The pattern he established for WGBH is a model now for educational television stations across the country. His habit is to take a vacation in the month following the auction and then return to begin work on the next year's.

This is a retiree's Cinderella story. Other retirees may not succeed as dramatically, but the options are there for the exercising.

Although organizations, social action groups, church and interest groups can open volunteer prospects to thousands of older people, many men and women may not be drawn to scheduled activity. There are individual activities, however, akin to organized volunteer work, that seem to develop among the healthy aged. In large city apartment houses where so many widowed live, and in retirement villages and communities, residents volunteer their services to each other. One helps with an income tax form, another with a shopping chore; one teaches ceramics, another keeps the books of the residents' association. The point of it all is to be involved with other people, doing something that provides personal satisfaction and wins someone else's approval. Efforts like these stimulate the healthy juices of life.

When job opportunities are slim and your parent sits idle and restless in his home, there's no better help you can give him than to urge him strongly and repeatedly to volunteer—to get out of the house and out of the doldrums.

Government-Sponsored Volunteer Programs

ACTION, a federal government agency, is the overall umbrella for a group of volunteer programs which bring older people in large numbers into community service.

RSVP (Retired Service Volunteer Program) is perhaps the best known of the government-sponsored programs for older volunteers. Elderly persons are recruited to work in federal hospitals, courts, libraries, and day-care centers. They may work as teaching assistants, tutors, counselors, bookkeepers, or arts and crafts instructors. Some RSVPers are volunteers in local offices on aging, rewarded with the knowledge that they are helping their own peers.

The Peace Corps still takes older men and women for overseas assignments, and VISTA (Volunteers in Service to America) takes them for assignments in underprivileged communities within the United States. Under SCORE (Service Corps of Retired Executives), ex-executives counsel on managerial problems, and ACE (Active Corps of Executives) is for experienced business people who can advise others on setting up and managing small businesses.

In addition to such national programs, there are numerous opportunities within any state or local government agency. A telephone call to the state office on aging will provide specific information on current opportunities for volunteers. Openings may include work in social service, health, or educational agencies. Almost every older person has something to offer: A linguist can help foreign students; a carpenter or plumber can assist in vocational education programs in the local high school; a lawyer, doctor, or other professional can, at the very least, give excellent career counseling to students; and a nurse can help in a public health clinic. (See the Appendix for listings.)

Continuing Education

Not so long ago, when the middle-aged man went to college to earn the degree he couldn't afford as a youngster, his picture in cap and gown made the front page of the newspapers. When a woman whose grandchildren were teenagers went to law school instead of to the garden club, she rated a feature story, with quotes from her proud family. The social revolution in the United States has been rapid and broad. It's hard to believe that less than a decade ago people adhered to their expected roles so rigidly that those who left the mold to get further formal education in their later years were newsworthy.

But today it is a common sight to see students of all ages mixed in the classrooms of many of the nation's campuses.

More than one out of every five colleges and universities has instituted special courses and programs for older students, retooled academic policy to begin to accommodate the hundreds of thousands of older people who are going back to school. To date, most of these are two-year community and junior colleges, but four-year schools are now following the same route.

Research projects and long-range studies have demonstrated beyond doubt that many older people maintain intellectual and learning ability at a high level. A mind that has been active throughout life usually remains active. Your parent, like most of his contemporaries, is probably better educated than his parents. This implies that he has more intellectual needs and a greater ability to fulfill them than preceding generations at the same age. If this analysis is true for him, he should have no problem linking up comfortably with whatever kind of educational program he wants. The opportunities for senior citizen schooling are numerous, and senior citizens can usually enroll free or with low tuition rates.

The Hawkeye Institute of Technology in Iowa, for example, in response to the local Gray Panthers chapter, designed 100 courses in which over 8,000 older people are currently enrolled. The Institute for Retired Professionals at the New School for Social Research in New York City has a student body of 600 retired people and a curriculum that covers sciences, the humanities, and the arts; it has sparked similar institutes in half a dozen other cities across the country. A much more ambitious continuing education operation is New York City Community College's Institute of Study for Older Adults, offering 160 courses at 60 different locations. The average age of the 5,000 people currently enrolled is seventy!

What do older people want to study? Everything and anything from videotaping to basic English, from home nursing to organizing older people for political action. Your parent will find a plethora of opportunities for education in his own locality, no matter where that is, with the promise of even more in the future.

The fruits of continuing education are many and sweet. One retired psychologist in New York, interested in new developments in neurology, took a course "to keep up." Now she has started a new career in a major hospital center, and, at sixty-seven, is pioneering in a new department as neuropsychologist. Her boss is in his thirties. They make a great team. A retired army colonel, first introduced to the arts in a San Francisco senior center, has become a sculptor and now attends a fine arts institute to study the history of art while he develops his new-found talent.

City and suburban campuses are usually accessible by public transportation, but getting to class may be a problem in rural or less-populated areas. There are probably drivers among these older students, however, and car pools for senior citizens are as natural as car pools for kids. It's also possible that a local agency or the school itself will provide a bus for these aspiring students.

To find out about education prospects, your parent can get in touch with local colleges and universities, the city or county board of education, or the state board of higher education. He can also write to the national associations of higher education for material. (See the Appendix.)

Recreation and Entertainment

Recreation is an essential means of refreshing the spirit when one is young and active and needs respite from work and responsibility. For older people it is equally essential as a substitute for work and responsibility. In the later years, recreation becomes a two-way street. It is at once a channel for using one's energies creatively and for receiving the satisfactions which recharge those energies.

Should you ever visit a nursing home or a home for the aged, you will be struck by the fact that the residents who seem alert and relatively content are actively engaged in doing something: a game of cards; a poetry reading or a current events discussion; embroidery or needlepoint; carpentry or painting. There are others who sit alone, their hands still, their faces vacant. It's true that they may not have the physical or mental resources for entering into some kind of activity, but it is also possible that they are people who were never inclined to do so and who never learned earlier to do anything beyond the requirements of their professional or homemaking careers. One middle-aged woman recently told us, "I've never played bridge in my life, but after visiting my mother-in-law in a senior residence, I decided to learn how to play bridge now, as a protection for my old age." Good idea!

Recreation can become an occupation for older people, a strong link with other human beings, a major source of self-satisfaction and feelings of self-competence. It is both pleasure and necessity to learn how to use leisure time so that it nourishes. Reading and television can fill time for the non-gregarious, but in an important sense—and especially for the shy and insecure—these diversions are nonproductive. Developing new interests, improving one's deftness at a game or craft, joining a movie or theater club or a group at the public library constitutes a basic ingredient in the recipe for continuing intellectual health. Participating in these groups assures companionship and bespeaks an openness to new people and new situations which is essential to maintaining emotional health.

If your parent has always been a joiner, he will probably continue to be one unless a strong shock—widowhood or other sharp loss, a severe illness, deepening money problems—knocks him off course. After such an event, however, you may be able to help him reestablish his connections and lead him back to those avenues which he sought previously. If your parent has always been a loner, antigroup, anti-new experience, you should try hard by any means you can think of to seduce or coerce him into testing some form of group experience, some means of expressing whatever creative abilities he may have.

If private instruction is too costly—and it generally is—a good place to learn new recreational skills or to sharpen stale ones is a local city or county recreation program. Most communities, in addition, have adult education programs, run as an adjunct to the public school system. There is an astonishing variety of courses scheduled. "I've taken crewel embroidery, needlepoint, advanced knitting, and three sessions in rugmaking at the Cambridge Adult Education Center, and I've loved it all," one seventy-year-old lady said to another in a doctor's waiting room. "But my husband said if I put another rug down on the floor, he'd throw it out, so now I'm taking flower arranging."

Local YMCAs and their counterparts generally have excellent adult education programs, emphasizing arts and crafts and other skills which don't require extraordinary talent but still enable the craft pursuer to turn out attractive and satisfying objects. Senior citizens' centers are often beehives, honeycombed with dozens of opportunities for creative and social activities; church groups and fraternal and professional organizations are other sites where your parent might find outlets for pursuing interests and hobbies and for directing his energies to a variety of recreational projects.

Museums have special benefits and reduced fees for senior citizens; in large cities they conduct full programs of lectures and events related to their collections. These are especially interesting for people who never before had the time to enjoy expanding their knowledge of art, science, history, or anthropology.

Social dancing brings a wonderful lift to the spirits. The music is soothing, and the physical effort minimal. For many of today's older couples, who courted across a series of dance floors, it evokes a pleasant part of their past. If your father claims he has two left feet and can't count, but your mother has been longing to join a dance group just for fun, suggest that she do exactly that. Your father may change his mind and gain confidence when he sees his peers perform. Senior residences and retirement communities feature social dancing, and it's great fun to watch the dancers—especially when a jitterbugging septuagenarian takes a whirl or two with a game partner.

Entertainment outside the home can sometimes be expensive and, for many older people, remains a special treat for special occasions. But discounts at movies, theaters, and concerts are becoming routine these days for people with senior citizen cards. In larger communities there are free concerts and plays in the parks or, on winter evenings, in the public libraries. Nearby colleges and high schools and community theater groups are happy to play to larger audiences and will welcome grandparents to their productions. If entertaining at home is costly, a more sedentary version of the old progressive dinner party may work. Each couple or person is responsible for a course, and so the cost to the host is minimal. Everybody takes a turn at hosting. What is important is not how much the meal costs, but that there is company to share it.

Making the days more interesting helps to make the long evenings seem shorter for those who are afraid to go out at night. Having participated in some daytime activity, they've probably made some new friends. The telephone at night can then become a social link to a whole new group of people. And watching television is welcome restful entertainment then, instead of a continuation of what they were doing all day.

There is obviously no end to the possibilities open to healthy people for enjoying their leisure at little or no expense. As in every other phase of life, however, attitude and initiative enable some to make the most of what is available, to create for themselves what is missing. If your parents need a nudge, put their names on some mailing lists for information about what is happening in their communities, and perhaps they'll take it from there.

Information on all the local recreational and entertainment opportunities can come from a call to the cultural activities aide in the office of the mayor or county executive. Often the commission on aging or the local library will have regular listings of current events and activities of special interest to older people.

Travel: Variety Is the Spice of Life

One of the national benefits of mandatory retirement, theoretically, was that it provided a cadre of financially secure older people who would change from producers to consumers. Retirees, who had worked hard all their lives and saved judiciously, would benefit from wise pension plans, good investments, and social security coverage. This good financial base, combined with unending leisure, would allow them to do as they wished, when and where they wished, with total pleasure surrounding every move.

While this pie-in-the-sky picture is a long way from the lives of most older people in the United States today, there are many who can afford some form of travel for fun and recreation.

And there's no question that reduced-fare charter flights and package tours by plane or bus have made domestic and foreign travel a reality for a generation that dreamed when it was growing up of traveling coast-to-coast or of seeing Paris, the Fiji Islands, or the Khyber Pass.

Nearby Travel

There are many elderly people who've never been very far away from home—never out of the city, county, or state, let alone to a foreign land. For them, planning a modest trip for a day or a week can be as exciting and stimulating as a foreign trip for the more affluent or sophisticated person. There's no part of the country without accessible resorts, interesting natural phenomena, museums, and historical landmarks. If your parents haven't been accustomed to travel, it is much easier to encourage a trip if both are living and not too old; they have each other as sure companions. But travel for the widowed or really elderly, though enticing, may also be frightening. In recent years, group travel arrangements have taken most of the burden away, and arranging a day's or weekend's junket for the single person or the elderly traveler is now realistic and appealing.

Trailer Travel

Despite rising gasoline costs, house trailers and campers continue to present a relatively inexpensive way to travel across the country or to visit a particular area and stay there and explore it for a while. In all regions of the country there are good facilities for people traveling in this four-wheeled fashion. Older people on limited incomes find it much less expensive than paying for hotel rooms and restaurant meals, and your parents will meet congenial company in privately operated camper parks and in the state and national parks across the country. The trailer or camper can lead to an infinite variety of recreational experiences: sightseeing in cities, exploring towns and byways, enjoying the outdoors. In Florida, for example, it's not unusual to see a land-sea recreation combination: a trailer park next to a waterway, with a trailer for "home," a car parked nearby for land transportation, and a boat in the water for cruising.

Traveling with camper or trailer is a happier experience for two persons than for one because it often requires long hours on the road. If your parents enjoy driving, they will find that this approach assures flexibility and variety in addition to economy. For information on sites which are attractive and safe and offer all necessary services, consult the travel guides listed in the Appendix.

World Travel

Wherever one travels around the country and around the world these days, older Americans are very much in sight and very obviously enjoying themselves. For a lover of ancient history, the Acropolis is just as compelling at seventy as at twenty, and the streets of London just as exciting for a student of English literature.

The adventurous and affluent can plan their own journeys through an individual travel agent or by linking up with one of the hundreds of package tours offered regularly by domestic and foreign airlines. Church, business, and professional groups and college and university alumni associations all have group tours, and there is sure to be an interesting itinerary for your parent among them.

Group tours organized especially for older people and catering to their needs might be more satisfying. The national associations of older people organize an infinite variety of group tours geared to a range of budgets and personal tastes. A unique advantage is that these tours are plotted at the slower pace older people usually prefer to follow, and allow plenty of time for rest and refreshment. Single women are especially comfortable traveling in this manner. Everything is taken care of, and companionship is assured.

If your parent can afford a trip and needs only your encouragement to go to a close-by resort or to a faraway strange and exotic place, send him off. It will do you both a world of good. Once bitten, he may become an avid tourist, each new experience the seed for the next. And remember that a trip is not just confined to the period of travel. It requires much pleasant discussion and planning for a long time in advance, including reading and learning about places to be visited, and, perhaps, dipping a bit into a foreign language. After the voyage there will be countless interesting anecdotes and happy recollections with the pleasing reinforcement of picture albums and slide shows.

CHAPTER 10

YOUR PARENT AT A CROSSROAD: Life-Changing Events

Profound life events don't just happen to an individual alone—they happen to his family, too. The chronic or catastrophic illness of an older parent carries his family along in the trauma. Grief at the death of a parent is a family experience. The aftermath of a parent's retirement or remarriage can spark strong reaction from adult children. Some families cope better than others with these life events. They cope when they have personal resources and strengths, access to outside resources if these are needed, and the insight which tells them there are no perfect situations or solutions. In this chapter we talk about some ways to make these intense life events less painful and disruptive than they might be.

Retirement: Blessing or Blight?

Not so very long ago, a gold watch was a prized possession, an expression of appreciation for years of satisfactory and respected service to a business enterprise. In its ritualistic way, it marked for the retiree the end of a long, fruitful era. And nobody thought much about what it was the beginning of.

A retirement ceremony today has different overtones. People think about the problems that lie ahead; psychologists and sociologists have pointed them out in books and magazine articles. The retiree who is feted often feels it marks the first step toward the end of his life. If he has no plans, no way of life marked out for his future years, the watch can become an object of loathing, a passport to discontent.

Yet these passports are thrust into the hands of hundreds of thousands of older Americans each year, as more and more business firms require mandatory retirement at age sixty-two or sixty-five. Many of these new retirees don't want to retire; they still feel they are performing at peak capacity and that they have a further contribution to make to their job, their profession, and their society. Often these feelings go side by side with a lack of preparation for what the retiree regards as the empty years ahead. For the retired individual, enforced retirement may not at all turn out to be the idyllic boon it was conceived to be.

Although more men than women have been subject to the arbitrary mandate to step aside, since fewer women have been in the labor force until now, women who have worked outside the home must also face the same problem. According to the Louis Harris and other surveys on attitudes toward aging, working women as a whole seem to be making a better adjustment to retirement than men. Perhaps the reason is that women are usually more geared to household activities and can transfer some of their creative energies to them more readily and with more satisfaction than a man.

The woman who has worked only in the home, or not worked very much outside of it, faces her own brand of woes when the last child leaves home or when a married child moves away, taking grandchildren from the area. Often, a woman in this situation has been devoting much of her time and energy to the care of an aged parent or parent-in-law whose death may rob her of a major focus and responsibility. In these years she is dealing with her own changed status and that of her husband—and the husband, similarly, has a double problem. Each has to deal not only with his or her own reactions to the new and difficult event, but with the other's. Retirement not only can disrupt the life of the individual, but can have distressing effects on the relationship of a married couple.

Studies of the impact of retirement on families indicate that couples who have previously adapted successfully to their marriage relationship will make a better adaptation to retirement than those who enter the retirement years with unresolved marital conflicts. A smaller income, more time closeted together, fewer outside opportunities for satisfactions, and possible health worries can threaten even a good marriage.

If your parents are experiencing retirement as a shock, the shock waves will reverberate through the family. The retiree may become despondent and depressed, may develop true symptoms of physical illness. Old frustrations may surface to muddy the waters, as may new ones created by empty time and empty hands. Your parent's sense of self-esteem may dwindle. One parent may not know how to give the other the support he needs. Each will need support.

You should be sensitive to the atmosphere between your parents at this time. Perhaps you can help with positive suggestions for work or recreation, shared or separate. (You'll find many such suggestions in Chapter 9.) You cannot be a counselor for their problems with each other, but if these problems seem temporarily destructive of their relationship, you might want to suggest that they seek professional counseling.

Voluntary Retirement

Those who retire voluntarily may be better prepared for retirement and, in many ways, may welcome it. Professional people and entrepreneurs who are self-employed can often choose the time of their retirement, unless poor health dictates an earlier date than they had envisaged. The act of choice maintains for them a sense of autonomy which mandatory retirement negates.

They may see retirement as a positive and not a negative state—one which gives them a more relaxed pattern of life and the opportunity to pursue activities and experiences which the pressures of their working years precluded. "I am becoming hungry for privacy, for the opportunity to savor life at my own gait, and I am choosing, hopefully, to attain a bit of serenity," said an Ohio congressman who chose to retire recently at age seventy. "I am at the right age and in the right mood to retire, and it's better to retire too soon than too late."[1]

Experience pinpoints some general precepts about retirement which you and your parent can think about. Carrying out some of these may be beyond individual control, but others can readily be applied to his postretirement years. Your parent will adjust better to retirement if:

• He has shown skill previously in handling major problems.
• He has looked forward to retirement as a period when, free of time pressure, he will follow the hobbies and interests which were out of his reach before.
• He has made plans for postretirement.
• He is involved in a number of regular activities, which include some emphasis on helping others.

The Shock Absorbers

Large corporations, professional societies, labor unions, and other groups offer educational seminars for employees who are about to retire. The content is generally quite thoughtful and tries to explore many aspects of the postretirement period: psychological problems, housing needs, financial management, the productive use of leisure time. Preretirement education can be very useful if your parent has access to it.

Many colleges and universities schedule regular workshops in "Third Age Living," which bring in batteries of psychologists, lawyers, vocational and avocational counselors to help the freshmen retirees carve out a new life-style. Your parent should check in his area.

Written material on retirement abounds. Insurance companies, associations of retired people, local mental health associations, and other aware groups have published thousands of pages on postretirement problems and their possible solutions. (See the Appendix.)

One insurance company has prepared *The Next Promotion,* a booklet which explores the psychological impact of retirement on formerly busy executives. Your father may have been a man who was a workaholic, brought home bundles of papers to read each night, and entertained only his "contacts," without having time for the people he claimed really to like. Like the "Chairman of the Bored" in this booklet, he may find himself depressed in retirement because he doesn't know what to do with himself all day and doesn't have any real friends to join. If he puts the same energy and creativity into planning his future days as he did into his past business, he may come up with quite a plan.[2]

Choices

A young woman recently told her father that all the choices she was called upon to make were exciting because the rest of her life would be determined by these choices. Each decision was an adventure: which college, which boy, which book to read, which language to study. My life is like a tree, she said. The trunk is flexible, and each choice I make and risk I take will make it strong or weak and will determine how many branches I can sustain. For you, she said to her sixty-year-old father, life is all set. You've made your choices, and there is very little you can do now to alter your style and direction, your branches, or the strength of the main trunk.

Many sixty-year-olds would be quick to accept her viewpoint. But for those still wrestling with decisions about self and lifestyle, about retirement and new careers, about housing and where to move, the decisions are as pivotal in determining the quality of the rest of their lives as the choices the young are called upon to make.

Your Role

The creative person will find his own solutions after retirement to the need for a new career of whatever kind. The creative child will try to inform and encourage his parent and will respect whatever decision he makes.

Your retired parent may be among the millions of over-sixty-five people who would like to continue to work full- or part-time, whether for income or for interest. He may prefer doing some kind of volunteer work, or he may choose to spend part of his time at a hobby of some sort. Perhaps he truly wants to stop any kind of organized activity and prefers watching television or keeping his days unplanned.

Your greatest contribution could be in helping to make possible the kind of life your parent chooses.

Think about his decision carefully in terms of his past life, his personality, and **his** expectation for his retirement years. Perhaps he has chosen the best move for him—for a time. Many people remain active after retirement, and many others prefer to stay inactive. Equal numbers in each group are happy and unhappy. If your parent seems happy doing what you think is nothing, don't make him feel guilty. If you feel he is doing too much and should "relax" more, don't nag him. Decisions about occupation and recreation after retirement are often subject to change.

Whatever the choice your parent makes, the primary test is whether it is suitable for him and not you. Consider a distinguished filmmaker who says that when he retires he plans to deliver newspapers door-to-door the way he did as a boy. "It will be so great watching the sun come up from my bicycle," he muses. "There won't be much traffic. I don't sleep late anymore, anyway. I'll toss the papers at the doorways and see how good my aim is. If I miss, I'll really be sure to walk the paper to the door. By the time I get back for breakfast, I'll be all set to sit down, read my own paper, and get ready for the next part of my day. I'll prepare my materials to help the kids in the high school who are making a movie. I'm not sure about the afternoon route, because I won't want to tie myself down for both ends of the day, but I will absolutely do the mornings. I can't wait."

If this were your father, would you be ready to accept this decision?

Chronic Illness

Whatever strains or upsets may ensue from your parent's retirement, they are dramatically different from the feelings that emerge when a hitherto healthy parent becomes seriously ill.

The illness may or may not be immediately life-threatening, but if it is chronic and prolonged and involves vital functions, then you and your stricken parent are nevertheless face-to-face with the prospect of death.

Indeed, the first time a child may face up to the fact that his parent may die comes, sometimes, when the parent first becomes chronically ill. Prolonged illness puts great strains on a family. Tempers run short, people feel guilty, sad, and depressed, sometimes angry. Lives have to be rearranged. When a hitherto healthy parent becomes chronically ill, families need to cope to avoid crisis.

Some adult children can't face up to it. They deny to themselves that their parent is seriously ill, is aging, and is going to die, because acknowledging this alters the whole hierarchy of the relationship. These children may cope with the daily problems, but they're looking the other way. "It's nothing," they say to the parent, "you're going to get better." The child may really believe this is true—because he wants to believe it.

But the parent who knows he has a severe chronic condition may view things differently from the child. Even if the illness is not immediately life-threatening, he may regard it as catastrophic. It doesn't really help, then, if your parent holds this view, to handle his distress lightly and make believe it is "nothing."

Saying "Yes, I know how you feel, it must make you sad, or miserable" is probably better than appearing to be totally insensitive to the depth of your parent's emotion. It is not unusual, however, for chronically ill patients themselves to go through a denial phase and say it's "nothing" before they become depressed or sad. The process of dealing with a serious chronic illness is, in fact, similar for the patient and for the family. Dr. Stuart Blauner, of the Burke Rehabilitation Center, White Plains, New York, describes this typical process: first denial, then realization and acceptance of the unwelcome events, then a kind of mourning for what has been lost.

Finally the patient and the family are ready to cope. If good communications are established between the patient and the doctor, the doctor and the family, and among the family members themselves, the stage is set for realistic decisions to be made. It may be a time when significant alterations may be required in everyone's life. "Don't decide everything at once," cautions Dr. Blauner. "Take one thing at a time. Don't be rigid about decisions that may need to be changed. Seek assistance from a social worker or psychologist, and don't be embarrassed to ask for help. Try to maintain a realistic outlook. Try not to gloss over tough problems, but do emphasize the day-to-day good events, to maintain morale."[3]

If your parents are together and one is stricken, you have to deal not only with the complex needs of the ill parent but with the ripple effects on the other parent. When an elderly person is exposed to catastrophic events involving the serious illness or death of a spouse, the seemingly well person himself becomes vulnerable to a catastrophic event. Statistics reveal that the first six months after the death of a spouse are the months of greatest risk for the surviving partner. It is therefore a time when caring children need to provide extra comfort and support to avoid compounding their tragedies.

It may also be a time when your relationships with other members of your family go awry. Brothers and sisters are particularly apt to argue and be angry with one another. Sibling rivalry is typically heightened during the chronic illness of parents, according to Dr. Blauner. It reflects itself in bickering and accusations, feelings of hostility as one or another child berates the others for not pulling their weight. While normal family behavior is frequently upset during critical moments, brothers and sisters seem to be particularly harsh on each other as they impose responsibility on one another. And even when they decide on sharing arrangements, undercurrents of displeasure continue to invade otherwise cordial relationships. Feelings of helplessnes are often responsible for this kind of behavior. Facing your feelings of helplessness and sharing them instead of burdening each other with impossible expectations may help relieve the emotional strain that builds up under such circumstances.

Crisis develops when people can't cope. What is a crisis in one family may not be a crisis in another. But why it's a crisis is not necessarily a reflection on an individual's abilities or on any family's character. Sometimes events can simply overwhelm the emotional, physical, or financial resources any one individual or any one family has to deal with the crisis—and that is a definition of catastrophe. For a community, a torrential flood, hurricane, or tornado can be catastrophic and cause a crisis for all its inhabitants. For a family the catastrophic illnesses such as

cancer, or severe kidney disease, or some of the serious degen-
erative diseases of the nervous system, of muscle structure, or
of any organ can precipitate crisis. Families need help to sustain
themselves through such traumas.

Get Help in Time

To make things better than they are means getting help in
time. You can get help in finding out what the alternatives are
for medical and nursing care, for example. Is it possible to keep
your parent at home, with services provided there? Is hospital
care essential, or can a nursing home provide care? Who will
pay for this, and how? This is the time to turn to the community
for assistance. Cancer Care, the American Cancer Society, family service agencies, a social worker, or a psychiatrist can help
you with your questions. (See Chapters 3 and 4.) Good counsel
and support can make all the difference in how a family weath-
ers a storm. If you cannot change the insidious course of the
disease, perhaps you can all get some emotional relief. This is
especially important during terminal illness that is painful or
unduly prolonged.

A California woman brought her aged invalid mother and
father home to live with her when she could no longer tolerate
emergency weekend trips to Atlanta, where the parents had
lived for many years. She had hired registered nurses and the
housekeepers to tend them, and, working at a full-time job,
tried to make arrangements which would provide more consistently and successfully for their many medical and nursing
needs.

"You don't need an educated person," she told us. "You just
need a good kind person to be with them. Then bring in the
specialists for particular tasks . . . each day if necessary."

Dr. Ewald Busse of the Duke University Medical Center, in
discussing training in psychology for workers dealing with the
dying, said this to a Cancer Care symposium: "Training is not
necessarily related to ability to judge a patient's feelings. For
example, a nurse's aide may be able to judge a patient's feelings
and respond more appropriately than the patient's doctor." It is
this attitude of caring that makes the difference for a terminally

ill patient. So many people abandon the dying as feeling people before they are beyond feeling.[4] "A difficult concept to accept is that at times the most helpful action may be holding a patient's hand and listening to him cry," says one practitioner. Dr. Leslie Libow of New York's Mt. Sinai Hospital's Section on Geriatric Medicine (Elmhurst Center) reports that "patients ask the same questions, no matter who is around, doctor, nurse, or homemaker. Often the more trained persons can avoid or escape the questions by not being around the patients. This leaves the homemaker and the family to contend with the situation."[5]

Dr. Busse has reported studies which found that "people in special units dealing with the catastrophically ill need more time off because of the emotional strain."[6] Thus, if you and family members are taking care of a catastrophically ill parent at home, you should, if at all possible, spell each other in chores and in bedside sitting for your ailing parent. When you are away from your parent and your obligation, try to conduct your life as normally as possible, with as much pleasure as possible. You should not feel guilty about enjoying yourself.

Death and Dying

How much easier it would be for you if your parent were quiet and accepting the end of life as death approaches. Whether this is possible is the sum of many things—but if your parent is angry, enraged, and hostile, that should be understandable to you. The professionals say that dying patients able to express this rage without fear of retribution from a doctor or disapproval from a family come sooner to an emotional acceptance of their fate than those who are encouraged to repress and who subsequently become profoundly depressed and withdrawn. The same is true of families.

Dr. Elisabeth Kübler-Ross, medical director of South Cook County Mental Health and Family Services, describes five stages of coping with death: denial, anger, bargaining, depression, and, finally, acceptance. If a patient is permitted to proceed through these stages, Kübler-Ross believes, the terminally ill individual can make peace with death and die with dignity and beauty. The family, too, must go through these stages to be able to accept the outcome and proceed with living.[7]

Young children today are being taught in school about the life process and the inevitability of death as part of that process. Those of us who are older have not had any "death education," and it is only through the recent efforts of such researchers as Kübler-Ross that we are learning to confront death instead of avoiding it as a fact of life. Many of us were left at home when our grandparent's funeral took place, or shushed away from the room where adults cried or grieved. Your doctor or your parent's doctor or nurse or health aide probably shares the same heritage, so that you may not get as much help from them as you would normally expect from professionals at a time of great stress. Religious families, with help from their clergymen, have been shown to have less traumatic problems with death than those who are skeptics. It has been suggested that rituals surrounding birth and death need to be designed for non-believers for the sake of their mental health.

In Britain, Dr. Cicely Saunders has been in the forefront of the movement to make death a more humane experience with her work at St. Christopher's Hospice in London. There, with nursing nuns, Dr. Saunders has created a haven for the terminally ill, where families are taught to work through their own fears, and patients are encouraged to express their feelings as they prepare for death. Together, the patients and their families approach the impending death with mutual emotional support. Now similar efforts are being initiated in this country. In New Haven, Connecticut, Dr. Sylvia Lack administers a hospice on the British model which has support from the National Cancer Institute. More hospices may follow. To help you overcome your own reluctance to deal with death and dying, we suggest you read Dr. Kübler-Ross's book *On Death and Dying*, James Agee's *A Death in the Family*, and others your librarian may suggest. They really help.

Burials and Funerals

Families who have never thought about burials and funerals can suddenly find themselves in a totally unanticipated whirlwind if someone unexpectedly dies. Even if they have considered alternatives but never resolved their thoughts into a plan of action, they're likely to have trouble. The most thoughtful elderly people will get their paperwork done ahead of time, leaving clear-cut instructions about their preferences. If this is done, the family is spared having to decide whose wishes to follow if there is disagreement among members.

One psychologist told us this: "Everybody is in the same boat. Everyone is going to die. Not being able to discuss your funeral or burial arrangements is really denying you're going to need them."

If discussing this with your parent is painful and difficult, you've got a problem. You'll have to decide such matters as burial or cremation, religious services or not, whether your generation will insist on certain practices in opposition to more traditional practices remaining older relatives prefer. Will you honor the wishes of the deceased, or the preferences of the living? Can you live with your decision, or will it be a constant source of guilt?

We are not offering you solutions to these very personal problems, only suggesting that you should think about them if you have not already done so.

Grief

How we deal with death tells a great deal about us—what we've faced and what we've avoided. Death is the ultimate crisis, the continuing mystery. The death of one parent leaves the other in jeopardy. The death of both parents leaves you an orphan. It puts you on the line; you are no longer someone's loved child. You're on your own psychologically.

No matter what you may have imagined before you've experienced the death of a parent, when it happens it is unique, overwhelming, elemental, and powerful. Everything in you surfaces—the love, the hate, the guilt, what you will miss, what you are free of. If you grieve, so much the better; if you repress your emotion, so much the worse. If you grieve too long, you're in trouble.

There is now a great deal of research on grief, particularly on how it affects the mental health of survivors. Ethnic and religious groups differ in how they grieve. Puritan heritage frowns on too much display of emotion, and those raised in its tradition have more psychological problems, it appears, than those who are free to express their emotions according to the mores of their group. The Catholics, with their wake, and the Jews, with their Shiva, emerge with fewer psychological scars. Freedom to cry without shame, to feel lost and alone, to express fears and love, to show resentment and anger, to express whatever it is that one feels—this is the liberating key from ceaseless mourning, prolonged, repressed guilt, and subsequent poor mental health.

Children, in mourning for one parent, should try to understand the needs and feelings of the remaining parent as well as their own. Some children are offended when a widow or widower expresses anger or hostility to the departed parent, and have no insight into the complex relationship that has just been ended. A surviving parent, on the other hand, can similarly impose a burden of guilt on a child who expresses anger or resentment about his departed parent. Most relationships are complex; too often in moments of stress one member of a grieving family may be too harsh in judging the others. With time and understanding, conflicting emotions can be worked through.

Unless other events or conditions intervene, you and your surviving parent will ultimately emerge from this period of mourning and grief to resume your lives. That may be easier for you than your parent.

Elderly people who lose a longtime partner may never really resume their lives in a meaningful manner. If they have been particularly dependent on each other, the loss is too profound for them to overcome at an advanced age. The survivor may quickly become ill and pass away, or become too frail or listless to maintain an independent life, a victim of grief which was never really resolved. But people with stronger emotional and physical resources, even quite old people, can still find the motivation to pick up and carry on if they have help.

Widows and Widowers

Being able to share one's sense of bewilderment and loss is an important part of the healing process for widows and widowers,

and this is often better accomplished with other people similarly situated than it is with one's children. For that reason,
retirement groups, family service associations, and mental
health associations offer workshops, sessions, or personal counseling for people who need a little extra boost to deal with their
problems.

Fannie Bakst, of the Widow's Consultation Service in New
York, led a workshop in Westchester not long ago for a coun-
tywide "Worry Clinic" on widowhood. The initial period of
being alone is a time of dealing with dilemmas, she said. Is it
time to start a new way of life, build a new personality, become a
new person?

"If I become a new person, should I feel guilty about enjoying something my husband hated, or was bored by—like the
ballet? Or should I continue to deprive myself of that pleasure
for his memory?" Anger is the probable outcome of that debate
with one's self, says Mrs. Bakst. If widowed persons don't get
rid of these conflicting feelings of anger and guilt, they end up
with physicial disabilities which are manifestations of their
inner turmoil. Children should not hinder the healthy efforts
of an adult parent to achieve a new life-style appropriate to his
new state.[8]

Whose advice to take is another dilemma. Is your father
being told one thing by you, another by his friends, and still
another by his aged sister? Should he learn how to cook, move
into a hotel, go on a cruise, or start looking for a new wife?
Denying that anything is different is a person's way of saying
that dealing with the difference is too much for him to face.
There is a tendency to hang onto familiar things and be afraid
to take the next step. But sooner or later the next step has to be
taken.

For women it is harder. Women really do suffer more as
widows. The fifth woman at a dinner party is a fifth wheel, as
Mrs. Bakst says. The fifth man is a social coup. A greater percentage of men than women can and do remarry. And the old
widows who remain are likely to have fewer coping resources.
Many older women may never have learned to drive, never had
advanced educations or interests or work outside the family to

sustain them. They may need financial advice and help from lawyers and banks and stockbrokers.

Intimate relationships with children seem to be different, also. Widowers tend to interfere less in their children's affairs than do widows. A widower will criticize much less than a widow how the grandchildren are being brought up or how his daughter is running the house.

Grandpa doesn't feel "slights" as much as Grandma does, is less sensitive to perceived hurts inflicted by unthinking children. Widowed men are less likely to depend on their children for emotional or social sustenance.[9]

Children cannot live their parents' lives. They can help make them better. They can treat them with respect, help them to have access to new opportunities for social activity, soothe some aches and pains, help to sustain them in crisis, and not get in their way when they adjust themselves to the new conditions. Sometimes parents remarry.

Remarriage

Families can certainly get stirred up when a parent remarries. Primal jealousies and more mundane problems of money and inheritance can spiral to distasteful levels when a new husband or wife takes up residence in a parental home.

Consider the prosperous merchant who, with his hardworking wife, developed a flourishing business in a Midwestern city. They had a single son, who helped in the business while he was growing up, but left after college to live and work in the East. The son became a college professor, earning a modest income but doing what he wanted to do. In the back of his mind he knew he had a cushion of security; following his parents' death he'd come into his inheritance. Sometime after his own child was born, the professor's mother became seriously ill and died after several years. His father was sorrowful and grieving. During the next two years, the professor added to his weekly teaching schedule regular weekend trips to St. Louis, to help his father with the business. Father rather expected this. He managed his own household, the business continued to prosper, but

Father was really lonely and dispirited. After a time he met a widow, somewhat younger than he. She was attractive and attentive. She made Father feel good. Life, it turned out, could be enjoyable for him. He married her. She helped in the business, made his home happy. The son no longer needed to make his weekend excursions. Father suddenly became ill and quickly died, leaving the entire business and inheritance to his new wife. Schemer, shouted the son! What about me?

What about you?

How will you feel if your parent remarries? Matters of money and inheritance can readily be handled through marriage contracts and other arrangements if people so desire, but can you view your parent as a private individual with needs and desires separate from the relationship with you? If you asked one of your own children to describe you to a stranger, would you be satisfied with his description, or would you think, "What does he really know about me and how I feel?"

Children can be severely judgmental about their parents. Just as you wanted your parent to have confidence in your choice of spouse, so should you have confidence in your parent's, unless the choice is obviously absurd or destructive. Even then you may have to bite your tongue and be silent, as many a parent has been when a child insisted on a disastrous marriage.

Of course old people make mistakes. There's no fool like an old fool, the saying goes, and it is perfectly possible that an aged man will fall victim to a scheming "gold digger." And of course there are elderly women so starved for companionship and affection they will fall into the arms of a clever con man who can divest them of all their financial assets. But this is not the rule.

Adult children do get upset about money. They are upset for themselves and their children, and upset when they think back on the sacrifices the dead parent made to accumulate the "nest egg" which is now being enjoyed (squandered?) by a stranger. A thoughtful parent should discuss with his children his contemplated financial commitment to a new partner and should make a new will which states clearly what portion of the estate will go to the new spouse and what portion to children and grandchildren. A friendly question from you is not out of order to determine that what your parent really intends has been legally secured for everyone.

In many families, the remarriage of a parent is a warm and welcomed event. Adult children will accept a parent as an independent adult, with an intimate personal life, pleasures and regrets, dreams and compromises that the parent alone can put value on. Children will not impose a burden of guilt on a widowed parent who chooses to remarry and is lucky enough to have found affection and companionship from another person. Or, more selfishly, they may even be happy the new spouse is relieving them of thinking about the daily events of a parent's life, or of feeling guilty when they don't. They may or may not develop a good relationship with the stepmother or -father, but at least their love for their own parent dominates the situation and softens any hostile feelings toward the stepparent which may emerge from time to time. Problems arise when all the relationships are in disarray. Petty problems become major problems. Major problems cause total rifts.

If you are having trouble accepting a stepparent who may be honorable and decent, and kind and loving to your parent, then perhaps you are the one who needs help. You should seek it before you attribute venal motives to a person who is adding a new and positive dimension to your parent's life.

Studies conducted in California have indicated that "after the age of sixty, only about one third of the elderly ... can depend on the companionship and nurturance of married life. The others must cope with widowhood or separation or face growing old as a single person." High morale often comes from the deepening relationship of old age, when incapacities or frailties cause one to make life more endurable for the other. Even in unhappy marriages, studies show, the "need for mutual assistance and interdependency in these long marriages may outweigh the long endured strains of persistent recriminations and hatred."[10]

Remarriage, unfortunately, runs the risk of being of short duration, and the burdens of providing nursing care for a relatively new partner sometimes give people pause before they undertake such commitments, or induce strain when they do.

Many older people are living together these days without

benefit of formal marriage. Like the young, they may be doing this on principle. Most of them, however, are avoiding the financial complications that can arise. More than inheritance is involved. For example, medicaid might be available to one partner and not the other. Married, the other person puts his or her financial security on the line. Like their grandchildren's generation, they may get tired of one another, or have trouble adjusting to the new relationship. They are saving themselves the trouble and expense of divorce. Don't snicker. They may be wise.

CHAPTER 11

DOING THE BEST YOU CAN

It's Your Problem, But It's Not Your Fault

Your problem is shared by many millions of people in our country, and as each year goes by, more join you.

In today's population, there are 22.4 million people over sixty-five, and although most of them are living independently, the characteristics of their age require some form of extra care and attention. More than 40 million people are in the forty-five-to-sixty-five-year-old bracket, and this, presumably, is the bulk of the caretaking generation—your generation.

The average adult child is in his fifties when his parents die. Probably a grandparent himself, he has spend a goodly portion of his most recent days taking care of his parents. It is not so rare now to find four-generation families where the burden of care for both the very young and the very old members of the family is focused on the middle generation.

Part of our anguish arises from the frustration of knowing that science and technology have lengthened life, while we ask ourselves, To what purpose? "It is a particularly frustrating irony that progress in man's search for a longer life should produce the 'problems of aging,'" says Herman B. Brotman in *Facts and Figures on Older Americans.* "In fact, the very successes of economic, social, medical and industrial progress that now permit such a large proportion of our population to reach old age, also have simultaneously produced the changes that make the elderly a generally 'dependent' group and have robbed them of their most important traditional functions, roles and statuses."[1]

Medical science has prolonged the life of the body, but often has not been able to prolong the adequate functioning of the body or of the mind—hence the old people unable to care for themselves who live out the last vacant years of their lives in nursing homes or with their overloaded families. Humane changes in labor laws and practices and the development of laborsaving devices have minimized the physical exhaustion and debilitation which used to send working people to earlier deaths. But these same developments have made the older worker obsolescent at an earlier age, consigning him willy-nilly to retirement from productive and gainful employment.

Broad social changes in values have stripped from the older person the respect which was formerly accorded him, and changes in communications techniques have robbed him of his traditional role of counselor, adviser, and sympathizer. The old used to have a positive role as teachers; now we learn from television programs, advice-giving newspaper columns, how-to books, and adult education courses. Sometimes the experience of the older person is no longer relevant to today's society.

We live in a country where there is unique upward mobility. Upward economic mobility often means lateral geographic mobility: In order to move up the economic ladder, people often have to move away from the places where they were born and where their parents remain. This dispersal of the younger generations has left many in the older generations isolated, without the lifeblood support that the young have traditionally given to the old. The young communicate by mail, by phone, by snapshot. They aren't there to give the morning smile that warms the day, to bring over the meal when the parent can't cook, to drive to buy what the parent can't get out to buy, to make the complicated phone call that the parent can no longer handle.

Small towns, where several generations of a family have remained to live and work, may still retain a way of life which fosters the easy giving and taking of affection, attention, and assistance among the generations. But more and more of America's children are too busy, too pressed, too distant, too tangled in their own problems to provide this close togetherness. The long-lived parent is all too often not an integral part of a family.

Although the great majority of elderly Americans cherish their independence, they also cherish the feeling of belonging. Even though the trend is toward providing social services in the home and thus avoiding institutional care, there is still some question about just how secure the older person feels when he is completely alone—even with a telephone reassurance call, a buddy doing the marketing, a Meal on Wheels for lunch or dinner. What happens during the night when a bad dream or a sudden pain intrudes on sleep, when a stroke or a paralyzing fall strikes at three o'clock in the morning? Old people who live alone are often fearful that these things will happen to them, that there will be no one to help, that they won't be able to reach the telephone, that they will die alone, without someone at their side. Living in separate quarters but in a setting with other people—with family or friends or in a senior residence—makes these fears less acute.

In the Israeli kibbutz where Bruno Bettelheim did some of his research for *Children of the Dream,* the kibbutzim realized some years ago that there were no old people participating. The kibbutz had been founded thirty years before, by a group of twenty-year-olds. They had grown older together, and had borne children, but they had not yet grown old. How should one deal with the problems of aging on a kibbutz? The children would have no models to follow as their own parents aged.

The kibbutzim decided to invite their own parents to join them. Those who came were assigned lighter tasks and continued to participate in productive activity as long as their health and spirit permitted. Except when they require the specialized services of the hospital in a nearby city, the oldest generation remains on the kibbutz, among family and friends, where the view from the window is familiar and a walk refreshes old memories. "Those who grow old on the kibbutz are never alone," says Bettelheim. "They remain, as before, in the middle of things, feeling needed. To the end of their natural days there is as much for them, or as little of importance to be done as they wish."[2]

In the Netherlands, an enlightened, caring population provides older people with apartment quarters on the village or town square so that they can live with the special services they require in a setting where they continue to be part of the central life of the community.

In England, the National Health Service provides special subsidies to families who continue to keep their elderly parents at home with them and also helps these families with a network of day-care centers for the parents.

But you do not live in England, in the Netherlands, or on an Israeli kibbutz. Your world is here, where the growing group of improperly tended older people is one of the nasty lags behind the general improvement in the quality of American life. Our society is certainly attempting to catch up through government research and action programs to help older people in countless ways. But the help still falls far short of what it needs to be.

What you must remember through the difficult times with your parent is that the problems you may face—sometimes overwhelming and insoluble—and the emotions that you and your parent may have—sometimes overpowering and destructive—aren't your fault. It's your problem, all right, and you are facing it as well as you know how, but you didn't cause it.

The Limits of Responsibility

A man in his late forties once proposed an ironic definition of middle age. It's the time of your life when you're in the middle, he said. You're caught between your responsibilities to your parents and your responsibilities to your children.

Somewhere along the way there will be sacrifices for you; of your time, your money, your energy, your peace of mind. Somewhere along the way there will be sacrifices required from your spouse and your children. And, sometimes, your parent may have to get the short end. Your parent, your family, and you are, in this mixture, the three intrinsic elements. You must be careful not to sacrifice any single element one-sidedly to the others. If you begin to feel overburdened and on edge, it's time to pay a little attention to your own needs and less to those of others. If your children legitimately find the homes of friends more attractive than yours because your resident mother endlessly voices her disapproval of their habits and life-styles, it's time to stop protecting her and to sit down with her for a frank discussion.

If your parent complains of insufficient attention, of being neglected, or even abandoned, you must look at it not only from his point of view but from the reality of what you are doing for him as you see it. If you are caring for your parent, you are not neglecting or abandoning him, even though he may tell you that you're not doing enough. Many aging parents do feel neglected or abandoned by their children, but the definition of neglect or abandonment is intrinsically personal. A parent in a nursing home may feel abandoned, even though children telephone and visit regularly. This parent's definition of not being abandoned is that he live with one of his children.

Unless you are an only child, caring for an older parent should be done on a shared family basis. The burden on one child alone can be too overpowering, and it is up to each family member to see to it that all share in some degree. All too often, one child is left alone to do it. "I work and I don't have time," a sister will say. "I can't afford to help," a brother says. Other family members who accept this statement are allowing injustice to prevail. In a demanding caretaking situation, there is no family member who cannot contribute something—a small amount of money if money is required, a few hours regularly to do some service for the parent or to give relief to the person who is the major caretaker. Sometimes it is not so simple to prod a neglecting child into the caretaking process. It probably is difficult for him to spare the money or to find the time. He probably does have negative feelings for the ailing parent which are strong enough to bar compassionate behavior. But other siblings should not allow a laggard to escape even some small form of responsibility without presenting the picture to him in strong, clear terms and suggesting realistic ways in which he can cooperate. The adult child who permits siblings to evade even some small responsibility may be reacting to his own emotional hang-ups and not to the realities of the situation.

Facing up to your parent's situation, whatever its dimensions, is the first order of business. If you avoid, postpone, or neglect, you're sure to find yourself in crisis, flailing about and miserable. It takes time and effort to plan; it takes communications to make things really work. You, your brothers or sisters, and your mother or father really need to talk with one another honestly to sort out the possibilities and select the most effective course of action. There's hardly a family in which one single decision will take care of the problem. As people age, they move through a series of crossroads, and their families with them. Each decision will be the basis for the next one, and even if each is made from the most informed and enlightened judgment, you may not be able to achieve the perfect solution. You can only do the best that you can.

The information in this book can help you even in the most difficult situations. It should lead you to investigate the specific resources available, alert you that any single solution is part of a whole process, and prepare you for the inevitability of change. It should convince you that there are concrete avenues of help for you. You may have to look for them. You may have to ask for them. But you don't have to invent them.

NOTES

CHAPTER ONE

1. Interview with Rabbi David Golovensky, New Rochelle, N.Y.
2. Interviews with Benjamin Kaplan, Jewish Association for Services for the Aged, New York; Alice Murphy, Catholic Charities of the Archdiocese of New York; and David Sambol, Federation of Protestant Welfare Agencies, Inc., New York.
3. Interview with Dr. Robert Butler, director, National Institute on Aging, Washington, D.C.
4. Interviews with Dr. George Maddox, director, Center for the Study of Aging and Human Development, Duke University, Durham, N.C.; and Dr. Eric Pfeiffer, professor of psychiatry, Duke University School of Medicine, Durham, N.C.
5. Interview with Dr. Robert Butler.
6. Interview with David Sambol.

CHAPTER TWO

1. Bertha G. Simos, "Adult Children and Their Aging Parents," *Social Work* 18 (1973):78.
2. Interviews with Alice Murphy, David Sambol, and Benjamin Kaplan.
3. Interview with Lottie L. Hook, Homemakers Home and Health Care Services, Washington, D.C.
4. Interview with George Bragaw, Health Services Administration, U.S. Public Health Service, Washington, D.C.
5. Interview with Jeanne Priester, Cooperative Extension Service, U.S. Department of Agriculture, Washington, D.C.

CHAPTER THREE

1. Margaret Clark and Barbara Gallatin Anderson, *Culture and Aging: An Anthropological Study of Older Americans* (Springfield, Ill.: Charles C Thomas, 1967), pp. 211, 222.

2. Interview with Judith Altholz, associate in psychiatric social work, Duke University, Durham, N.C.
3. Bertha G. Simos, "Adult Children and Their Aging Parents," *Social Work* 18 (1973):80.
4. Olga Knopf, *Successful Aging* (New York: Viking, 1975), p. 33.
5. Warner A. Wick, "The Aging Society and the Promise of Human Life," in Bernice L. Neugarten and Robert J. Havighurst, eds., *Social Policy, Social Ethics and the Aging Society* (forthcoming).
6. National Council on the Aging, *A National Directory of Housing for Older People* (Washington, D.C.: NCOA, 1969).
7. Interview with Dr. Donald Watkin, director, Nutrition Program, Administration on Aging, Washington, D.C.
8. Amanda A. Beck, *Michigan Aging Citizens: Characteristics, Opinions, and Service Utilizations* (Ann Arbor, Mich.: University of Michigan–Wayne State University, 1975).

CHAPTER FOUR

1. Barbara Price, social worker, Department of Social Services, Fairfax County, Va.
2. Minna Field, *The Aged, the Family and the Community* (New York: Columbia University Press, 1972), p. 60.
3. Daphne Krause, executive director, Minneapolis Age and Opportunity Center, quoted in the *Congressional Record*, September 9, 1975, p. S15522.
4. Olga Knopf, *Successful Aging* (New York: Viking, 1975), p. 44.
5. Interview with Judith Altholz, associate in psychiatric social work, Duke University, Durham, N.C.
6. Interview with Dr. Leah Robinson Warner, clinical psychologist, Virginia Beach, Va.
7. Alvin I. Goldfarb, "Institutional Care of the Aged," in Ewald W. Busse, ed., *Behavior and Adaptation in Late Life* (Boston: Little, Brown, 1969), p. 308.
8. Jean Baron Nassau, *Choosing a Nursing Home* (New York: Funk & Wagnalls, 1975), and pamphlets of the Association of American Homes for the Aging and American Health Care Association.
9. Interview with David Sambol, director, Division on Aging, Federation of Protestant Welfare Agencies, Inc., New York.
10. Interview with Harold Mawhinney, director, Miriam Osborn Memorial Home, Rye, N.Y.
11. Beverly A. Yawney and Darrell L. Slover, "Relocation of the Elderly," *Social Work* 18 (1973):90, 91.
12. Interview with Harold Mawhinney.

CHAPTER FIVE

1. Olga Knopf, *Successful Aging* (New York: Viking, 1975), p. 25.
2. Gladys Ellenbogen, *Private Health Insurance Supplementary to Medicare*, working paper prepared for the U.S. Senate Special Committee on Aging, December 1974, p. 27.

3. Gaylord A. Nelson, U.S. Senator, "High Drug Prices: Brand Names vs. Generic," statement, June 11, 1973.
4. Interview with Geneva Mathiasen, former executive director, National Council on the Aging, Washington, D.C.

CHAPTER SIX

1. Robert Butler, *Why Survive? Being Old in America* (New York: Harper & Row, 1975), p. xii.
2. Francis W. Peabody, "The Care of the Patient," *Journal of the American Medical Association* 88 (1927):887. Quoted in William Morgan and George L. Engel, *The Clinical Approach to the Patient* (Philadelphia: W. B. Saunders, 1969), p. 2.
3. Interview with Dr. Edward Fischel, professor of medicine, Albert Einstein College of Medicine, Bronx, N.Y.

CHAPTER SEVEN

1. Raymond Harris, "Special Features of Heart Disease in the Elderly Patient," in *Working with Older People: A Guide to Practice*, Vol. IV, *Clinical Aspects of Aging* (Rockville, Md.: U.S. Public Health Service, 1974), p. 92.
2. The information on heart disease came from interviews with Dr. Robert Stivelman, assistant clinical professor of medicine, University of Southern California, Los Angeles, Calif., and Dr. Ira Gelb, associate clinical professor of cardiology, Mt. Sinai School of Medicine, New York.
3. Harris, p. 89.
4. *High Blood Pressure: What to Do When Your Numbers Are Up*, reprint from Consumer Reports (Mt. Vernon, N.Y.: Consumers Union, 1974).
5. American Cancer Society pamphlets.
6. Robert Butler, *Why Survive? Being Old in America* (New York: Harper & Row, 1975), p. 205.
7. Interview with Dr. Harold Rifkin, chief, Division of Diabetes, Montefiore Hospital and Medical Center, Bronx, N.Y.
8. Information from interview with Dr. Maclyn McCarty, vice-president, Rockefeller University, New York, and from Oscar J. Balchum, "The Bronchopulmonary System," in *Working with Older People: A Guide to Practice*, Vol. IV, *Clinical Aspects of Aging* (Rockville, Md.: U.S. Public Health Service, 1974), pp. 113–124.
9. Arthritis Foundation pamphlets.
10. *Arthritis: The Basic Facts* (New York: Arthritis Foundation, 1974).
11. *Facts about Osteoporosis* (Bethesda, Md.: National Institute of Arthritis and Metabolic Disease, U.S. Department of Health, Education and Welfare, 1970).
12. New York League for the Hard of Hearing pamphlets, and *Hearing Loss: Hope Through Research* (Bethesda, Md.: National Institute of Neurological Diseases and Stroke, U.S. Department of Health, Education and Welfare, 1973).

13. American Society for the Prevention of Blindness, American Foundation for the Blind.
14. Interview with Mother M. Bernadette de Lourdes, administrator, St. Joseph's Manor, Trumbull, Conn.

CHAPTER EIGHT

1. Information from interviews with Dr. Elliot Weitzman, professor and chairman, Department of Neurology, Montefiore Hospital and Medical Center, Bronx, N.Y., Dr. Steven Mattis, chief clinical neuropsychologist, Montefiore Hospital and Medical Center, Bronx, New York, and Dr. Robert Terry, chairman, Department of Pathology, Albert Einstein College of Medicine, Bronx, N.Y.
2. Robert Butler, *Why Survive? Being Old in America* (New York: Harper & Row, 1975), pp. 175–176.
3. *Ibid.*, p. 176.
4. Caroline S. Ford, "Confused and Disoriented Elderly," in *Working with Older People: A Guide to Practice*, Vol. III, *The Aging Person: Needs and Services* (Rockville, Md.: U.S. Public Health Service, 1974), p. 50.
5. Interviews with Dr. Steven Mattis and with Mother M. Bernadette de Lourdes, administrator, St. Joseph's Manor, Trumbull, Conn.

CHAPTER NINE

1. Margaret Clark and Barbara Gallatin Anderson, *Culture and Aging: An Anthropological Study of Older Americans* (Springfield, Ill.: Charles C Thomas, 1967), pp. 415–433.
2. Bernice Neugarten, "Successful Aging in 1970 and 1990," in Eric Pfeiffer, ed., *Successful Aging,* report of a conference, June 7–9, 1973, Center for the Study of Aging and Human Development, Duke University, Durham, N.C.

CHAPTER TEN

1. Congressman Charles A. Mosher of Ohio, quoted in the *Wall Street Journal,* January 2, 1976.
2. *The Next Promotion* (Hartford, Conn.: Connecticut Mutual Life Insurance Company, 1960).
3. Interview with Dr. Stuart Blauner, Burke Rehabilitation Center, White Plains, N.Y.
4. Ewald Busse, quoted in *Catastrophic Illness in the Seventies* (New York: Cancer Care, Inc., 1971), p. 88.
5. Leslie Libow, quoted in *Ibid.*, p. 89.
6. Busse, quoted in *Ibid.*, p. 89.
7. Elisabeth Kübler-Ross, quoted in *Ibid.*, pp. 14–18.
8. Fannie Bakst, "Worry Clinic" Workshop, Westchester County (N.Y.) Mental Health Association, 1975.

9. Margaret Clark and Barbara Gallatin Anderson, *Culture and Aging: An Anthropological Study of Older Americans* (Springfield, Ill.: Charles C Thomas, 1967), p. 279.
10. *Ibid.*, p. 242.

CHAPTER ELEVEN

1. Herman B. Brotman, *Facts and Figures on Older Americans: An Overview* (Washington, D.C.: Administration on Aging, U.S. Department of Health, Education and Welfare, 1971), p. 1.
2. Bruno Bettelheim, *Children of the Dream* (New York: Macmillan, 1969), p. 318.

APPENDIX A   WHERE TO WRITE

FEDERAL GOVERNMENT PROGRAMS INFORMATION

U.S. DEPARTMENT OF HEALTH, EDUCATION AND WELFARE
WASHINGTON, D.C. 20201

Write to the address above for the following booklets:

SOCIAL SECURITY ADMINISTRATION
Introducing Supplemental Security Income (SSA 74-11015)
Supplemental Security Income for the Aged, Blind and Disabled (SSA 75-11000)
Pocket Guide to Supplemental Security Income (SSA 74-11014)
Your Claim for Supplemental Security Income (SSA 74-11010)
Questioning the Decision on Supplemental Security Income Claims (SSA 74-11008)
Important Information about Your Supplemental Security Income Payments (SSA 75-11011)
Your Social Security (SSA 75-10035)
Estimating Your Social Security Retirement Check (SSA 75-10047)
You Can Work and Still Get Social Security Checks (SSA 75-10092)
Higher Social Security Payments (SSA 75-10324)
Disabled? Find Out about Social Security Disability Benefits (SAA 73-10068)
Your Right to Question the Decision Made on Your Claim (SSA 73-10058)

SOCIAL AND REHABILITATION SERVICE
A Citizen's Handbook: Social Services (SRS 75-23038)

ADMINISTRATION ON AGING *(Some selections from a wide variety of booklets)*
Older Americans and Community Colleges: An Overview. DHEW Publication No. (OHD) 74-20191
Handle Yourself with Care: Accident Prevention for Older Americans. DHEW Publication No. (OHD/AoA) 73-20805
To Find the Way to Serve in Your Community. DHEW Publication No. (SRS) 73-20807
Are You Planning on Living the Rest of Your Life? DHEW Publication No. (OHD/AoA) 73-20803

Brighter Vistas: Church Programs for Older Adults. DHEW Publication No. (OHD) 74-20188

MEDICARE

Your Medicare Handbook (SSA 74-10050)
A Brief Explanation of Medicare (SSA 75-10043)
Basic Facts about Medicare (SSA 75-10014)
Medicare Benefits in a Skilled Nursing Facility (SSA 75-10041)
Home Health Care under Medicare (SSA 75-10042)
Your Right to Question Your Medical Insurance Payment (SSA 73-10079)
Your Right to Question the Decision on Your Hospital Insurance Claim (SAA 75-10085)

INTERNAL REVENUE SERVICE

In addition to IRS Publication No. 17, which gives general information for individual tax returns, there are special pamphlets which can be particularly helpful to people over sixty-five:

Retirement Income Credit, Publication No. 4804-00715
The Federal Gift Tax, Publication No. 048-004-00813-1
Tax Benefits for Older Americans, Publication No. 4804-00766
Tax Information on Selling Your Home, Publication No. 4804-00714
Tax Information on Pension and Annuity Income, Publication No. 048-004-00804-1

These can be obtained by writing to the Superintendent of Documents, U.S. Government Printing Office, Washington, D.C. 20402. Prices in 1975 ranged from 45 to 60 cents for each pamphlet.

CONSUMER INFORMATION

Protection for the Elderly (Consumer Bulletin No. 9). Federal Trade Commission, 6th and Pennsylvania Ave. N.W., Washington, D.C. 20508. Free from this address, or for 15 cents from the U.S. Government Printing Office, Washington, D.C. 20402.
Consumer Guide for Older People. Administration on Aging, Washington, D.C. 20201. Publication SRS 72-20801. Free.
An Index of Selected Federal Publications of Consumer Interest (1974). Includes information on budgets, finance, insurance, clothing. Consumer Information Public Documents Distribution Center, Pueblo, Colorado 81009.
How to Pay Less for Prescription Drugs. How to Find a Doctor for Yourself. From *Consumer Reports.* Reprint Department, Consumers Union, Orangeburg, New York 10962.

CRIME PREVENTION

Preventing Crime Through Education: How to Spot a Con Artist. NRTA/AARP, 1901 K Street N.W., Washington, D.C. 20049. Free.

EDUCATION

For information on nearby colleges and universities with continuing education courses for older people, write to the American Association of State Colleges and Universities and the American Association of Community and Junior Colleges. Each is located at One Dupont Circle, Washington, D.C. 20036.

HEALTH

Blue Cross/Blue Shield publications: *Secrets of Good Health,* by Jane E. Brody and Richard Enquist, and *The Modern Family Guide to Good Health.* Check your local Blue Cross office.

Health Aspects of Aging. American Medical Association, 535 North Dearborn Street, Chicago, Illinois, 60610. Price: 20 cents.

Write to the Office of Communications and Public Affairs, Health Services Administration, U.S. Public Health Service, 5600 Fishers Lane, Rockville, Md. 20852 for pamphlets on particular health-care problems and common diseases.

Your Guide to Good Health. Metropolitan Life Insurance Co., One Madison Ave., New York, New York 10010.

Day after Tomorrow. A preretirement health counseling booklet issued by the New York State Department of Health, Albany, New York. Chronic Diseases and Geriatrics Monograph No. 2-1958.

The national health organizations listed in Appendix B: "Where to Turn" distribute many pamphlets giving information about the diseases in which they specialize. (See pages 267–268.)

HOUSING

A Guide for Selection of Retirement Housing. Published by the National Council on Aging, 1828 L Street N.W., Washington, D.C. 20036.

The National Directory of Retirement Residences, by Noverre Musson. Published by Frederick Fell. Available in public libraries and bookstores.

Guide to Retirement Living, by Paul Holter. Published by Rand McNally. Available in public libraries, bookstores, or through The Map Store, 1636 Eye Street N.W., Washington, D.C. 20006.

RURAL

Farmers Home Administration, U.S. Department of Agriculture, Washington, D.C. 20250. Help for those over sixty to build or buy homes, and information about rental units in rural areas.

Rural Housing Alliance, 1346 Connecticut Avenue, N.W., Washington, D.C. 20036.

Cooperative Extension Service, U.S. Department of Agriculture. Check your phone book for local listing.

LEGAL AND FINANCIAL MANAGEMENT

You, the Law and Retirement (OHD/AoA 73-20800). For sale by the Superintendent of Documents, U.S. Government Printing Office, Washington, D.C. 20402. Price: 45 cents.

Dollars and Sense after Sixty, by Louis L. Himber. Division on Aging, Federation of Protestant Welfare Agencies, 281 Park Avenue South, New York, New York 10010. Free.

Tax Facts for Older Americans. A detailed description of tax regulations affecting older residents in each of the fifty states. AARP/NRTA, 1909 K Street N.W., Washington, D.C. 20049. Free.

Your Retirement Income Tax Guide. AARP, P.O. Box 2400, Long Beach, California 90801. Free.

Protecting Older Americans against Overpayment of Income Taxes: A Checklist of Itemized Deductions. Special Committee on Aging, U.S. Senate, Room G225, Dirksen Building, Washington, D.C. 20510. Free. For sale as No. 5270–2228 by the Superintendent of Documents, U.S. Government Printing Office, Washington, D.C. 20402, for 35 cents.

Continental Association of Funeral and Memorial Societies (125 member groups), 1828 L Street N.W., Washington, D.C. 20036. Information on holding down funeral costs.

NURSING HOMES

Nursing Home Care. Published by the Social and Rehabilitation Service, U.S. Department of Health, Education and Welfare, Washington, D.C. 20201. Try here for a copy at no cost, by writing for SRS Booklet No. 73–24902. For 30 cents you can get one from the U.S. Government Printing Office by asking for Booklet No. 1761–00032.

American Association of Homes for the Aging, a national association of non-profit, nonproprietary homes, publishes a directory describing all the nursing homes, intermediate-care homes, and housing projects which belong to the association. Copies cost $20 each, but may be found in public libraries. In addition, affiliated associations in twenty states have their own statewide listings. For information, write: Membership Service Department, AAHA, 1050 17th St. N.W., Washington, D.C. 20036.

American Health Care Association (formerly American Nursing Home Association) is another national organization of nursing homes—including those with day-care programs—and mental health institutions. About three-fourths of the members are proprietary institutions, and the rest are nonprofit. AHCA has affiliated associations in every state but North Dakota, and each will have a list of member homes and institutions in its state. AHCA publishes a brochure called *Thinking about a Nursing Home,* available from the national office or from the state affiliates, which contains a long checklist to use in investigating a nursing home. Write: American Health Care Association, 1200 Fifteenth Street N.W., Washington, D.C. 20005.

An informative book on the subject is *Choosing a Nursing Home,* by Jean Baron Nassau. Published in 1975 by Funk & Wagnalls.

NUTRITION

The U.S. Department of Agriculture (USDA) publishes several pamphlets giving good nutrition information to older people and others. You may be able to get them free from the USDA. If not, you can order them at small cost from the U.S. Government Printing Office. For the Department of Agriculture, write Office of Communication, USDA, Washington, D.C. 20250. If what you want isn't available there, write Superintendent of Documents, U.S. Government Printing Office, Washington, D.C. 20402.

Food Guide for Older Folks. USDA Home and Garden Bulletin No. 17. (U.S. Government Printing Office No. 1011-03321. Price: 40 cents.)

Cooking for Two. USDA Program Aid No. 1043. (U.S. Government Printing Office No. 0100–03327. Price: $1.25.)

Nutrition: Food at Work for You. USDA Home and Garden Bulletin No. 1 Family Fare, Separate 1. (U.S. Government Printing Office No. 0100-1517. Price: 20 cents.)

Food Is More Than Just Something to Eat. (Obtainable from USDA only.)

Food for Fitness. USDA Leaflet No. 424. (U.S. Government Printing Office No. 0100-02882. Price: 15 cents.)

Other good nutrition publications:

Cooking for One in the Senior Years. Cooperative Extension, New York State College of Human Ecology, Cornell University, Ithaca, New York 14853. Price: 20 cents.

Meal Planning for the Golden Years. General Mills, Inc. Nutrition Service Department 5, 9200 Wayzata Boulevard, Minneapolis, Minnesota 55440.

Food Hints for Mature People, by Charles Glen King with George Britt. Public Affairs Pamphlet No. 336. Public Affairs Committee, Inc., 381 Park Avenue South, New York, New York 10016. Price: 25 cents.

Many national health associations and professional societies publish and distribute free general and specific nutrition information:

Allergy Foundation of America, 801 Second Avenue, New York, New York 10017.

American Diabetes Association, 18 East 48th Street, New York, New York 10017.

American Dietetic Association, 620 North Michigan Avenue, Chicago, Illinois 60611.

American Heart Association, 44 East 23rd Street, New York, New York 10010.

American Medical Association, 535 North Dearborn Street, Chicago, Illinois 60610.

National Academy of Sciences, Food and Nutrition Board, National Research Council, Washington, D.C. 20418.

National Heart and Lung Institute, Office of Heart Information, National Institutes of Health, Bethesda, Maryland 20014.

Nutrition Foundation, Inc., 99 Park Avenue, New York, New York 10016.

PHYSICAL FITNESS

The Fitness Challenge in the Later Years: An Exercise Program for Older Americans.
You may be able to obtain this at no cost from the U.S. Department of
Health, Education and Welfare, Administration on Aging, Washington,
D.C. 20201, by writing for Publication OHD/AoA 73-20802. If not, write
to the Superintendent of Documents, U.S. Government Printing Office,
Washington, D.C. 20402. Price: 70 cents.
Aiming for Dynamic Fitness. Action for Independent Maturity, 1909 K Street
N.W., Washington, D.C. 20006.

RETIREMENT

There is an enormous literature on retirement and all its aspects, pleasures,
and problems. You'll find many books in local public libraries. Low-cost and
no-cost pamphlets also abound, and you can request them from a variety of
sources.

Here are some books you may find on library shelves: *Complete Guide to
Retirement,* by Thomas Collins; *Where to Retire on a Small Income,* by Norman
Ford; *Retirement: A Time to Live Anew,* by Harry Hepner; *Second Wind: Handbook for Happy Retirement,* by Philip Kelly; *High Old Time: Or How to Enjoy Being
a Woman Over 60,* by Lavinia Russ.

The Public Affairs Committee's small pamphlets are informative and cost
under $1. Write: Public Affairs Committee, Inc., 381 Park Avenue South,
New York, New York 10016 for:

After 65: Resources for Self-Reliance, by Theodore Irwin. Public Affairs Pamphlet No. 501.
Getting Ready to Retire, by Kathryn Close. Public Affairs Pamphet No. 182.

Life insurance companies are frequent sources of material which advises on
retirement. Try these:

Begin Now to Enjoy Tomorrow. Mutual Benefit Life, Box 520, Newark, New
Jersey 07101.
Planning for Retirement. Consumer and Community Services, Institute of Life
Insurance, 277 Park Avenue, New York, New York 10017.
The Next Promotion. Connecticut Mutual Life Insurance Company, Hartford,
Connecticut.

You might also try:

Not Quite Ready to Retire, by William David. Macmillan, 1970.
Self-Marketing Tips for Unemployed Professionals. The Catholic University of
America, 620 Michigan Avenue, N.E., Washington, D.C. 20064. Free.
Retirement: A Medical Philosophy and Approach. Department of Health Care
Services, Division of Socioeconomic Activities, American Medical Associ-
ation, 535 North Dearborn Street, Chicago, Illinois 60610.

Write: the Publications Office, Andrus Gerontology Center, University of Southern California, University Park, Los Angeles, California 90007, for its pamphlet series. Price: 50 cents each; $2.50 for series.
Is My Mind Slipping?
Nutrition for Health and Enjoyment in Retirement
Getting Ready for Retirement
What About the Generation Gap?
Health and Physical Fitness in Retirement
Sex, Romance and Marriage after 55.

The American Association of Retired Persons/National Retired Teachers Association (AARP/NRTA) publishes a series of eleven booklets for retirement planning, available at no charge, which includes: *Retirement Housing Guide; Retirement Psychology Guide; Retirement Job Guide;* etc. Write: AARP/NRTA, 215 Long Beach Boulevard, Long Beach, California 90801, and ask for the Better Retirement Books Series.

The AARP/NRTA also has an excellent small, free booklet which gives a bibliography of dozens of books and pamphlets written for the prospective or actual retiree. These publications are available in public libraries, bookstores, and through publishing houses.

SAFETY

Handle Yourself with Care. Administration on Aging, Washington, D.C. 20201. Free.

SENIOR CITIZENS' CENTERS

Both the National Council on Aging and the National Council of Senior Citizens publish a directory of senior citizens' centers across the country. Check your local library or write directly to the NCOA or NCSC (addresses on page 267).

SEXUAL PROBLEMS

Butler, Robert and Lewis, Myrna. *Sex After Sixty.* New York: Harper & Row, 1976.
Dickinson, Peter. *The Fires of Autumn: Sexual Activity in the Middle and Later Years.* New York: Drake, 1974.
The Sex Information Council of the United States (SEICUS) at 122 East 42 Street, New York, New York 10017, recommends these books on sexual counseling for older people:
Felstein, Ivor. *Sex and the Longer Life.* London: Allen Pane/Penguin Press, 1970.
Rubin, Isadore. *Sexual Life after Sxity.* New York: Basic Books, 1965.

TRAVEL

For information on special tours for older people, both in the United States and abroad, write to:

NRTA/AARP Travel Service, 555 Madison Avenue, New York, New York 10022.

Tour Department, National Council of Senior Citizens, Inc., 1511 K Street N.W., Washington, D.C. 20005.

There are several comprehensive guides to the 20,000 camper and trailer parks and sites, both public and private, across the United States. You will find them in public libraries and bookstores. Here are some:

Camp Grounds and Trailer Park Guide, published by Rand McNally. One volume is a guide to the entire country; another covers the East. Write to The Map Store, 1636 Eye Street N.W., Washington, D.C. 20006.

Woodall's Trailering Parks and Campgrounds, published by the Woodall Publishing Company, 500 Hyacinth Place, Highland Park, Illinois 60035.

Woodall's Travel-Camping in the Four Seasons is a travel guide to points of interest, with descriptions of nearby sites and parks.

Private Campgrounds, U.S.A., by Glenn and Dale Rhodes, describes only private locations. Published by Camping Maps, U.S.A., P.O. Box 2652, Palos Verdes Peninsula, California 90274.

In addition, members of the American Automobile Association can send for *Camping Directories,* four guides to the four major regions of the country. These are available at no cost. Check the nearest AAA office or write: Travel Services, AAA, 8111 Gatehouse Road, Falls Church, Virginia 22042.

National Recreation and Parks Association, 1700 Pennsylvania Avenue N.W., Washington, D.C. 20006, has a great deal of information about opportunities for recreation.

VISION

Directory of Low Vision Facilities in the United States. Published by the National Society for the Prevention of Blindness, Inc., 79 Madison Avenue, New York, New York 10016. The society also publishes information pamphlets, such as *First Aid for Eye Emergencies, Cataract: What It Is and How It Is Treated, Glaucoma: Sneak Thief of Sight, Your Eyes: For a Lifetime of Sight, Television and Your Eyes, The Aging Eye: Facts on Eye Care for Older Persons.*

The American Foundation for the Blind, 15 West 16th Street, New York, New York 10011, will give information on services available for aging blind persons. Among the pamphlets it publishes are *Aids and Appliances, Blindness and Diabetes, Facts about Blindness: How Does a Blind Person Get Around?*

VOLUNTEER PROGRAMS

ACTION is the coordinating agency for the federal government's volunteer programs for older Americans. It includes the Retired Senior Volunteer Programs (RSVP), the Foster Grandparent Program, the Service Corps of Retired Executives (SCORE), the Peace Corps, Volunteers in Service to America (VISTA), and the Senior Companion Program.

For information about these programs, write: ACTION, Washington, D.C. 20525, or call ACTION's toll-free telephone number: 800–424–8580. Regional offices are located in Boston, New York City, Philadelphia, Atlanta, Chicago, Dallas, Kansas City, Denver, San Francisco, and Seattle. Look up ACTION under U.S. Government in the local telephone book.

Senior Aides offers part-time community service work in about three dozen urban and rural areas. Write: National Council of Senior Citizens, 1511 K Street N.W., Washington, D.C. 20005.

Senior Community Service Aides also offers part-time work in community service agencies and, in addition, puts older people into part-time jobs helping other older people. Write: National Council on the Aging, 1828 L Street N.W., Washington, D.C. 20036.

Senior Community Aides is a similar program, sponsored by the AARP/ NRTA. Write to them at 1909 K Street N.W., Washington, D.C. 20006.

The national office of Common Cause, at 2030 M Street N.W., Washington, D.C. 20036, can tell you whether there is an office near your parent.

To find out about Volunteers with Vision, write: Division for the Blind and Physically Handicapped, Library of Congress, Washington, D.C. 20542.

The National Center for Voluntary Action, 1735 Eye Street N.W., Washington, D.C. 20006, has free pamphlets about volunteer work.

WIDOWHOOD

On Being Alone and *Your Retirement Guide.* Both published by the AARP/ NRTA, 215 Long Beach Boulevard, Long Beach, California 90802. Free.

What Do I Do Now? A pamphlet for beneficiaries published by the Continental Life Insurance Co. CNA Plaza, Chicago, Illinois 60685.

WORK AFTER RETIREMENT

The Small Business Administration has many pamphlets for those thinking about starting a new business. Write: Management Assistance, Small Business Administration, Room 250, 1030 Fifteenth Street N.W., Washington, D.C. 20417 for:

SBA Form 115A and 115B, a list of publications from which you can choose the most helpful.

SMA 71, a checklist of important considerations for people going into business.

General Information Kit for Starting a Business, a package for those going into business.

Green Thumb offers part-time jobs in rural areas. Check the Farmers Union, 1012 Fourteenth Street N.W., Washington, D.C. 20004.

APPENDIX B WHERE TO TURN

NATIONAL ORGANIZATIONS OF AND FOR OLDER PEOPLE

American Association of Retired Persons/National Retired Teachers Association, 1909 K Street N.W., Washington, D.C. 20006

Gray Panthers, 3700 Chestnut Street, Philadelphia, Pennsylvania 19104

The National Caucus on the Black Aged, Inc., 1730 M Street N.W., Suite 811, Washington, D.C. 20036

National Council of Senior Citizens (NCSC), 1511 K Street N.W., Washington, D.C. 20036

National Council on the Aging (NCOA), 1828 L Street N.W., Washington, D.C. 20006

National Organization for Women (NOW), Task Force on Older Women, 434 66th Street, Oakland, California 94609

Senior Advocates International, 1825 K Street N.W., Washington, D.C. 20006

NATIONAL HEALTH ORGANIZATIONS

Alexander Graham Bell Association for the Deaf, 3417 Volta Place, Washington, D.C. 20007

American Cancer Society, 219 East 42nd Street, New York, New York 10021

American Diabetes Association, 18 East 48th Street, New York, New York 10017

American Foundation for the Blind, 15 West 16th Street, New York, New York 10011

American Heart Association, 44 East 23rd Street, New York, New York 10010

American Lung Association, 1740 Broadway, New York, New York 10019

American Medical Association, 535 North Dearborn Street, Chicago, Illinois 60610

American Occupational Therapy Association, Inc., 6000 Executive Boulevard, Rockville, Maryland 20852

American Physical Therapy Association, 1740 Broadway, New York, New York 10019

American Psychiatric Association, 1700 18th Street N.W., Washington, D.C. 20009

Arthritis Foundation, 1212 Avenue of the Americas, New York, New York 10036

Association of Rehabilitation Facilities, 5530 Wisconsin Avenue N.W., Washington, D.C. 20015, (For information about rehabilitation centers across the country serving older people.)

Cancer Care, One Park Avenue, New York, New York 10016

National Association for Mental Health, 1800 North Kent Street, Arlington, Virginia 22209

National Association for Visually Handicapped, 305 East 24th Street, New York, N.Y. 10010

National Association of the Deaf, 814 Thayer Avenue, Silver Spring, Maryland 20910

National Association of Hearing and Speech Agencies, 814 Thayer Avenue, Silver Spring, Maryland 20910

National Society for the Prevention of Blindness, Inc., 79 Madison Avenue, New York, New York 10016

NATIONAL HELPING ASSOCIATIONS

(Write to find the nearest local agency.)

Family Service Association of America, 44 East 23rd Street, New York, New York 10010

American Red Cross, 17th and D Streets N.W., Washington, D.C. 20006

The Salvation Army, National Headquarters, 120 West 14th Street, New York, New York 10011

Eastern Headquarters
120 West 14th Street, New York, New York 10011

Central Headquarters
860 North Dearborn Street, Chicago, Illinois 60610

Southern Headquarters
P.O. Box 5236, Atlanta, Georgia 30307

Western Headquarters
P.O. Box 3846, San Francisco, California 94119

Volunteers of America, 340 West 85th Street, New York, New York 10024

FOR HELP IN THE HOME

(Write to find the nearest local agency.)

Homemakers Home and Health Care Services, 3651 Van Rick Drive, Kalamazoo, Michigan 49001

National Council for Homemaker—Home Health Aide Services, Inc., 67 Irving Place, New York, New York 10003

Visiting Nurses, National League for Nursing, 10 Columbus Circle, New York, New York 10019

DENOMINATIONAL SOCIAL WELFARE AGENCIES

Check local telephone book listings for organizations such as Catholic Charities, Jewish Social Service Agency, Protestant Welfare Agency.

GOVERNMENT AGENCIES ON AGING

FEDERAL:

The Administration on Aging, Office of Human Development, U.S. Department of Health, Education and Welfare, Washington, D.C. 20201

STATE:

Alabama: Commission on Aging, 740 Madison Avenue, Montgomery, Alabama 36104, Tel. (205) 269-8171

Alaska: Office on Aging, Department of Health and Social Services, Pouch H, Juneau, Alaska 99801, Tel. (907) 586-6153

American Samoa: Government of American Samoa, Office of the Governor, Pago Pago, Samoa 96920

Arizona: Bureau on Aging, Department of Economic Security, Suite 800, South Tower, 2721 North Central, Phoenix, Arizona 85004, Tel. (602) 271-4446

Arkansas: Office on Aging, P.O. Box 2179, Hendrix Hall, 4313 West Markham, Little Rock, Arkansas 72203, Tel. (501) 371-2441

California: Office on Aging, Health and Welfare Agency, 455 Capital Mall, Suite 500, Sacramento, California 95814, Tel. (916) 322-3887

Colorado: Division of Services for the Aging, Department of Social Services, 1575 Sherman Street, Denver, Colorado 80203, Tel. (303) 892-2651

Connecticut: Department of Aging, 90 Washington Street, Room 312, Hartford, Connecticut 06115, Tel. (203) 566-2480

Delaware: Division of Aging, Department of Health and Social Services, 2407 Lancaster Avenue, Wilmington, Delaware 19805, Tel. (302) 571-3480

District of Columbia: Office of Services to the Aged, Department of Human Resources, 1329 E Street N.W. (Munsey Building), Washington, D.C. 20004, Tel. (202) 638-2406

Florida: Division on Aging, Department of Health and Rehabilitation Services, 1317 Winewood Boulevard, Building 3, Tallahassee, Florida 32301, Tel. (904) 488-4797

Georgia: Office of Aging, Department of Human Resources, 618 Ponce de Leon Avenue, Atlanta, Georgia 30308, Tel. (404) 894-5333

Guam: Office of Aging, Social Services Administration, Government of Guam, P.O. Box 2816, Agana, Guam 96910

Hawaii: Commission on Aging, 1149 Bethel Street, Room 311, Honolulu, Hawaii 96813

Idaho: Office on Aging, Department of Special Services, Capitol Annex No. 7, 509 North 5th Street, Room 100, Boise, Idaho 83720, Tel. (208) 384-3833

Illinois: Department on Aging, 2401 West Jefferson Street, Springfield, Illinois 62706, Tel. (217) 782-5773

Indiana: Commission on the Aging and the Aged, Graphic Arts Building, 215 North Senate Avenue, Indianapolis, Indiana 46202, Tel. (317) 633-5948

Iowa: Commission on the Aging, 415 West 10th (Jewett Building), Des Moines, Iowa 50319, Tel. (515) 281-5187

Kansas: Services for the Aging Section, Division of Social Services, Social and Rehabilitative Services Department, State Office Building, Topeka, Kansas 66612, Tel. (913) 296-3465

Kentucky: Aging Program Unit, Department for Human Resources, 403 Wapping Street, Frankfort, Kentucky 40601, Tel. (502) 564-4238

Louisiana: Bureau of Aging Service, Division of Human Resources, Health and Social and Rehabilitative Services Administration, P.O. Box 44282, Capital Station, Baton Rouge, Louisiana 70804, Tel. (504) 389-6713

Maine: Bureau of Maine's Elderly, Department of Health and Welfare, State House, Augusta, Maine 04330, Tel. (207) 622-6171, ask for 289-2561

Maryland: Commission on Aging, State Office Building, 1123 North Eutaw Street, Baltimore, Maryland 21201, Tel. (301) 383-2100

Massachusetts: Executive Office of Elder Affairs, State Office Building, 18 Tremont Street, Boston, Massachusetts 02109, Tel. (617) 727-7751

Michigan: Offices of Services to the Aging, 1026 East Michigan, Lansing, Michigan 48912, Tel. (517) 373-8230

Minnesota: Governor's Citizens Council on Aging, Suite 204, Metro Square Building, 7th and Robert Streets, St. Paul, Minnesota 55101, Tel. (612) 296-2544

Mississippi: Council on Aging, P.O. Box 5136, Fondren Station, 2906 North State Street, Jackson, Mississippi 39216, Tel. (601) 354-6590

Missouri: Office of Aging, Division of Special Services, Department of Social Services, The Broadway State Office Building, Jefferson City, Missouri 65101, Tel. (314) 751-2075

Montana: Aging Services Bureau, Department of Social and Rehabilitative Services, P.O. Box 1723, Helena, Montana 59601, Tel. (406) 449-3124

Nebraska: Commission on Aging, State House Station 94784, 300 South 17th Street, Lincoln, Nebraska 68509, Tel. (402) 471-2307

Nevada: Division of Aging, Department of Human Resources, Room 300, Nye Building, 201 South Fall Street, Carson City, Nevada 89701, Tel. (702) 882-7855

New Hampshire: Council on Aging, P.O. Box 786, 14 Depot Street, Concord, New Hampshire 03301, Tel. (603) 271-2751

New Jersey: Office on Aging, Department of Community Affairs, P.O. Box 2768, 363 West State Street, Trenton, New Jersey 08625, Tel. (609) 292-3765

New Mexico: State Commission on Aging, Villagra Building, 408 Galisteo Street, Santa Fe, New Mexico 87501, Tel. (505) 827-5258

New York: Office for the Aging, New York State Executive Department, 855 Central Avenue, Albany, New York 12206, Tel. (518) 457-7321

New York City: Office for the Aging, Room 5036, 2 World Trade Center, New York, New York 10047, Tel. (212) 488-6405

North Carolina: Governor's Coordinating Council on Aging, Administration Building, 213 Hillsborough Street, Raleigh, North Carolina 27603, Tel. (919) 829-3983

North Dakota: Aging Services, Social Services Board, State Capitol Building, Bismarck, North Dakota 58501, Tel. (701) 224-2577

Ohio: Commission on Aging, 34 North High Street, 3rd Floor, Columbus, Ohio 43215, Tel. (614) 466-5500

Oklahoma: Special Unit of Aging, Department of Institutions, Social and Rehabilitative Services, Box 25352, Capitol Station, Sequoyah Memorial Building, Oklahoma City, Oklahoma 73125, Tel. (405) 521-2281

Oregon: Program on Aging, Human Resources Department, 315 Public Service Building, Salem, Oregon 97310, Tel. (503) 378-4728

Pennsylvania: Office for the Aging, Department of Public Welfare, Capital Associates Building, 7th and Forster Streets, Harrisburg, Pennsylvania 17120, Tel. (717) 787-5350

Puerto Rico: Gericulture Commission, Department of Social Services, Apartado 11697, Santurce, Puerto Rico 00910, Tel. (809) 725-8015, (Overseas Operator)

Rhode Island: Division on Aging, Department of Community Affairs, 150 Washington Street, Providence, Rhode Island 02903, Tel. (401) 528-1000, ask for 277-2858

South Carolina: Commission on Aging, 915 Main Street, Columbia, South Carolina 29201, Tel. (803) 758-2576

South Dakota: Program on Aging, Department of Social Services, St. Charles Hotel, Pierre, South Dakota 57501, Tel. (605) 224-3656

Tennessee: Commission on Aging, S & P Building, Room 102, 306 Gay Street, Nashville, Tennessee 37201, Tel. (615) 741-2056

Texas: Governor's Committee on Aging, Southwest Tower, 8th Floor, 211 East 7th Street, Austin, Texas 78711, Tel. (512) 475-2717

Trust Territory of the Pacific: Office of Aging, Community Development Division, Governor of the Trust Territory of the Pacific Islands, Saipan, Mariana Islands 96950

Utah: Division of Aging, Department of Social Services, 345 South 6th East, Salt Lake City, Utah 84102, Tel. (801) 328-6422

Vermont: Office on Aging, Department of Human Services, 56 State Street, Montpelier, Vermont 05602, Tel. (802) 828-3471

Virginia: Office on Aging, Division of State Planning and Community Affairs, 9 North 12th Street, Richmond, Virginia 23219, Tel. (804) 770-7894

Virgin Islands: Commission on Aging, P.O. Box 539, Charlotte Amalie, St. Thomas, Virgin Islands 00801, Tel. (809) 774-5884

Washington: Office on Aging, Department of Social and Health Services, P.O. Box 1788—M.S. 45-2, 410 West Fifth, Olympia, Washington 98504, Tel. (206) 753-2502

West Virginia: Commission on Aging, State Capitol—Room 420-26, 1800 Washington Street, East Charleston, West Virginia 25305, Tel. (304) 348-3317

Wisconsin: Division on Aging, Department of Health and Social Services, State Office Building, Room 686, One West Wilson Street, Madison, Wisconsin 53702, Tel. (608) 266-2536

Wyoming: Aging Services, Department of Health and Social Services, Division of Public Assistance and Social Services, State Office Building, Cheyenne, Wyoming 82002, Tel. (307) 777-7561

RIGHTS OF HOSPITAL AND NURSING HOME PATIENTS

Most state departments of health publish bills of rights for patients in hospitals and nursing homes, and you can obtain copies from your own state health department. You and your parent should be familiar with these rights. In general, they will follow those printed here.

HOSPITAL PATIENT'S BILL OF RIGHTS

The patient should have the right:

1. To considerate and respectful care.
2. To receive, upon request, the name of the physician responsible for coordinating his care.
3. To know the name and function of any person providing health-care services to the patient.
4. To obtain from his physician complete current information concerning his diagnosis, treatment, and prognosis in terms the patient can reasonably be expected to understand. When it is not medically advisable to give such information to the patient, the information shall be made available to an appropriate person in his behalf.
5. To receive from his physician information necessary to give informed consent prior to the start of any procedure or treatment or both, and which, except for those emergency situations not requiring an informed consent, shall include as a minimum the specific procedure or treatment or both, the medically significant risks involved, and the probable duration of incapacitation, if any. The patient shall be advised of medically significant alternatives for care or treatment, if any.
6. To refuse treatment to the extent permitted by law and to be informed of the medical consequences of his action.
7. To privacy to the extent consistent with providing adequate medical care to the patient. This shall not preclude discreet discussion of a patient's case or examination of a patient by appropriate health-care personnel.
8. To privacy and confidentiality of all records pertaining to the patient's treatment, except as otherwise provided by law or third-party-payment contract.
9. To a response by the hospital, in a reasonable manner, to the patient's request for services customarily rendered by the hospital consistent with the patient's treatment.
10. To be informed by his physician or a delegate of the physician of the patient's continuing health-care requirements following discharge; and to be informed by the hospital, before transferral to another facility, of the need for, and alternatives to, such a transfer.
11. To know the identity, upon request, of other health-care and educational institutions that the hospital has authorized to participate in his treatment.
12. To refuse to participate in research or human expermentation without his consent.
13. To examine and receive an explanation of his bill, regardless of source of payment.
14. To know the hospital rules and regulations that apply to his conduct as a patient.

15. To treatment without discrimination as to race, color, religion, sex, national origin, or source of payment.

NURSING-HOME PATIENTS BILL OF RIGHTS

The nursing home must assure that each patient:

1. Is fully informed, as evidenced by the patient's written acknowledgment, prior to or at the time of admission, and during stay, of these rights and of all rules and regulations governing patient conduct and responsibilities.
2. Is fully informed, prior to or at the time of admission, and during stay, of services available in the facility, and of related charges, including any charges for services not covered by sources of third-party payments or not covered by the facility's basic per-diem rate.
3. Is fully informed, by a physician, of his medical condition unless medically contraindicated (as documented, by a physician, in his medical record), and is afforded the opportunity to participate in the planning of his medical treatment and to refuse to participate in experimental research.
4. Is transferred or discharged only for medical reasons, or for his welfare or that of other patients, or for nonpayment for his stay (except as prohibited by sources of third-party payment), and is given reasonable advance notice to ensure orderly transfer or discharge, and such actions are documented in his medical record.
5. Is encouraged and assisted, throughout his period of stay, to exercise his rights as a patient and as a citizen, and to this end may voice grievances and recommend changes in policies and services to facility staff and/or to outside representatives of his choice, free from restraint, interference, coercion, discrimination, or reprisal.
6. May manage his personal financial affairs, or is given at least a quarterly accounting of financial transactions made on his behalf should the facility accept his written delegation of this responsibility to the facility for any period of time in conformance with state law.
7. Is free from mental and physical abuse, and free from chemical and (except in emergencies) physical restraints, except as authorized in writing by a physician for a specified and limited period of time, or when necessary to protect the patient from injury to himself or to others.
8. Is assured confidential treatment of his personal and medical records, and may approve or refuse their release to any individual outside the facility, except in the case of his transfer to another health-care institution.
9. Is treated with consideration, respect, and full recognition of his dignity and individuality, including privacy in treatment and in care for his personal needs.
10. Is not required to perform services for the facility that are not included for therapeutic purposes in his plan of care.
11. May associate and communicate privately with persons of his choice, and send and receive his personal mail unopened, unless medically contraindicated.
12. May meet with and participate in activities of social, religious, and community groups at his discretion, unless medically contraindicated.

13. May retain and use his personal clothing and possessions as space permits, unless to do so would infringe upon rights of other patients, and unless medically contraindicated.
14. If married, is assured privacy for visits by his/her spouse; if both are inpatients in the facility, they are permitted to share a room, unless medically contraindicated.

BIBLIOGRAPHY

BOOK LIST

Beauvoir, Simone de. *The Coming of Age*. New York: Putnam, 1972.

Bettelheim, Bruno. *The Children of the Dream*. New York: Macmillan, 1969.

Bird, Brian. *Talking With Patients*. Philadelphia and Montreal: J. B. Lippincott, 1955.

Brody, Elaine M., et al. *A Social Work Guide for Long-term Care Facilities*. Rockville, Md.: National Institute of Mental Health, 1974.

Busse, Ewald W., and Pfeiffer, Eric, eds. *Behavior and Adaptation in Late Life*. Boston: Little, Brown, 1969.

Butler, Robert N. *Why Survive? Being Old in America*. New York: Harper & Row, 1975.

Clark, Margaret, and Anderson, Barbara Gallatin. *Culture and Aging: An Anthropological Study of Older Americans*. Springfield, Ill: Charles C Thomas, 1967.

David, William. *Not Quite Ready to Retire*. New York: Collier Books, 1970.

Field, Minna. *The Aged, the Family and the Community*. New York: Columbia University Press, 1972.

Galton, Lawrence. *Don't Give Up on an Aging Parent*. New York: Crown, 1975.

Griesel, Elma, and Horn, Linda. *Citizen's Action Guide: Nursing Home Reform*. Philadelphia: Gray Panthers, 1975.

Harris, Louis, and Associates, Inc. *The Myth and Reality of Aging in America*. Washington, D.C.: National Council on the Aging, 1975.

Horowitz, Milton J. *Educating Tomorrow's Doctors*. New York: Appleton-Century-Crofts, 1964.

Ingraham, Mark H., and Mulanaphy, James M. *My Purpose Holds: Reactions and Experiences in Retirement of TIAA–CREF Annuitants*. New York: Teachers Insurance and Annuity Association–College Retirement Equities Fund, 1974.

Kahn, Samuel. *Essays on Longevity*. New York: Philosophical Library, 1974.

Knopf, Olga. *Successful Aging*. New York: Viking, 1975.

Korim, Andrew S. *Older Americans and Community Colleges: A Guide for Program Implementation*. Washington, D.C.: American Association of Community and Junior Colleges, 1974.

McKinney, John C., and de Vyver, Frank T., eds. *Aging and Social Policy*. New York: Meredith, 1966.

Morgan, William L., Jr., and Engel, George L. *The Clinical Approach to the Patient*. Philadelphia, London, and Toronto: Saunders, 1969.

Moss, Bertram B. *Caring for the Aged*. New York: Doubleday, 1966.

Nassau, Jean Baron. *Choosing a Nursing Home*. New York: Funk & Wagnalls, 1975.

Percy, Charles H. *Growing Old in the Country of the Young*. New York: McGraw-Hill, 1974.

Pfeiffer, Eric, ed. *Successful Aging*. Durham, N.C.: Center for the Study of Aging and Human Development, Duke University, 1974.

Poe, William D. *The Old Person in Your Home*. New York: Scribner, 1969.

Rosow, Irving. *Social Integration of the Aged*. New York: Free Press, 1967.

Sheldon, Alan; McEwan, Peter J. M.; and Ryser, Carol Pierson. *Retirement Patterns and Predictions*. Rockville, Md.: National Institute of Mental Health, Section on Mental Health of the Aging, 1975.

Simon, Alexander, and Epstein, Leon J. *Aging in Modern Society* (February 1968, Psychiatric Research Report No. 23). Washington, D.C.: American Psychiatric Association.

Teeling-Smith, George. *You and the National Health Service*. London: Arrow, 1975.

Wintrobe, Maxwell, et. al., eds., *Harrison's Principles of Internal Medicine*, 7th ed. *Part One: The Physician and the Patient*. New York: McGraw-Hill, 1974.

Working with Older People: A Guide to Practice. Vol. I, *The Practitioner and the Elderly*. Vol. II, *Biological, Psychological and Sociological Aspects of Aging*. Vol. III, *The Aging Person: Needs and Services*. Vol. IV, *Clinical Aspects of Aging*. Rockville, Md.: Bureau of Health Services Research, Division of Long-term Care, U.S. Public Health Service, 1974.

ARTICLES

Atar, David. "Aging in Kibbutz Society," *Gerontology* 1 (1975).

Davis, Catherine Clayton. "Fairhaven's Senior Freshmen." *American Education* 2 (1975): 6–10.

Juris Doctor (March 1975): Articles by Jonathan A. Weiss, Laura Villafane, Marlene Adler Marks, and Stephen Singular.

Kohlberg, Lawrence. "Stages and Aging in Moral Development." *Gerontologist* 13 (1973): 497–502.

Lawton, M. Powell, and Gottesman, Leonard E. "Psychological Services to the Elderly." *American Psychologist* 29 (1974): 689–693.

Simos, Bertha G. "Adult Children and Their Aging Parents." *Social Work* 18 (1973): 78–85.

Yawney, Beverly A., and Slover, Darrell L. "Relocation of the Elderly," *Social Work* 18 (1973): 86–95.

DIRECTORIES

Directory of Senior Centers and Clubs: A National Resource 1974. Issued by the National Institute of Senior Centers of the National Council on the Aging, Washington, D.C.

A National Directory of Housing for Older People: Including a Guide for Selection 1969–70. Issued by the National Council on the Aging, Washington, D.C.

CONFERENCE AND ORGANIZATIONAL REPORTS

Beck, Amanda A. *Michigan Aging Citizens: Characteristics, Opinions, and Service Utilizations.* Ann Arbor, Mich.: Institute of Gerontology, University of Michigan–Wayne State University, 1975.

Catastrophic Illness in the Seventies: Critical Issues and Complex Decisions. Proceedings of the Fourth National Symposium. New York: Cancer Care, Inc., of the National Cancer Foundation, 1971.

Epidemiology of Aging. Summary report and selected papers from a research conference on epidemiology of aging, Elkridge, Md., June 11–13, 1972. DHEW Publication No. (NIH) 75-711. Bethesda, Md.: National Institutes of Health, 1972.

Home Health Care Benefits under Medicare and Medicaid. A report to the Congress by the U.S. Comptroller General, Washington, D.C., July 1974.

Pfeiffer, Eric, ed. *Successful Aging.* Report of a conference at the Center for the Study of Aging and Human Development, June 7–9, 1974. Duke University, Durham, N.C.

Planning for the Later Years. Washington, D.C.: Social Security Administration, U.S. Department of Health, Education and Welfare, 1967.

Regulating Nursing Home Care: The Paper Tigers. Report of the New York State Moreland Act Commission, Albany, N.Y., October 1975.

Social Policy, Social Ethics, and the Aging Society. Selected papers from a conference at the Center for Continuing Education, University of Chicago, June 1975.

Towards a New Attitude on Aging: A Report on the Administration's Continuing Response to the Recommendations of the Delegates to the 1971 White House Conference on Aging. Washington, D.C.: U.S. Department of Health, Education and Welfare, 1973.

PAMPHLETS

After a Life of Labor: A Pioneering Union's Program for Retirees. International Ladies Garment Workers Union, 1710 Broadway, New York, N.Y. 10019.

Arthritis: The Basic Facts. The Arthritis Foundation, 1212 Avenue of the Americas, New York, N.Y. 10036 (1974).

Facts about Osteoporosis. National Institute of Arthritis and Metabolic Diseases, Bethesda, Md. 20014 (1970).

Hearing Loss: Hope Through Research. National Institute of Neurological Diseases and Stroke, U.S. Department of Health, Education and Welfare (1973).

High Blood Pressure: What to Do When Your Numbers Are Up. Consumer Reports reprint. Consumers Union, Mount Vernon, N.Y. (October 1974.)

How to Spot a Con Artist. NRTA/AARP/AIM, 1909 K Street, N.W., Washington, D.C. 20049.

The Next Promotion. Connecticut Mutual Life Insurance Co., Hartford, Conn. 06115.

Reading Is for Everyone. The Library of Congress, Division for the Blind and Physically Handicapped, Washington, D.C. 20542 (1974).

Social Security and Medicare Explained. Commerce Clearing House, Inc., 4025 West Peterson Ave., Chicago, Ill. 60646 (1974).

What Do I Do Now? For Beneficiaries. Continental Assurance Co., CNA Plaza, Chicago, Ill. 60685.

SELECTED MATERIALS

Selected materials from the Administration on Aging: *Basic Concepts of Aging, Information and Referral Services, Transportation and the Aging, Home Delivered Meals, Increasing Mobility among Isolated Elderly, Traffic Accidents and Older Drivers, Let's End Isolation, Protective Services for the Aged, Facts and Figures on Older Americans* (a series of statistical portraits of older Americans).

Selected hearings and materials from the U.S. Senate Special Committee on Aging, the House Committee on Government Operations, the House Committee on Labor and Public Welfare, the Older Americans Amendments of 1975.

Selected materials from the U.S. Bureau of the Census, Washington, D.C.

Selected materials from the U.S. Public Health Service, including *Comprehensive Care Service in Your Community, Preliminary Analysis of Select Geriatric Day Care Programs* and *Adult Day Care in the United States.*

Selected materials from the U.S. Department of Labor, Manpower Administration, Washington, D.C. 20210.

Selected materials from the National Council of Senior Citizens, Legal Research and Services for the Elderly, including Georgia M. Springer, *Protective Services for Older Persons in Pennsylvania,* 1975, and John J. Regan and Henry Schwartz, *A Protective Services Program for the Elderly in Maryland,* 1974.

Selected materials from the National Council on the Aging, including *Industrial Gerontology,* quarterly, and *Perspective on Aging,* a regular periodical for member agencies and individuals, Washington, D.C., 1973–76.

Selected materials describing programs and activities offered through state agencies on aging in most of the fifty states.

INTERVIEWS

Altholz, Judith
    Associate in Psychiatric Social Work, Center for the Study of Aging and Human Development, Duke University, Durham, North Carolina

Bakst, Fannie
  Widows Consultation Service, New York, New York
Beattie, Walter M.
  Director, All-University Gerontology Center, Syracuse University, Syracuse, New York
Mother M. Bernadette de Lourdes, O. Carm.
  Administrator, St. Joseph's Manor, Trumbull, Connecticut
Bernstein, Dr. Ira
  Optometrist, White Plains, New York
Blauner, Dr. Stuart
  Director, Cardio-Pulmonary Units, The Burke Rehabilitation Center, White Plains, New York
Bragaw, George
  Public Affairs Officer, Health Services Administration, U.S. Public Health Service, Washington, D.C.
Breslau, Ruth
  Executive Director, Jewish Council for the Aging of Greater Washington, Washington, D.C.
Briscoe, Betty, R.N.
  Program Specialist, Institutional and Medical Care Section, Montgomery County Health Department, Montgomery County, Maryland
Brook, Major Marjorie
  Assistant Director of Social Services, Salvation Army, New York, New York
Brown, Betty
  Information and Research Coordinator, Commission on Aging, Montgomery County, Maryland
Brown, Roberta
  Social Science Analyst, Administration on Aging, Washington, D.C.
Browne, James
  Public Affairs Officer, Social Security Administration, U.S. Department of Health, Education and Welfare, Washington, D.C.
Butler, Dr. Robert
  Psychiatrist and Researcher, Director, National Institute on Aging, Washington, D.C.
Calhoun, Erma
  Information and Referral Specialist, Commission on Aging, Montgomery County, Maryland
Callahan, Lois
  Director of Information, American Cancer Society, Washington, D.C.
Cochran, Clay
  Executive Director, Rural Housing Alliance, Washington, D.C.
Codell, Michael
  Director of Information, American Health Care Association, Washington, D.C.
Cooper, Norma
  Director, Freda Mohr Center, Jewish Family Service, Los Angeles, California
Elowitz, Gertrude
  Director, Older Persons Service, Community Service Society of New York, New York, New York

Engelmann, Erika
　　Social Worker, Jewish Social Service Agency, Montgomery County, Maryland
Feiden, Elaine
　　Director, Crisis Intervention, Westchester County Mental Health Association, White Plains, New York
Fischel, Dr. Edward E.
　　Professor of Medicine, Albert Einstein College of Medicine, Bronx, New York, and Director, Department of Medicine, Bronx-Lebanon Hospital Center, Bronx, New York
Forman, Evelyn H.
　　Community Coordinator, New York State Department of Mental Hygiene, New Rochelle, New York
Gaffin, Philip
　　Director of Information, Visiting Nurse Association, Washington, D.C.
Gates, O. J.
　　Director, City–County Commission on Aging, Portland, Oregon
Gelb, Dr. Ira
　　Associate Clinical Professor of Cardiology, Mt. Sinai School of Medicine, New York, New York
Golovensky, Dr. David
　　Rabbi, Congregation Beth El, New Rochelle, New York
Gordon, Benjamin
　　Staff Economist, Select Committee on Small Business, U.S. Senate, Washington, D.C.
Griesel, Elma
　　Staff Associate, National Paralegal Institute, Washington, D.C.
Gutner, Thomas
　　Director of Information, American Association of Homes for the Aging, Washington, D.C.
Hook, Lottie L.
　　Service Coordinator, Homemakers Home and Health Care Services, Washington, D.C.
Jackson, Hobart C.
　　Executive Director, Stephen Smith Geriatric Center, Philadelphia, Pennsylvania
Kahanovitz, Varda
　　Kibbutz Magan Michael, Israel
Kaplan, Benjamin
　　Director of Administration, Jewish Association for Services for the Aged, Federation of Jewish Philanthropies, New York, New York
Kaplan, Frances
　　Public Affairs Officer, U.S. Department of Health, Education and Welfare, Washington, D.C.
Lewis, Robert
　　Executive Director, Farmers Union, Washington, D.C.
Livingston, Joanne H., R.N.
　　Nurse Surveyor, Institutional and Medical Care Section, Montgomery County Health Department, Montgomery County, Maryland

McCarthy, Joseph
   Assistant Vice-President, Institute of Life Insurance, Washington, D.C.
McCarty, Dr. Maclyn
   Vice-President, the Rockefeller University, New York, New York
McCleave, Kathleen D.
   Social Worker, Cass County Council on Aging, Cassapolis, Michigan
Maddox, Dr. George
   Director, Center for the Study of Aging and Human Development, Duke
   University, Durham, North Carolina
Mathiasen, Geneva
   Former Executive Director, National Council on the Aging, Washington,
   D.C.
Mattis, Dr. Steven
   Chief Clinical Neuropsychologist, Montefiore Hospital and Medical
   Center, and Associate Clinical Professor of Neurology, Albert Einstein
   College of Medicine, Bronx, New York
Mawhinney, Harold
   Director, Miriam Osborn Memorial Home, Rye, New York
Murphy, Alice
   Director, Service for the Aging, Catholic Charities, New York, New York
Nagelschmidt, Joseph
   Director of Information, Blue Cross/Blue Shield, Washington, D.C.
Nelson, Gaylord A.
   U.S. Senator from Wisconsin, U.S. Senate, Washington, D.C.
Odell, Charles
   Commissioner on Aging, State of Connecticut, Hartford, Connecticut
Patterson, Joyce
   Information Officer, Food and Nutrition Service, U.S. Department of
   Agriculture, Washington, D.C.
Pfeiffer, Dr. Eric
   Project Director, Older Americans Resources and Service Program, and
   Professor of Psychiatry, Duke University, Durham, North Carolina
Pothier, William R.
   Executive Director, San Francisco Senior Center, San Francisco, Califor-
   nia
Price, Barbara
   Social Worker, Department of Social Services, Fairfax County, Virginia
Priester, Jeanne
   Program Leader, Cooperative Extension Service, U.S. Department of
   Agriculture, Washington, D.C.
Rhodes, Kay
   Home Economist, Cooperative Extension Service, Montgomery County,
   Maryland
Rifkin, Dr. Harold
   Chief, Division of Diabetes, Montefiore Hospital and Medical Center,
   Bronx, New York, and Clinical Professor of Medicine, Albert Einstein
   College of Medicine, Bronx, New York
Robbins, Ira
   Director, Beth Shalom Home, Richmond, Virginia

Rockwell, Evelyn
    Casework Supervisor, Cancer Care Inc., New York, New York
Sambol, Irving
    Director, Division on Aging, Federation of Protestant Welfare Agencies, Inc., New York, New York
Seidman, Irene
    Director, Foster Grandparents Program, New Rochelle, New York
Simko, John
    Supervisor, Interview Unit, Veterans Services Division, Washington Regional Office, Veterans Administration, Washington, D.C.
Stern, Eve
    Coordinator for Information and Referral, Westchester County Office for the Aging, White Plains, New York
Stewart, Sally Ann
    Information Specialist, American Red Cross, Washington, D.C.
Stivelman, Dr. Robert
    Clinical Assistant Professor of Medicine (Cardiology), University of Southern California and Director, Cardiovascular Stress Laboratory, Mt. Sinai Medical Center, Los Angeles, California
Terry, Dr. Robert
    Chairman, Department of Pathology, Albert Einstein College of Medicine, Bronx, New York
Trobe, Adele
    Manhattan Borough Director, Jewish Association for Services for the Aged, Federation of Jewish Philanthropies, New York, New York
von Euler, Mary
    Staff Attorney, Legal Research Services for the Elderly, National Council of Senior Citizens, Washington, D.C.
Warner, Dr. Leah Robinson
    Clinical Psychologist, Virginia Beach, Virginia
Watkin, Dr. Donald
    Director, Nutrition Program, Administration on Aging, Washington, D.C.
Weitzman, Dr. Elliot
    Professor and Chairman, Department of Neurology, Montefiore Hospital and Medical Center, and Albert Einstein College of Medicine, Bronx, New York
Winston, Dr. Ellen
    Chairman, National Voluntary Organizations for Independent Living for the Aging, and former Executive Director, National Council for Homemaker–Home Health Aide Services, Inc., Raleigh, North Carolina
Wyman, June
    Information Officer, Food and Nutrition Service, U.S. Department of Agriculture, Washington, D.C.

INDEX

[Also check Appendixes A and B for resources.]